D0078465

OXFORD THEOLOGICAL MONOGRAPHS

Editorial Committee

OXFORD THEOLOGICAL MONOGRAPHS

THE PRINCIPLE OF RESERVE IN THE WRITINGS
OF JOHN HENRY NEWMAN
R. C. Selby (1975)

THE COSMIC CHRIST IN ORIGEN AND
TEILHARD DE CHARDIN
A Comparative Study
J. A. Lyons (1982)

THE HIDDEN GOD
Samuel E. Balentine (1983)

PROTESTANT REFORMERS IN ELIZABETHAN
OXFORD
C. M. Dent (1983)

REVELATORY POSITIVISM?
Barth's Earliest Theology and
the Marburg School
Simon Fisher (1988)

THE COMMUNION OF SAINTS
Radical Puritan and Separatist Ecclesiology 1570–1625
S. Brachlow (1988)

PROBABILITY AND THEISTIC EXPLANATION
Robert Prevost (1990)

VERBAL ASPECT IN NEW TESTAMENT GREEK
Buist M. Fanning (1990)

"WORKING THE EARTH OF THE HEART"
The Messalian Controversy in History, Texts, and Language
to AD 431
Columba Stewart, OSB (1991)

BEAUTY AND REVELATION IN THE THOUGHT OF
SAINT AUGUSTINE
Carol Harrison (1992)

THE MURATORIAN FRAGMENT AND THE
DEVELOPMENT OF THE CANON
Geoffrey Mark Hahneman (1992)

Kierkegaard
as
Negative Theologian

DAVID R. LAW

CLARENDON PRESS · OXFORD
1993

Oxford University Press, Walton Street, Oxford OX2 6DP
Oxford   New York   Toronto
Delhi   Bombay   Calcutta   Madras   Karachi
Kuala Lumpar   Singapore   Hong Kong   Tokyo
Nairobi   Dar es Salaam   Cape Town
Melbourne   Auckland   Madrid
and associated companies in
Berlin   Ibadan

Oxford is a trade mark of Oxford University Press

Published in the United States
by Oxford University Press Inc., New York

British Library Cataloguing in Publication Data
Data available
ISBN 0-19-826336-8

Library of Congress Cataloging-in-Publication Data
Law, David R.
Kierkegaard as negative theologian/David R. Law.
(Oxford theological monographs)
Includes bibliographical references and index.
1. Kierkegaard, Søren, 1813-1855.   2. Negative theology—History of
doctrines—19th century.   3. Knowledge, Theory of (Religion)—
History—19th century.   I. Title.   II. Series.
BX4827.K5L42   1993
231' .4—dc20
ISBN 0-19-826336-8

1 3 5 7 9 10 8 6 4 2

Typeset by BP Integraphics Ltd, Bath, Avon
Printed in Great Britain
on acid-free paper by
Bookcraft (Bath) Limited
Midsomer Norton, Avon

To my mother and father
Gwendoline and Dennis

PREFACE

A WORK of this nature owes a great deal to many people and institutions and I am pleased to be able to express my gratitude here. My thanks go first to those institutions which have provided me with the opportunity to pursue my research and to complete this book. A Major State Studentship awarded by the Department of Education and Science enabled me to embark upon the research which led to an earlier version of this work being accepted by Oxford University for the D.Phil. degree in October 1989. I am also indebted to the trustees of the 'Michael Foster Memorial Scholarship' and to the Deutscher Akademischer Austauschdienst for enabling me to pursue this research in Tübingen and thereby add a breadth and depth to my work which would have otherwise been lacking. The final version of this book was completed in the idyllic surroundings of St Mary's College, St Andrews, and I am very grateful to the Senatus Academicus of the University of St Andrews for appointing me to the Gifford Research Fellowship which made this possible. I would also like to express my gratitude to the Principal and Masters of St Mary's for receiving me so warmly and for making my stay in St Andrews so agreeable and rewarding.

I should also like to acknowledge the assistance given to me by Revd Dr D. G. Rowell, who first introduced me to Kierkegaard in an undergraduate tutorial. I am particularly indebted to my supervisor, Revd Professor J. Macquarrie, who guided me through my research and helped me to penetrate the maze of Kierkegaard's thought.

Finally, I would like to acknowledge the incalculable assistance provided by my family. Above all, I am indebted to my wife Claudia for her support and encouragement over the years. My thanks also go out to Paul and Uschi for their many kindnesses. Last but certainly not least, I would like to acknowledge the help of my parents, to whom this book is dedicated.

D. R. L.

St Mary's College, St Andrews
5 December 1991

CONTENTS

Abbreviations   x

Bibliographical Note   xi

1. INTRODUCTION   1

2. DIALECTICS   35

3. EPISTEMOLOGY   71

4. TRUTH   90

5. THE STAGES OF EXISTENCE   124

6. GOD   162

7. CHRISTOLOGY   182

8. KIERKEGAARD AS NEGATIVE THEOLOGIAN   206

Bibliography   218

Index   225

ABBREVIATIONS

ASKB	*Auktionsprotokol over Søren Kierkegaards Bogsamling* (The Auctioneer's Sales Record of the Library of Søren Kierkegaard)
CA	*The Concept of Anxiety*
CD	*Christian Discourses*
CH	*The Celestial Hierarchy*
CI	*The Concept of Irony*
CUP	*Concluding Unscientific Postscript*
DN	*The Divine Names*
E/O	*Either/Or*
ET	English Translation
FT	*Fear and Trembling*
JC	*Johannes Climacus*
JP	*Journals and Papers*
MT	*The Mystical Theology*
Paed.	*Paedagogus*
Pap.	*Papirer* (Kierkegaard's untranslated Danish Journals and Papers)
PF	*Philosophical Fragments*
Protr.	*Protrepticus*
PV	*The Point of View*
R	*Repetition*
SD	*The Sickness unto Death*
SLW	*Stages on Life's Way*
Str.	*Stromateis*
TC	*Training in Christianity*

BIBLIOGRAPHICAL NOTE

QUOTATIONS from Kierkegaard's works are taken from the Princeton University Press translations; quotations from Kierkegaard's *Journals and Papers* are taken from the Indiana University Press translations. I am grateful to Princeton University Press and Indiana University Press for kindly granting permission to quote from these works. I am also indebted to SPCK for permission to quote from their translations of Pseudo-Dionysius and Meister Eckhart in the Classics of Western Spirituality Series, and to Element Books for allowing me to quote from *Meister Eckhart: Sermons and Treatises*, i–ii, trans. M. O'C. Walshe (Shaftesbury, Dorset, 1979).

Where possible, reference is made to English translations of works used or cited by Kierkegaard. If Kierkegaard cites a page number, this is retained and the English equivalent given in brackets.

Translations of foreign secondary literature are my own unless otherwise stated.

I

Introduction

THE purpose of this work is to examine whether and to what extent Kierkegaard can be understood as a negative theologian. This will involve two things. First, we shall be concerned to examine what we have chosen to term the 'apophaticism' of Kierkegaard's thought. Secondly, we shall be concerned with ascertaining whether any apophatic motifs we might discover allow us to speak of Kierkegaard as a negative theologian.

'Apophaticism'[1] is not a term that appears either in Kierkegaard's works or in his journals. It is introduced here as a hermeneutical tool to articulate what we believe to be an underlying strand in Kierkegaard's thought. The term derives from the theology of Dionysius the Areopagite, where apophatic theology—that is, the negation of all positive terms predicated of God—constitutes the second moment in the human being's progression towards knowledge of God. Following Dionysius' usage, we here employ the term to designate those elements of Kierkegaard's thought which emphasize the inadequacy and incapacity of human thought, knowledge, and language to grasp the reality of God; the hiddenness and incomprehensibility of God; and the mystery of the Incarnation. The bulk of this work will be concerned with ascertaining to what extent, if any, such 'apophatic motifs' are present in Kierkegaard's pseudonymous works.

This work falls into five parts. First, we deal in this introductory chapter with the historical background to Kierkegaard's apophaticism. This will involve an examination of the nature of

[1] Although Kierkegaard does not himself employ the term 'apophaticism' he does make use of what at first sight seems to be a related term, namely 'negativity'. This term bears some resemblance to 'apophaticism' but should not be regarded as a simple synonym. Kierkegaard employs it to describe that which breaks up directness, immediacy, and immanence. Thus in perception, for example, negativity is the intrinsic uncertainty and unreliability of the information provided to us by our senses. A *positive* result, in this case an act of perception on the basis of which knowledge can be constructed, can only come about by passing through and overcoming this negativity (*CUP* 38, cf. 74–8).

negative theology and a consideration of Kierkegaard's knowledge
of negative theology and negative theologians.

The second part, which comprises Chapter 2 only, consists of an
analysis of the methodological foundations of Kierkegaard's
thought. Here we attempt to show that apophaticism is an implicit
factor in his 'qualitative' or 'existential dialectics'.

The third section comprises Chapters 3–5. This deals with what
we might describe as the *anthropological* basis of Kierkegaard's
apophaticism. That is, an examination is undertaken of those
elements in human existence which preclude the human being from
establishing a direct and immediate relationship with God. In
Chapters 3 and 4 we will ascertain that objective knowledge and
truth are unattainable for the human being and that the subjective
forms he or she constructs in their place are always threatened by
uncertainty. Chapter 5 will deal with Kierkegaard's theory of stages
or spheres of existence and will show that we only make progress in
our God-relationship when we realize the depth of the gulf that
separates us from him. All these factors impose a fundamental
limitation on the human being which makes impossible a direct
and objective relationship with God. Indeed, our discussion of
religiousness A and B in Chapter 5 will reveal that it is only when he
accepts this limitation and the hiddenness of God it entails that the
human being can come to establish a relationship with God.

The fourth part of our investigation comprises Chapters 6 and 7.
Here we are concerned with the *theological* basis of Kierkegaard's
apophaticism. This will involve an analysis of Kierkegaard's
understanding of God and his Christology. The attempt is made to
show that Kierkegaard develops a theology in which God remains
hidden both before *and* after his revelation of himself in the
Incarnation.

Finally, in Chapter 8 the results of our analysis of the apophatic
motifs in Kierkegaard's thought will be compared and contrasted
with the thought of the negative theologians and an answer given to
our question: is Kierkegaard a negative theologian?[2]

---

[2] By no means do we claim that this concluding chapter is a definitive discussion of
the relation between Kierkegaard and the negative theologians. The main aim of this
work is to show that the principles of negative theology can be detected in
Kierkegaard's thought. Consequently, our comparison of Kierkegaard with the
negative theologians is general rather than specific, and scope exists for a *detailed*
examination of Kierkegaard's position in relation to the thought of individual
negative theologians.

Before we can embark upon a detailed discussion of the apophatic elements of Kierkegaard's thought, however, there are certain preliminary issues that must be dealt with. These concern the methodology to be employed in our investigation and problems concerning the interpretation of Kierkegaard's works. Once we have dealt with these issues we devote the remainder of this chapter to a discussion of the nature of negative theology and consider to what degree Kierkegaard was aware of and influenced by it.

I. METHODOLOGY

There are many different ways of interpreting Kierkegaard's works. Aage Henriksen[3] cites three methods:

(i) *The literary method.* This concentrates on the literary form of Kierkegaard's works.

(ii) *The content method.* This is based on an examination of the thoughts and ideas contained in the works. This method falls into two parts. Either the works are treated as part of a totality. Or they are treated as the products of Kierkegaard's spiritual development.

(iii) *The psychological method.* This aims at explaining Kierkegaard's works on the basis of his personality.

In his book, *Kierkegaard's Pseudonymous Authorship*, Mark Taylor also cites three methods for dealing with Kierkegaard's thought:

(i) *The biographical-psychological method.*[4] This corresponds to Henriksen's psychological method.

(ii) *The historical-comparative method.*[5] This attempts to establish Kierkegaard's place in the history of theology and philosophy by comparing him with other thinkers.

(iii) *The descriptive-thematic method.*[6] This method interprets Kierkegaard's thought on its own terms. Taylor divides this method into two. The first division, 'descriptive studies', attempts to describe the content of Kierkegaard's works. The second division, 'thematic

---

[3] A. Henriksen, *Methods and Results of Kierkegaard Studies in Scandinavia* (Copenhagen, 1951), 11.

[4] M. C. Taylor, *Kierkegaard's Pseudonymous Authorship: A Study of Time and the Self* (Princeton, NJ, 1975), 27–8.

[5] Taylor, *Kierkegaard's Pseudonymous Authorship*, 30–3.

[6] Ibid. 34–6.

studies', attempts to isolate and interpret a particular concept or theme present in Kierkegaard's thought.

In the bulk of this study we will employ the descriptive-thematic method. By means of a detailed examination of the text we shall attempt to draw out the apophatic strand underlying Kierkegaard's thought. Only in the final chapter will we switch to the historical-comparative method and attempt to show how Kierkegaard's apophaticism can be interpreted in terms of negative theology.

II. PROBLEMS CONCERNING THE INTERPRETATION OF KIERKEGAARD'S THOUGHT

Every Kierkegaard interpreter has to resolve three problems before he can embark upon an analysis of Kierkegaard's thought. First, he must answer the question of whether it is at all valid to engage in an interpretation of Kierkegaard's work. Secondly, he must resolve the much-debated question of the relationship between Kierkegaard and his pseudonyms as well as the relationship between the pseudonymous works themselves.[7] Thirdly, he must establish to what degree a systematic plan or structure underlies Kierkegaard's philosophy.

Is an investigation of the kind to be undertaken in this book or, indeed, any investigation of Kierkegaard's work, valid? In Kierkegaard's opinion the answer is 'no'. He ends the *Concluding Unscientific Postscript* with the words, 'And, oh, that no half-learned man would lay a dialectic hand upon this work, but would let it stand as it now stands!'[8] The reason for this, as will become clear in our discussion of indirect communication in Chapter 2, is that Kierkegaard wishes to communicate existential truths. The danger facing the interpreter is that of taking these truths and translating them into a series of objective propositions. Thereby the dialectical tension of the works, whereby the reader is confronted with questions to which he must make a personal, existential

---

[7] Because we have limited our discussion to the apophaticism of Kierkegaard's *pseudonymous* authorship, we shall leave out of consideration the difficult question of the relationship between Kierkegaard's pseudonymous and non-pseudonymous works.

[8] *CUP* 554.

response, is eliminated and replaced with a simple communication of information. On this basis, then, the only valid interpretation of Kierkegaard's works would seem to be that which adopts his own techniques of indirect communication and pseudonymous publication!

However, although Kierkegaard may have been averse to analyses of the kind to be undertaken in this book, he has, in my opinion, no right to dictate or predetermine the work of the interpreter of his thought. It is the legitimate task of the interpreter of any author to attempt to uncover the fundamental presuppositions upon which a work is based. Due to the deliberate opaqueness of much of Kierkegaard's work this is perhaps more necessary in his case than it is with many other authors. For this reason we feel justified in examining Kierkegaard's works in a direct manner and in occasionally employing non-Kierkegaardian terms as a means of throwing light upon the deeper structures of his thought.

What is the relation between Kierkegaard and his pseudonyms? Should we treat Kierkegaard's works as representative of his own position or merely of that of the fictitious characters that populate his works? This is one of the most disputed questions in Kierkegaard scholarship and we cannot possibly do justice to it here. The position taken in this study falls into two parts. First, although Kierkegaard may not personally occupy the positions advocated in his works, they nevertheless form an integral part of his thought. In this sense we can ascribe them to him even if he himself has rejected them as possibilities for his own existence. Secondly, it is to a certain degree irrelevant whether Kierkegaard himself subscribed to the positions described in his works. It is not the personality of the man that is important—although this can of course shed light on his thought—but the philosophy he has developed and whether this stands up to scrutiny.

The third question is: to what degree is Kierkegaard systematic? It is important to resolve this question, since if Kierkegaard is unsystematic, then a systematic interpretation of his works would seem necessarily to result in a distortion of his position. There are three positions among Kierkegaard scholars on this issue. First, there are those who argue that Kierkegaard is intentionally unsystematic and that it is therefore an error to attempt to draw out the philosophical principles that underlie his thought. To these belong Torsten Bohlin[9] and Josiah Thompson, the latter of whom argues that Kierkegaard's works demonstrate 'not the adequacy of a new philosophy but the nullity of all philosophy'.[10]

Secondly, there are those who argue that Kierkegaard confronts us not with a system but with a method or procedure. To these belong Hermann Diem,[11] Regis Jolivet,[12] and Gregor Malantschuk.[13] These all understand the coherence and unity of Kierkegaard's works to be, as Jolivet puts it, that of 'a unity of movement, like the continuity of flight or, better still, of an organic growth whose stages are marked by crises which are at once necessary and unpredictable'.[14] Louis Pojman makes a similar point in his assertion that Kierkegaard's interests are not theoretical but practical. Kierkegaard is concerned 'to help men and women *exist*, not learn to speculate on "existence"'.[15] Amongst these scholars we might also include Wilhelm Anz, who argues that Kierkegaard writes 'epigrammatically'. That is, Kierkegaard expresses various experiences in brief formulae which acquire their meaning not through a methodologically established conceptual language but through their practical use.[16]

Thirdly, there are those scholars who attribute a higher degree of systematization to Kierkegaard. Thus George Price believes that 'the authorship has the unity of a pattern imposed upon it from the beginning', in which each work has its proper place.[17] Similarly, Johannes Sløk holds that Kierkegaard's works are held together as a coherent whole by his examination from every conceivable angle of the problem of how the human being is to live a genuine existence.[18]

---

[9] Cited in Taylor, *Kierkegaard's Pseudonymous Authorship*, 22.

[10] J. Thompson, 'The Master of Irony', in J. Thompson (ed.), *Kierkegaard: A Collection of Critical Essays* (New York, 1972), 113, 163.

[11] H. Diem, *Kierkegaard's Dialectic of Existence*, trans. H. Knight (Edinburgh, 1959), 4.

[12] R. Jolivet, *Introduction to Kierkegaard*, trans. W. H. Barber (London, 1950), 93.

[13] G. Malantschuk, *Kierkegaard's Thought*, ed. and trans. H. V. and E. H. Hong (Princeton, NJ, 1971), 359.

[14] Jolivet, *Introduction*, 111; cf. Malantschuk, *Kierkegaard's Thought*, 359.

[15] L. P. Pojman, *The Logic of Subjectivity: Kierkegaard's Philosophy of Religion* (Tuscaloosa, Ala., 1984), 23 (original emphasis).

[16] W. Anz, *Kierkegaard und der deutsche Idealismus* (Tübingen, 1956), 6.

[17] G. Price, *The Narrow Pass: A Study of Kierkegaard's Concept of Man* (London, 1963), 26, cf. 31–2.

[18] J. Sløk, *Die Anthropologie Kierkegaards* (Copenhagen, 1954), 13.

Dunning, on the other hand, believes that 'it is the inner/outer relation that provides an Ariadne's thread, enabling the interpreter to find a coherent statement in the pseudonymous texts as a whole.'[19] Paul Sponheim is another scholar who argues that Kierkegaard is far more systematic than many are prepared to give him credit for. He argues that Kierkegaard's work is dominated by a dialectic between 'diastasis', i.e. the separation of God and the human being, and 'synthesis', i.e. the bringing together of God and the human being.[20] Finally, we might also include Mark Taylor in this group. He sees in Kierkegaard's thought 'a basic vision of the nature of the self and of what it means to attain authentic selfhood', and detects 'a singular intention of the authorship . . . to lead the reader to actualize genuine selfhood in his personal existence'.[21] Taylor, however, emphasizes that this unity should be described only as 'coherence' and not as 'systematization'.[22]

The view taken in this study is very similar to Taylor's. In my opinion Kierkegaard is *not* systematic if this is understood in the Hegelian sense of attempting to incorporate every dimension of human existence into a philosophical system. However, if it is taken to mean philosophical coherence and consistency, we believe that the term 'systematic' can be legitimately applied to Kierkegaard. In Kierkegaard's case, of course, the philosophy in question is a philosophy of existence. To be coherent and consistent here means leaving unresolved questions and unfilled gaps in one's 'system'. Although this may create the impression of inconsistency and incoherence, it is in fact the expression of a truly coherent system, since it takes existence together with its contingency and finitude seriously.

In view of this basic coherence and consistency in Kierkegaard's works, we believe that it is legitimate to embark upon an attempt to give a coherent and consistent account of his thought. In addition to this, two other arguments for a systematic account of Kierkegaard's thought can be cited. First, as Walter Schulz points out, 'a systematic interpretation must be undertaken if a discussion of Kierkegaard's works as a whole is to succeed, since it is only by means of a unifying

[19] S. N. Dunning, *Kierkegaard's Dialectic of Inwardness* (Princeton, NJ, 1985), 3.
[20] P. Sponheim, *Kierkegaard on Christ and Christian Coherence* (Westport, Conn., 1968), 9 and *passim*.
[21] Taylor, *Kierkegaard's Pseudonymous Authorship*, 23.   [22] Ibid. 22–3.

interpretation that the historical significance of Kierkegaard's work can be grasped.'[23] Secondly, as Mark Taylor remarks,

Given the nature and the intention of the pseudonymous writings, we would be delinquent if we only allowed Kierkegaard to speak, and ourselves remained listeners. To be sure, we must listen to his pseudonyms. But it is also our responsibility to speak—to respond to Kierkegaard. We must offer our contribution to his Socratic dialogue. Quite naturally this involves a risk, the risk of misunderstanding and of being misunderstood. But not to respond is a greater risk and a deeper misunderstanding of Kierkegaard's writings.[24]

In what follows we will attempt a systematic elucidation of Kierkegaard's thought with reference to the theme of apophaticism. We hope that what emerges, although running the risk of misunderstanding and error, may make some contribution to our comprehension of this difficult thinker.

III. THE NATURE OF NEGATIVE THEOLOGY

We now wish to embark upon a brief survey of a selection of negative theologians in order to ascertain the nature of negative theology. Thereby a basis will be provided for the consideration of our question: can Kierkegaard be understood as a negative theologian?

An exhaustive survey of the whole of negative theology is, of course, not possible here. For this reason we shall restrict our discussion to a small selection of Christian negative theologians. We have selected Clement of Alexandria, Dionysius the Areopagite, and Meister Eckhart, although reference will also be made to other theologians where relevant.

1. *Clement of Alexandria*

For Clement of Alexandria, God is utterly transcendent. He is 'the absolutely first and oldest principle',[25] and is 'above both space, and

---

[23] W. Schulz, 'Søren Kierkegaard: Existenz und System', in H.-H. Schrey (ed.), *Søren Kierkegaard* (Darmstadt, 1971), 298.

[24] Taylor, *Kierkegaard's Pseudonymous Authorship*, 343.

[25] *Str.* v. 81. 4 (ii. 269). References to Clement of Alexandria consist of two sets of numbers. The first set refers to Otto Stählin's Greek edition of Clement's works:

time, and name, and conception'.[26] He is formless,[27] invisible,[28] and 'incapable of being circumscribed'.[29] Because God is so utterly transcendent, he is 'not a subject for demonstration, [and] cannot be the object of science',[30] for 'the science of demonstration . . . depends on primary and better known principles. But there is nothing antecedent to the Unbegotten.'[31] God is, therefore, 'a Being difficult to grasp and apprehend, ever receding and withdrawing from him who pursues'.[32]

The consequence of this is that human language is incapable of expressing anything essential about God. 'Human speech', Clement writes, 'is by nature feeble, and incapable of uttering God'.[33] Consequently, 'God is not capable of being taught by man, or expressed in speech',[34] but is 'above all speech, all conception, all thought, [and] can never be committed to writing'.[35]

Does this mean that we are condemned to silence? On one level this is indeed the case, for, as we have seen, human concepts are incapable of grasping the transcendent God. On another level, however, it is possible to speak intelligibly and meaningfully of God, provided that this discourse is always conditioned by the limitations imposed by God's transcendence. That is, we can legitimately apply positive terms to God as long as we are aware that these do not express the divine essence but are merely aids to the human understanding.

And if we name it, we do not do so properly, terming it either the One, or the Good, or Mind, or Absolute Being, or Father, or God, or Creator, or Lord. We speak not as supplying his name; but for want, we use good names, in order that the mind may have these as points of support, so as not to err in

---

Clemens Alexandrinus, ed. O. Stählin (Die griechischen christlichen Schriftsteller der ersten drei Jahrhunderte), i (2nd edn., Leipzig, 1936), ii (3rd edn., Berlin, 1960), iii (Leipzig, 1909). The second set, which is in parentheses, refers to the *Ante-Nicene Christian Library* translation, from which the quotations are taken: *The Writings of Clement of Alexandria*, i–ii, trans. W. Wilson, Ante-Nicene Christian Library (Edinburgh, 1867–89).

26 *Str.* v. 71. 5 (ii. 264); cf. ii. 6. 1 (ii. 4); *Paed.* i. 71. 1 (i. 161).
27 *Str.* v. 71. 4 (ii. 264); v. 81. 6 (ii. 270).
28 *Str.* v. 74. 4 (ii. 265); v. 78. 3 (ii. 267).
29 *Str.* v. 74. 4 (ii. 265); cf. v. 81. 5 (ii. 270); ii. 81. 1 (ii. 48); iv. 151. 2 (ii. 210).
30 *Str.* iv. 156. 1 (ii. 212). 31 *Str.* v. 82. 3 (ii. 270).
32 *Str.* ii. 5. 3 (ii. 4). 33 *Str.* vi. 166. 1 (ii. 404).
34 *Str.* v. 71. 5 (ii. 264); cf. v. 78. 3 (ii. 267); v. 79. 1 (ii. 268).
35 *Str.* v. 65. 2 (ii. 260); cf. v. 79. 1 (ii. 268).

other respects. For each one by itself does not express God; but all together
are indicative of the power of the Omnipotent.[36]

Clement permits positive or 'cataphatic' theology, then, but only as
a concession to human incapacity. This, however, is only the first
step on the way to knowledge of the Divine.[37] If we wish to make
progress in our spiritual quest, we must go on to 'perceive spiritual
things'.[38] To achieve this, we must strip away this positive
terminology in order to get closer to the underlying divine mystery.
To achieve this, Clement develops a form of negative theology.

Clement's negative theology is made up of two movements. The
first movement is only partially apophatic.[39] It consists in sweeping
away accidental, non-essential elements accruing to our concept of
God. This takes place in two stages. First, there is what he describes
as 'the mode of purification by confession'.[40] That is, the human
being confesses his inability to progress towards the goal of his
epistemological quest, namely, the transcendent God, by means of
his own powers and acknowledges the absolute primacy of this
goal.

This sets the scene for the second stage in Clement's religious
epistemology, namely, an 'analysis' whereby the individual strips
away the qualities and attributes that have been predicated of
God.[41] This process of eliminating cataphatic terminology enables
the individual to see 'face to face, by those sole pure and incorporeal
applications of the intellect'.[42] 'Analysis', then, enables the intellect
to develop a purer concept of God that is stripped of material and
non-essential accretions.

Although an advance on cataphatic knowledge, this purified
knowledge is not the final step in the human being's epistemological
quest. If he wishes to progress further, however, this cannot be on
the basis of his own powers. These he has exhausted in the process
of analysis. If he is to make further progress he therefore needs
divine assistance,[43] which God provides by graciously sending his
Son. As Clement puts it, 'It remains that we understand, then, the

---

[36] *Str.* v. 82. 1–2 (ii. 270).   [37] See *Str.* v. 73. 1 (ii. 264).
[38] *Str.* v. 73. 2 (ii. 265).
[39] The terms 'apophatic' and 'cataphatic' are, as far as I have been able to ascertain,
not employed by Clement. Because they so adequately describe Clement's position,
however, we will apply them to his thought when appropriate.
[40] *Str.* v. 71. 2 (ii. 263).   [41] *Str.* v. 71. 2–3 (ii. 263).
[42] *Str.* v. 74. 1 (ii. 265); cf. v. 74. 2 (ii. 265).   [43] See, e.g., *Str.* v. 71. 5 (ii. 264).

Unknown, by divine grace, and by the word alone that proceeds from him'.[44] God's sending of his Son has two important results for the individual's progress towards knowledge of the Divine.

Firstly, it halts the process of analysis by which the human intellect progressed towards a purer concept of God. Thus instead of revealing God, it reveals to us what God is not. As Clement puts it,

If, then, abstracting all that belongs to bodies and things called incorporeal, we cast ourselves into the greatness of Christ, and thence advance into immensity by holiness, we may reach somehow to the conception of the Almighty, knowing not what he is, but what he is not.[45]

God's revelation in Christ thus shows to the human being that the knowledge acquired through analysis is not knowledge of God.

Secondly, at the same time as showing the inadequacy of human knowledge, Christ nevertheless opens up the possibility of knowing God. This is because as the Son of God he is an expression of the Godhead. He is 'the first principle of all things',[46] Clement writes, and is 'the true Only-begotten'.[47] He 'was imaged forth from the invisible God first, and before the ages',[48] and participated in the creative act through which God brought the universe into being.[49] Consequently, Christ is the 'image of God . . . the genuine Son of Mind, the Divine Word, the archetypal light of light'.[50]

Because he is the Divine Word and the image of God, the incarnate Christ is able to act as a mediator between God and humankind, and provides the human being with knowledge of God. He is, as Clement puts it, the great High Priest through whom we have converse with God[51] and humanity's guide, instructor, and teacher.[52] Christ is able to perform this task of mediation because, in contrast to the Father, he is 'susceptible of demonstration and of description'.[53] Consequently, he is the means whereby the human being comes to know God or, as Clement puts it, 'The face of God is the Word by whom God is manifested and made known.'[54]

---

[44] *Str.* v. 82. 4 (ii. 270); cf. v. 71. 5 (ii. 264); vi. 166. 3 (ii. 404).

[45] *Str.* v. 71. 3 (ii. 264).   [46] *Str.* v. 38. 7 (ii. 244).

[47] *Str.* vii. 16. 6 (ii. 417).   [48] *Str.* v. 38. 7 (ii. 244).

[49] Ibid.   [50] *Protr.* x. 98. 4 (i. 91).   [51] *Str.* vii. 13. 2 (ii. 415).

[52] *Str.* v. 1. 3 (ii. 220); *Paed.* i. 55. 2 (i. 151); i. 56–8 (i. 151–2); *Str.* v. 7. 8 (ii. 224); iv. 162. 5 (ii. 215); v. 1. 4 (ii. 220); vi. 122. 1 (ii. 375); v. 85. 2 (ii. 272). His pre-incarnate instruction consisted in giving philosophy to the Greeks (*Str.* vii. 6. 4 (ii. 410) and speaking to Israel through Moses and the prophets (*Paed.* i. 56. 2–1. 60. 1 (i. 151–3)).

[53] *Str.* iv. 156. 1 (ii. 212).   [54] *Paed.* i. 57. 2 (i. 152); cf. *Str.* v. 73. 2 (ii. 265).

For Clement, then, Christ's mission is double-sided. On the one hand, he brings human attempts at acquiring knowledge of God to a standstill. Christ halts the process of analysis, thereby removing the knowledge of God which the human being believes he possesses or, more precisely, showing that human knowledge of God is not knowledge of what God is but of what he is not. On the other hand, because he himself is the expression or 'face' of God, Christ both is and provides knowledge of God. He alone, then, is the means whereby the human being comes to know God.

The ultimate goal of the knowledge or 'gnosis' imparted by and through Christ is to bring about the most intimate possible relationship with God. This is, of course, something that is never fully achieved in this life. Nevertheless, by means of the gnosis imparted to him by Christ, the true believer or 'gnostic', as Clement prefers to describe him, is able to gain glimpses of the Divine Mystery and to progress as far as is possible in this life towards knowledge of the Divine. Clement describes the gnostic's relationship with God in two ways.

(a) The Divine Vision

Christ and the gnosis he brings enables the gnostic to leave behind the material world and to penetrate through to the abode of the Divine. Clement speaks of the gnostic 'cleav[ing] the heaven by knowledge . . . passing through the spiritual Essences . . . [where] he touches the highest thrones'.[55] This is brought about by the gnostic's attachment to Christ. 'And this takes place', Clement writes, 'whenever one hangs on the Lord by faith, by knowledge, by love, and ascends along with him to where the God and guard of our faith and love is.'[56] The ultimate goal of this ascent is 'to gaze on God, face to face, with knowledge and comprehension'.[57]

(b) Deification

Clement speaks not only of the gnostic enjoying the beatific vision of God, but also of his deification. This deification comes about through the person and teaching of Christ. It is the consequence of the gnostic's being stamped with Christ's image or, as Clement puts

---

[55] *Str.* vii. 82. 5 (ii. 467); cf. v. 83. 1 (ii. 271).   [56] *Str.* vii. 56. 1 (ii. 447).
[57] *Str.* vii. 57. 1 (ii. 447); cf. vii. 13. 1 (ii. 415); vi. 102. 23 (ii. 363).

it: 'Let us listen to the Word and take on the impress of the truly saving life of our Saviour, henceforward cultivating the heavenly citizenship in accordance with which we are being deified.'[58] The result of being impressed with Christ's image is that 'there is now a third divine image, made as far as possible like the Second Cause, the Essential Life, through which we live the true life'.[59] This third divine image is the gnostic, who, divinized through Christ's salvific work, is 'destined to sit on thrones with the other gods that have been first put in their places by the Saviour'.[60]

2. Dionysius the Areopagite

Like Clement, Dionysius emphasizes the transcendence of God. First, God is the 'Super-Essential Godhead' (*huperousios thearchia*) or simply 'the Super-Essential' (*huperousia*).[61] That is, God is not at the apex of a hierarchy of being but transcends this hierarchy altogether.[62] Secondly, God is 'the One'. This term expresses God's transcendence by making clear that God is not subject to the plurality common to existent beings. Furthermore, it is a Oneness which encompasses both plurality *and* oneness. If this were not the case, Dionysius argues, then to describe God as the One would be to impose a limit upon him by distinguishing him from plurality. God's oneness, then, is something that utterly transcends our conception of it.

---

[58] *Paed.* i. 98. 3. This translation is taken from J. Patrick, *Clement of Alexandria* (Edinburgh, 1914), 116, which in this instance is more adequate than that of the *Ante-Nicene Library*, i. 181; cf. vi. 114. 5–6 (ii. 371).

[59] *Str.* vii. 16. 6 (ii. 417).

[60] *Str.* vii. 56. 6 (ii. 447); vii. 82. 2 (ii. 467); *Prot.* i. 8. 4 (i. 24). The gnosis Christ imparts, however, is not available to all human beings (*Str.* v. 35. 5 (ii. 242); v. 80. 3 (ii. 268); vi. 116. 1 (ii. 372); vi. 129. 4 (ii. 380)) but only to those who are worthy of it (*Str.* vii. 55. 6 (ii. 446)).

[61] There is some disagreement amongst scholars as to how these terms are best to be translated into English. Rutledge opts for 'Divinity' or 'Deity': D. Rutledge, *Cosmic Theology—The Ecclesiastical Hierarchy of Pseudo-Denys: An Introduction* (London, 1964), p. x. The problem with this is that it does not really express the idea of transcendence that is present in Dionysius' terminology. Stiglmayr's *Urgottheit* (cited in Rutledge, *Cosmic Theology*, p. x) is in my opinion a far more adequate translation because it expresses the idea of primary source or origin that is present in the term *thearchia*. The best English translation, although rather cumbersome, is in my opinion Rolt's 'Super-Essential Godhead'. The advantage of this is that it makes clear the utter transcendence of God. It is this term that we will employ here.

[62] *Dionysius the Areopagite: The Divine Names and the Mystical Theology*, trans. and intro. C. E. Rolt (London, 1940), 4.

The Super-Essential Godhead does not, however, remain in absolute transcendence but goes on to express itself immanently. This it does by *creating*. According to Dionysius, the various factors which are present in undifferentiated form in the Godhead are subject to the urge to *differentiate* themselves. That is, they are not content to remain submerged within the transcendent Godhead but desire to actualize themselves individually and concretely. Thus plurality, for example, is not prepared to remain submerged in God's transcendent Oneness but strives to differentiate or actualize itself, i.e. to realize itself as *plural*. To satisfy the urge for differentiation, the Godhead *creates*.[63]

To fulfil the creative urge two other undifferentiated categories are differentiated, namely, particularity and universality. In the Godhead itself these are continually welling up and falling back into the Godhead.[64] This continues until the point is reached where they both merge into each other. This 'merging' of particularity and universality results in the creation of the universe.[65]

This act of creation manifests itself on many different levels. The first level is the fusion of particularity with the most universal of all universals, namely, being. This fusion posits the existence of the universe as a whole. Higher forms of being are then created through the further addition of universals to the primary synthesis. There thus occurs a progression in which life is added to primary being, consciousness to life, rationality to consciousness, and so on.[66]

This ever greater differentiation of the elements contained in the Super-Essential results in the positing of a hierarchy of being. At the top is the 'Celestial hierarchy', i.e. the angels. Then comes the human being in the 'ecclesiastical hierarchy', and below him the animal and plant world.

Dionysius also describes the act of creation 'in terms of light, of light manifesting itself in varying degrees of concentration and brilliance'.[67] God expresses himself by giving being to creatures in much the same way as a light can express itself at different levels of brightness. The brightest manifestation of the light occurs in those beings which stand closest to the source of the light. Each manifestation of the light then passes the light down through itself to lower forms of being.

[63] Ibid. 6.   [64] Ibid. 12.   [65] Ibid. 17–18.   [66] Ibid. 25.
[67] Rutledge, *Cosmic Theology*, 10.

It [the Godhead] bestows the gift of its own light on the most senior beings and, because of their premier rank, it uses them as intermediaries to pass that same light harmoniously along to beings of lower order in a way which is adapted to the capacity of each rank to look upon the divine.[68]

At each stage the light is modified according to the ability of the recipient to receive it. As the light filters down the scale of being, the matter in which it manifests itself becomes increasingly 'opaque' and less suitable for its manifestation.[69] The result of this is that the divine light becomes 'dimmer' or less evident at each descent in the hierarchy of being.

The act of creation has two important results for our discussion. First, it posits a dialectic within the Godhead between what Rolt calls 'the Ultimate Reality' and 'the Manifested Appearance' of God.[70] On the one hand, there is that aspect of the Godhead which expresses itself in relation to Creation. On the other hand, the Super-Essential side of the Godhead still remains intact and continues to occupy its pre-creational state of absolute transcendence. As Macquarrie puts it: 'God has two aspects. There is the aspect that is turned towards us and that manifests itself in creation, time and history. But there is also, as it were, the "far side" of God, God as he is in himself, incomprehensible to our minds.'[71] The outward-looking aspect of the Godhead manifests itself above all in the Trinity. Again, like the Absolute Godhead itself, the Trinity has two aspects. The first aspect is that which faces the Absolute Godhead. Here the distinctness between the Trinitarian Persons disappears in the Super-Essential unity of undifferentiated Godhead. The second aspect of the Trinity is that which is turned towards the created world. Here the Persons of the Trinity manifest themselves in differentiated form, although they still retain undifferentiation. Their undifferentiation manifests itself in the creative energy that proceeds indivisibly from all of them. As differentiated Persons, however, they are responsible for splitting this creative energy into its component parts.[72]

The second important result of the act of creation is that, like God, creatures have two sides. On the one hand, there is the fact that they

---

[68] Dionysius, CH xiii. 3 (301A); cf. DN iv. 1 (693B). All translations are taken from Pseudo-Dionysius: The Complete Works, Classics of Western Spirituality, trans. C. Luibheid (London, 1987).

[69] CH xiii. 3 (301A–301B).   [70] Rolt, Dionysius the Areopagite, 7.

[71] J. Macquarrie, In Search of Deity: An Essay in Dialectical Theism (London, 1984), 80.

[72] Rolt, Dionysius the Areopagite, 17.

flow from and are themselves expressions of the Super-Essential. On the other hand, there is the fact that they are distanced from the source of the Super-Essential. There thus arises a dialectic between the Super-Essential in its true form and its expression in existent beings. To return to Dionysius' light metaphor, we could say that there is a dialectic between the divine light's true brightness and its brightness in the creature. It is the goal of all creatures to close the distance between their expression of the Super-Essential and the Super-Essential itself.[73]

The task of theology is to allow the human being to overcome the distance that exists between him and the Super-Essential Godhead. Dionysius sees this as coming about in three movements, namely cataphatic theology, apophatic theology, and mystical theology.

(a) Cataphatic Theology

This form of theology is the subject of *The Divine Names* and, so Dionysius tells us, his now lost *Theological Representations*.[74] It is concerned with examining positive descriptions and affirmations about God and developing a concept of God on their basis. There seem to be three forms of cataphatic theology. First, there is the form that is based on the application of the deductive method to the term 'God'. The theologian begins with the highest concept, i.e. God, and by means of deduction, establishes an exhaustive analysis of the permutations of this concept. Dionysius describes this method as a 'descent': 'In the earlier books[75] my argument travelled downward from the most exalted to the humblest categories, taking in on this downward path an ever-increasing number of ideas which multiplied with every stage of the descent.'[76] Secondly, cataphatic theology can construct a concept of God based on terms drawn from everyday experience.

We cannot know God in his nature, since this is unknowable and is beyond the reach of mind or of reason. But we know him from the arrangement of everything, because everything is, in a sense, projected out from him, and this order possesses certain images and semblances of his divine paradigms.[77]

---

[73] *DN* iv. 4 (700A–700B).   [74] *MT* iii (1032D–1033A).
[75] That is, *The Divine Names*, *The Theological Representations*, and *The Symbolic Theology*. The latter two have not survived.
[76] *MT* iii (1033C), cf. ii (1025B).   [77] *DN* vii. 3 (869C–869D).

We can know God, then, in the things in which he manifests himself.

Thirdly, we can know God on the basis of what he has revealed of himself in the Bible.[78]

Dionysius regards cataphatic theology as necessary to set us on the road towards the comprehension of God. However, it only gives us a comprehension of the 'manifested appearance' of God, i.e. that side of God which is turned towards us. The 'far side' of God, the Super-Essential Godhead, remains concealed.

(b) Apophatic Theology

This form of theology is the subject of Dionysius' little work entitled *The Mystical Theology*. Unlike cataphatic theology, apophatic theology is aimed not at the Godhead's appearance in creation but at the ultimate reality that lies behind it. Indeed, the goal of apophatic theology is to bring the human being into union with the Super-Essential Godhead. Consequently, it does not aim to establish an objective definition of God by means of 'descent' but attempts to trace the terms and concepts we have back to their source in the Super-Essential. Dionysius describes this process as an 'ascent': 'But my argument now rises from what is below up to the transcendent, and the more it climbs, the more language falters, and when it has passed up and beyond the ascent, it will turn silent completely, since it will finally be at one with him who is indescribable.'[79] The means by which this 'ascent' is achieved is the negation of those positive terms which provided us with our initial conception of God. In the fifth chapter of *The Mystical Theology* Dionysius provides a comprehensive list of such negations. As Hella Theill-Wunder points out,[80] these fall into three groups. First, Dionysius negates concepts drawn from the physical world. He sets up polar concepts such as greatness and smallness and rejects their applicability to God. Secondly, Dionysius rejects terms which are based on or related to the concept of being. Terms such as being and non-being, eternity and time, etc., are rejected as inadequate descriptions of the Super-Essential. Thirdly, Dionysius negates traditional descriptions of God such as power, wisdom, and divinity. Again, these terms are simply not capable of grasping the transcendent mystery that is God.

---

[78] *DN* i. 2 (588C–589A).   [79] *MT* iii (1033C), cf. ii (1025B).
[80] H. Theill-Wunder, *Die archaische Verborgenheit* (Munich, 1970), 149–53.

(c) Mystical Theology

Now Dionysius' wholesale negation of these terms might seem to be wholly destructive. It might appear as if it involved abandoning God altogether. This, however, is not the case. On the contrary, negation is precisely the means by which the human being comes into union with God and returns to the Super-Essential source from which he emerged. There are two reasons for this. First, negation functions very much like a sculptor at work on a block of marble. It sweeps away external material in order to reveal the hidden form beneath.[81] Secondly, it moulds our souls into the form necessary for true knowledge of God, namely 'silence and unknowing'.[82] In this state of unknowing, the barriers between the soul and God are broken down. By putting aside language and thought, the self grasps, by a means that it is impossible to articulate, a glimpse into the mystery that is God. In this mystic state of 'unknowing', it has achieved true knowledge. It has discovered that there is ultimately no distinction between itself and the Super-Essential Godhead. With this the individual has transcended himself and come into union with God.

3. *Meister Eckhart*

As was the case with Clement and Dionysius, Meister Eckhart places considerable weight on God's transcendence. He describes this transcendence in a number of different ways. First, 'God is something that necessarily transcends being.'[83] Being, Eckhart argues, is limited by time and space.[84] 'God', however, 'works beyond being, in breadth, where he can move, and he works in non-being: before there was being, God was working.'[85] Consequently, 'if I say that God is a being, that is not true: he is a transcendent being, and a superessential nothingness.'[86] God, then,

---

[81] *MT* ii (1025A–1025B).   [82] See *MT* iii (1033B).

[83] *Meister Eckhart: Sermons and Treatises*, i–ii, tr. and ed. M. O'C. Walshe (Shaftesbury, Dorset, 1979), ii. 67. 149. The first Arabic numeral refers to the sermon, the second to the page number. Not all of Eckhart's sermons are contained in Walshe. For this reason reference will sometimes be made to: *Meister Eckhart: The Essential Sermons, Commentaries, Treatises, and Defense*, Classics of Western Spirituality, trans. and intro. E. Colledge and B. McGinn (London, 1981). It should be noted that Walshe numbers the sermons differently from Colledge and McGinn.

[84] *Eckhart: Sermons*, trans. Walshe, ii. 67. 149.   [85] Ibid. ii. 67. 150.

[86] Ibid. ii. 96. 332.

although the source of being and possessing being within himself, is far beyond being.

Secondly, God is *pure intellect*. This is Eckhart's primary description of God. In his opinion, intellect precedes being. Being is merely God's 'forecourt'.[87] 'Intellect', however, 'is the temple of God,'[88] i.e. the very fundament of God. As intellect God is most truly himself. He is completely self-sufficient, a 'silent desert' which communes only with itself.[89]

The Godhead does not remain enclosed in its transcendence, however, but emerges out of itself into the world. This it does by *creating*. The basic principle of this act of creation is God's knowing of himself. First, the Godhead knows itself in its own reflection, namely, its Word, Logos, or Son.[90] Secondly, it knows itself in the eternal ideas of the creatures.

Like Dionysius, Eckhart conceives of this creative process in terms of a procession from and a return to God. This procession[91] occurs in two stages. First, it occurs within the Godhead itself. Eckhart describes this as *bullitio*, literally 'boiling'. The Godhead is conceived as a dynamic, seething cauldron of pure divinity. It is this 'boiling' that results in the first procession, namely, the emanation of the Trinitarian Persons.[92] This 'boiling' continues within the Trinity itself and between the Trinity and the Absolute Godhead.

The second procession from the Godhead is described by Eckhart as *ebullitio*, literally 'a boiling over'. Here the idea seems to be that the dynamism of the Godhead is so great that it spills out of the cauldron, so to speak. It is this 'boiling' or 'spilling over' that results in the creation of the universe.

But creation does not only flow out from the Godhead, it also contains the urge to return to and become one with its source.[93] According to Eckhart, the soul possesses an element which corresponds to the intellect that is the temple of the Divine Essence.[94] This element, which Eckhart describes variously as a 'little spark' (*vünkelin*), 'little castle' (*bürgelin*), or as *synteresis*,[95]

[87] Ibid. ii. 67. 152.　　[88] Ibid.　　[89] Cf. ibid. ii. 58. 95.

[90] J. Quint, *Meister Eckhart: Deutsche Predigten und Traktate* (Munich, 1979), 24.

[91] *Eckhart: Sermons*, trans. Walshe, ii. 51. 87; *Eckhart: Essential Sermons*, trans. Colledge and McGinn, Sermons 22 and 53.

[92] *Eckhart: Sermons*, trans. Walshe, i. 33. 249.

[93] *Eckhart: Essential Sermons*, trans. Colledge and McGinn, Sermon 53, p. 205.

[94] Quint, *Meister Eckhart*, 25.

[95] See *Eckhart: Sermons*, trans. Walshe, i, Introduction, pp. xli–xlii.

can, if cultivated in the correct manner, bring the human being into union with God.[96]

To bring about the successful cultivation of the divine spark within the human being, everything that obscures or hinders it must be swept away. 'Union', Eckhart states, 'comes only by the joining of like to like.'[97] Only when God and the human being stand naked before each other, stripped of every attribute, can union come about. To achieve this two movements are necessary.

The first movement consists of the removal by the human being of those 'creaturely' elements he has acquired through his having come into existence. This involves 'detachment', a process of stripping away the external and non-essential elements of our personality such as moods and emotions, so that the spirit may come 'to stand as immovable against whatever may chance to it of joy and sorrow, honour, shame and disgrace, as a mountain of lead stands before a little breath of wind'.[98]

The second movement calls upon the human being to remove thought, ideas, and beliefs. The temple of the soul must be free of images, just as the eye must be free of colour if it is to see colour.[99] As Eckhart puts it, 'For God to be perceived by the soul, she must be blind.'[100] It is to achieve this intellectual and cognitive 'blindness' that Eckhart employs negative theology.

The first stage in acquiring knowledge of God is to establish certain positive terms and descriptions of him. In Sermon 53 Eckhart gives a list of such terms. These are granted to us, he asserts, in order that 'through these we should first learn how we ought to pray to God'.[101] Despite this, these terms are fundamentally inadequate and must be left behind if we are to make progress towards the Divine Ground in which we have our being. The reason for this inadequacy is that no term is capable of describing the transcendence that is God. In Eckhart's opinion, God is without name[102] and 'the brightness of the divine nature is beyond words'.[103] Indeed, Eckhart goes so far as to state that 'by chattering about [God] you are lying and so

[96] Quint, *Meister Eckhart*, 27.
[97] *Eckhart: Sermons*, trans. Walshe, i. 8. 72, cf. ii. 60. 103.
[98] *Eckhart: Essential Sermons*, trans. Colledge and McGinn, 'On Detachment', 288.
[99] *Eckhart: Sermons*, trans. Walshe, i. 19. 160.   [100] Ibid.
[101] *Eckhart: Essential Sermons*, trans. Colledge and McGinn, Sermon 53, p. 204.
[102] *Eckhart: Sermons*, trans. Walshe, ii. 51. 53; 96. 332.
[103] *Eckhart: Essential Sermons*, trans. Colledge and McGinn, Sermon 53, p. 203.

committing a sin'.[104] All predication of God is a distortion of what God truly is. Consequently, 'If you understand anything of him, that is not he, and by understanding anything of him you fall into misunderstanding.'[105] Such images are a necessary starting-point on our journey back to the Divine Source from which we originated, but if we are to reach our goal, they must be left behind, including the Trinity and even the term 'God' itself.[106]

The next stage in acquiring knowledge of God is thus to abandon cataphatic theology and progress towards an intuitive understanding of God which transcends both thought and language. To achieve this Eckhart employs two apophatic methods. First, he negates positive terms commonly applied to God. A striking example of this is to be found in Sermon 96. Here he writes:

> If I now say God is good, it is not true; rather, I am good, God is not good. I will go further and say I am better than God: for what is good can become better, and what can become better can become best of all. Now God is not good, therefore he cannot become better. And since he cannot become better, therefore he cannot become best; for these three, good, better and best, are remote from God, since he is above them all.[107]

By means of such negations, Eckhart hopes to push the reader beyond human conceptions of goodness to an intuitive understanding that transcends such conceptions.

Secondly, Eckhart employs paradox as a means of breaking down our dependence on images and concepts.[108] This involves setting up a concept that is diametrically opposed to the original positive term employed by cataphatic theology. In the oscillation between the two poles of the paradox, the human being is forced to go beyond both terms to a deeper understanding which both encompasses and transcends them. Paradox brings reason to its outermost boundaries and points beyond reason and conceptuality to that mysterious realm in which God dwells.

The human being who completes the two movements of detachment and negation has achieved the following four things.

He has penetrated through his external, non-essential self to his true self, 'the ground of the soul', in which the spark of the Divine Intellect dwells.

[104] *Eckhart: Sermons*, trans. Walshe, ii. 96. 333.   [105] Ibid.
[106] Ibid. ii. 96. 331.   [107] Ibid. ii. 96. 332.
[108] C. Smith, *The Way of Paradox: Spiritual Life as Taught by Meister Eckhart* (New York, 1987), 27.

He discovers that the divine spark of the soul is in essence one with the Divine Intellect.[109] The soul 'breaks through' (*durchbricht*) to its ground and 'this breaking-through guarantees to me that I and God are one'.[110]

Through the sweeping away of the non-essential elements of the self and the discovery of his unity with God, he allows the Father to give birth to the Son in his soul and thereby becomes himself God's Son.[111]

He has stripped God of concepts. God is perceived *ohne mittel*, that is, without a medium.[112] Our relationship to God is mediated neither by language, thought, nor images. As Eckhart puts it: 'But when all images are detached from the soul and she sees nothing but the one alone, then the naked essence of the soul finds the naked, formless essence of divine unity, which is superessential being, passive, reposing in itself.'[113]

The individual who has successfully completed the two movements of detachment and negation is described by Eckhart as the 'just man'.[114] He has swept aside all that stands between himself and God, and merges into him without distinction: 'God must really become I and I must really become God, so fully one that this "he" and "I" become and are one "is", and in that "isness" work one work eternally.'[115] As one with God, the human being participates in and contributes to the thinking of God's thoughts. He shares in the Divine Knowledge, perceiving the world *sub specie aeternitatis*, i.e. according to the eternal ideas which lie behind the world's existent form.[116]

Summing up our survey, we can reduce negative theology to three fundamental characteristics.

1. *The transcendence of God.* Negative theologians place great emphasis on the gulf between God and the human being. Much of

[109] Quint, *Meister Eckhart*, 28.

[110] *Eckhart: Sermons*, trans. Walshe, ii. 87. 275.

[111] Ibid. ii. 65. 135; *Eckhart: Essential Sermons*, trans. Colledge and McGinn, Sermons 22 (pp. 192, 196), 53 (p. 205); The Book of Benedictus (*Eckhart: Essential Sermons*, trans. Colledge and McGinn, 229, 243).

[112] *Eckhart: Sermons*, trans. Walshe, ii. 96. 334.   [113] Ibid. ii. 96. 331.

[114] Ibid. ii. 59. 97.

[115] Ibid. ii. 96. 334; cf. i. 13. 117; ii. 53. 64; 65. 134.

[116] Quint, *Meister Eckhart*, 25–6.

their thought is devoted to how we overcome this gulf without undermining God's transcendence.

2. *The inadequacy of human language and reason.* Because God is so utterly transcendent, human concepts are incapable of expressing his nature. As we have seen, this prompts the negative theologians to attempt to progress beyond the limitations of human language and reason. This takes place in two stages:

(*a*) Cataphatic theology. The negative theologians begin by accepting or developing a cataphatic theology. Cataphatic theology is concerned with establishing and developing concepts which express God's attributes and qualities. This is achieved by applying to God concepts which are derived from human experience such as 'goodness', 'wisdom', 'light', etc., in a qualitatively higher way and attempting to purify them of their material and non-essential accretions. We thus come to some comprehension of what God is by envisaging human attributes transposed on to a divine plane.

(*b*) Apophatic theology. For the negative theologian, however, cataphatic theology is not enough. If we wish to make progress in our comprehension of God, he argues, we must penetrate through the images, concepts, and symbols of affirmative theology to the pure and absolute Divinity that lies behind them. The means by which this is achieved is the negation of those terms established by the cataphatic approach. Thus Meister Eckhart can write: 'You should love [God] as he is: a non-God, a non-spirit, a non-person, a non-image.'[117]

3. *Union with the Divine.* Negative theology is more than merely epistemology. It is, as Lossky points out, 'an existential attitude which involves the whole man'.[118] By sweeping aside positive concepts and images, negative theology provides the framework for a relationship between the human being and God. This anthropological dimension of negative theology is expressed in a variety of different ways. These can be reduced to two basic principles. First, negative theologians conceive of the underlying principle of the universe as a procession from and return to God. The act of creation is a procession from God, but within creation there exists an urge to return to its divine source. This leads us on to

[117] *Eckhart: Sermons*, trans. Walshe, ii. 96. 335.
[118] V. Lossky, *The Mystical Theology of the Eastern Church* (Cambridge, 1957), 39.

the second principle, namely, *union*. The urge of the creature to
return to its source is expressed in the human being as the desire to
become one with God. Negative theology plays a vital role here
because it is the means by which the individual ascends to a greater
comprehension of and *eo ipso* closer union with God.

If our thesis that Kierkegaard can be understood as a negative
theologian is correct, we should expect to find some reflection of
these fundamental apophatic principles in his works. Before we go
on to discuss the apophatic motifs in Kierkegaard's thought,
however, we should first turn our attention to the question of his
knowledge of negative theology.

IV. KIERKEGAARD'S KNOWLEDGE OF
NEGATIVE THEOLOGY

If our thesis that Kierkegaard can be understood as a negative
theologian is valid, we would expect to find some reference, on the
one hand, to Neoplatonism, since this seems to have exerted an
influence on the negative theologians, and, on the other hand, to
negative theology itself. On both counts, however, our expectations
are disappointed.

References to Neoplatonism are very rare both in Kierkegaard's
works and in his journals. Plotinus is mentioned only once in the
pseudonymous works, namely in *E/O* i. 300, where Kierkegaard, or
rather 'A', speaks of Plotinus' views concerning resurrection.[119] In
the *Journals* Plotinus appears slightly more frequently. In *JP* ii. 1594
Kierkegaard quotes, in the course of a discussion of Hegel's concept
of movement, a passage from Plotinus cited from G. O. Marbach's
Geschichte der Philosophie des Mittelalters.[120] Brief mention is
also made of Plotinus in *JP* iii. 3325, where Kierkegaard speaks of
Plotinus with reference to Plato and the trilogy of 'music, love,
philosophy'.[121] According to Hong and Hong, the reference to
Alexandrians in *Pap*. V B 40: 8, which was deleted from the final

---

[119] According to Hong and Hong, *E/O* i. 646 n. 46, Kierkegaard is referring to
Enneads iii. 4. 2.

[120] G. O. Marbach, *Geschichte der Philosophie des Mittelalters* (Leipzig, 1841)
(*ASKB* 643), 82.

[121] According to Hong and Hong, *JP* iii. 870 n. 972, Kierkegaard is referring to
Marbach's *Geschichte der Philosophie des Mittelalters*, 58, 63–4.

copy of *Philosophical Fragments*,[122] 'refers to Tennemann, vi, 383–95, 403–23, with an emphasis on Plotinus'.[123]

Direct references to Neoplatonism in general, as opposed to specific Neoplatonist authors, are even more rare. In the pseudo-nymous works the only passage is *E/O* i. 300, already cited above. However, indirect evidence for Kierkegaard's acquaintance with Neoplatonism can be found in his library. He possessed A. Kirchhoff's edition of *Plotini De Virtutibus et adversus gnosticos libellos*.[124] He also owned a number of works in which Neoplatonists were included: Tennemann, *Geschichte der Philosophie*;[125] H. E. F. Guerike, *Handbuch der Kirchengeschichte*;[126] Gottfrid Arnold, *Unparteysche Kirchen- und Ketzer-Historie*;[127] Marbach, *Geschichte der Philosophie*;[128] Hegel, *Geschichte der Philosophie*.[129] It must be pointed out, however, that although Kierkegaard owned these works, they are not cited with regard to Neoplatonism in his *Journals and Papers*. Their importance as a pointer to Kierkegaard's acquaintance with Neoplatonism is therefore limited.

References to negative theology itself are also very sparse in Kierkegaard's authorship. The terms 'negative theology', 'apophatic theology', and '*via negativa*' do not, as far as I have been able to ascertain, appear anywhere in Kierkegaard's works or journals. He does, however, very occasionally employ the term *via negationis*.[130]

[122] See *PF*, supplement, 187.

[123] *PF* 335 n. 20; W. G. Tennemann, *Geschichte der Philosophie*, i–xi (Leipzig, 1798–1819) (*ASKB* 815–26).

[124] A. Kirchhoff (ed.), *Plotini De Virtutibus et adversus gnosticos libellos* (Berlin, 1847) (*ASKB* 600).

[125] Tennemann, *Geschichte der Philosophie*, vi. 19–187 (Plotinus), 202–47 (Porphyry), 284–352 (Proclus).

[126] H. E. F. Guerike, *Handbuch der Kirchengeschichte*, i–ii (3rd edn., Halle, 1838) (*ASKB* 158–9); ET: H. E. F. Guericke, *A Manual of Church History*, trans. W. G. T. Shedd (Edinburgh, 1857), 99–101, 159, 244, 247 (all references are to the ET).

[127] Gottfrid Arnold, *Unparteysche Kirchen- und Ketzer-Historie* (Frankfurt am Main, 1699–1700) (*ASKB* 154–5), ii. 4. 54 (Proclus), iii. 1. 2 (Porphyry).

[128] Marbach, *Geschichte der Philosophie*, 54–91 (Plotinus), 91–4 (Porphyry), 98–118 (Proclus).

[129] G. W. F. Hegel, *Geschichte der Philosophie*, i–iii, ed. L. Michelet (Berlin, 1836) (*ASKB* 557–9); ET: *Hegel's Lectures on the History of Philosophy*, trans. E. S. Haldane and F. H. Simson, i–iii (London, 1955), see esp. ii. 374–453 (Neoplatonism), 404–31 (Plotinus), 431–2 (Porphyry), 432–50 (Proclus).

[130] Niels Thulstrup suggests that Kierkegaard knew this term, together with its positive counterpart the *via eminentiae*, 'through lectures in dogmatics covering standard material and most likely through Karl Hase, *Hutturus Redivivus*, para. 59,

Thus in his doctorate on the concept of irony, he says that he made use of the *via negationis* in developing the first part of his dissertation.[131] Later in the same work he uses the term to describe the way Socrates 'assisted the beautiful in and for itself to extricate itself (*via negationis*) from those determinations of being in which it had heretofore been available'.[132] Kierkegaard also employs the term in his discussion of paradox in *Philosophical Fragments*. Here he writes that the paradox is inaccessible both to the *via negationis* and the *via eminentiae*.[133] Finally, the *Sickness unto Death* shows that Kierkegaard is aware of negative theology and the method it employs. Here he writes that,

Sin is the one and only predication about a human being that in no way, either *via negationis* or *via eminentiae*, can be stated of God. To say of God (in the same sense as saying that he is not finite and, consequently, *via negationis*, that he is infinite) that he is not a sinner is blasphemy.[134]

It would seem, then, that Kierkegaard had at least some knowledge of negative theology and was very occasionally prepared to employ it in his own works.

Other evidence for Kierkegaard's knowledge of negative theology emerges when we examine his works for mention of individual negative theologians. In the following, we wish to examine Kierkegaard's acquaintance with these theologians.

1. Clement of Alexandria

An examination of Kierkegaard's pseudonymous works reveals a single direct reference to Clement of Alexandria in *Repetition*[135] and two indirect references to the same author in the *Concept of Anxiety* and *Concluding Unscientific Postscript*.[136] In each case Kierkegaard refers to Clement's statement that he wrote deliberately obscurely in order that the heretics should not understand the truths about which he was writing.[137] This statement is also cited in a journal entry

where the argument is summarized' (*Philosophical Fragments* (Swenson trans.), 220). K. Hase, *Hutturus Redivivus oder Dogmatik der Evangelisch-Lutherischen Kirche* (4th edn., Leipzig, 1839) (*ASKB*[8] 581). (Our references are to the 7th edn., Leipzig, 1848.)

[131] *CI* 222.   [132] *CI* 255.   [133] *PF* 44.   [134] *SD* 122.

[135] *R* 225. According to Hong and Hong, *R* 374, the reference is to *Str.* v. 9.

[136] *CA* 18; *CUP* 65; cf. *CA* 19.

[137] Passages of this kind occur throughout Clement's works. According to the editors of the *Concept of Anxiety*, Reidar Thomte and Albert B. Anderson, Clement 'states several times that he presents Christian doctrine in a concealed form, in order

made in 1840–1,[138] and in Kierkegaard's intended reply to Heiberg's review of *Repetition*.[139] Indeed, it is the reason that Kierkegaard eventually decided not to publish this reply.[140] It clearly made an impression on Kierkegaard, for we find him citing it again in a journal entry made (probably) in 1850.[141]

In addition to these references to Clement's esotericism, Kierkegaard also mentions Clement with regard to other issues. In a journal entry made in 1851 he criticizes Clement for wishing to 'substitute the purely human—reflection, scientific scholarship, etc.—for what the apostles had directly through the spirit'.[142] In another journal entry, made three years later, Kierkegaard cites Clement with regard to the opposition the individual suffers on becoming a Christian.[143]

Kierkegaard also owned several works that dealt with Clement. His main source was probably Friedrich Böhringer's *Die Kirche Christi und ihre Zeugen oder die Kirchengeschichte in Biographieen*,[144] which was the work Kierkegaard primarily consulted for his knowledge of the Church Fathers. However, although this work is cited frequently in the *Journals and Papers*,[145] Kierkegaard only once mentions it directly[146] with reference to

that the uninitiated might not misuse and abuse it. He does not refer to heretics' (*CA* 227 n. 39). In ch. 7 of the *Stromateis*, however, Clement does refer to heretics, although not exactly in the manner formulated by Kierkegaard. In this passage Clement writes that 'The Scriptures have conceived to Gnostics; but the heresies, not having learned them, dismiss them as not having conceived' (*Str.* vii. 94. 3 (ii. 477)).

[138] *JP* ii. 1724.

[139] *Urania Aarbog for 1844*, ed. J. Heiberg (Copenhagen, 1843) (*ASKB* U. 57). R 301 (*Pap.* IV B 112).

[140] *Pap.* IV B 109 (quoted in *R*, supplement, 282–3: 'N.B. Since I wrote that little book "so that the heretics would not be able to understand it," it would be stepping out of character to explain it in somewhat greater detail.' This, however, does not prevent Kierkegaard from publishing an attack on Heiberg in a footnote in the *Concept of Anxiety* (*CA* 18–19).

[141] *JP* iii. 2878.   [142] *JP* ii. 2080.   [143] *JP* iv. 3861.

[144] F. Böhringer, *Die Kirche Christi und ihre Zeugen oder die Kirchengeschichte in Biographieen*, i–vi (Zurich, 1842–55), (*ASKB* 173–7), 76–103. Kierkegaard does not seem to have owned vol. vi, which appeared in 1855, the year of his death.

[145] *JP* i. 21, 399, 531, 532, 542, 616; ii. 1196–9, 1269, 1483, 1894, 2080; iii. 2617, 2899, 3162, 3212, 3615, 3642; iv. 4046, 4047, 4210, 4295, 4470, 4670, 4671, 4765–4771; vi. 6741.

[146] This reference occurs in *JP* ii. 2080, a journal entry made in 1854 and therefore of no influence on the development of Kierkegaard's apophaticism. The reference, moreover, is not to Clement's negative theology, but to his views on martyrdom. See Böhringer, *Kirche Christi*, i. 83–4.

Clement and alludes to it on only one other occasion.[147] Nevertheless, certain passages in Böhringer that deal with Clement's
apophaticism may have exerted an influence upon Kierkegaard.
Thus we find Böhringer writing that for Clement, 'God . . . is not
knowable, not demonstrable. Only in the Logos, the Word, has he
revealed himself.'[148] Böhringer also refers to Clement's intention to
attract those receptive to the truth and to educate them in stages,
while at the same time wishing to hold at a distance those unworthy
of the truth.[149] This may have helped to mould Kierkegaard's theory
of indirect communication.

Another work Kierkegaard owned and used extensively is Wilhelm Gottfried Tennemann's *Geschichte der Philosophie*.[150] This
work, however, only contains brief references to Clement[151] and
does not deal with his negative theology. Kierkegaard also used
Neander's *Denkwürdigkeiten aus der Geschichte des christlichen
Lebens*,[152] which contains a chapter on Clement. However, although Kierkegaard occasionally cites this work,[153] he does not
mention it with reference to Clement.

Chapters or sections on Clement can also be found in a number of
other works owned by Kierkegaard. Thus we find mention of Clement in Arnold,[154] Marbach,[155] Hase,[156] Guerike,[157] Hegel,[158]
and Schleiermacher.[159] However, Kierkegaard cites none of these
works when dealing with Clement, nor do they contain any reference
to the apophatic elements of Clement's thought.

---

[147] *JP* iv. 3861. Kierkegaard is here referring to Böhringer, *Kirche Christi*, i. 82.

[148] Böhringer, *Kirche Christi*, i. 85.   [149] Ibid. i. 83, cf. 85.

[150] References to Tennemann occur in *JC* 167 n.; *FT* 123 n.; *CA* 151 n.; *JP* i. 42, 258;
ii. 1430, 2280; iii. 2339, 2348, 2361, 3295; iv. 4248, 4511, 4512, 4844, 4847; v. 5572, 5595,
5596, 5598, 5600, 5618, 5639.

[151] Tennemann, *Geschichte der Philosophie*, vii. 94–5, 138, 184, 318.

[152] August Neander, *Denkwürdigkeiten aus der Geschichte des christlichen
Lebens*, i–iii (Berlin, 1823–4) (*ASKB* 179–80). References to Clement can be found on
28, 32, 37, 47–9, 52, 61–2, 71, 79 (using 4th edn., Gotha, 1865).

[153] See *JP* i. 264; ii. 1403.   [154] Arnold, *Unparteysche . . . Historie*, ii. 2. 5.

[155] Marbach, *Geschichte der Philosophie*, 160.

[156] K. Hase, *Kirkehistorie*, trans. C. Winther and T. Schorn (Copenhagen, 1837)
(*ASKB* 160–6); ET: *A History of the Christian Church*, trans. C. E. Blumenthal
and C. P. Wing (London, 1855), 91–2.

[157] Guerike, *Manual*, 104–5, 149, 196, 223, 226, 312, 372.

[158] Hegel, *Lectures on the History of Philosophy*, i. 242, 289, 294.

[159] F. Schleiermacher, *Der christliche Glaube nach den Grundsätzen der
evangelischen Kirche*, i–ii (3rd edn., Berlin, 1835) (*ASKB* 258); ET: *The Christian
Faith*, ed. H. R. MacKintosh and J. S. Stewart (Edinburgh, 1989), 62 n. 134. All
references are to the English edition.

2. *Basil*

Kierkegaard was certainly aware of Basil and cites him on a number of occasions in journal entries made between 1851 and 1854.[160] None of these entries deals with Basil's apophaticism, however. Kierkegaard's main source for his knowledge of Basil seems to have been Böhringer.[161] Neander's *Denkwürdigkeiten* also contains references to Basil,[162] but although Kierkegaard occasionally used this work,[163] he does not cite it when dealing with Basil. Arnold,[164] Tennemann,[165] Hase,[166] Guerike,[167] and Schleiermacher[168] also make brief mention of Basil but Kierkegaard does not refer to these works when dealing with him.

3. *Gregory of Nyssa*

Kierkegaard makes little mention of Gregory of Nyssa. In a journal entry made in 1850 he quotes with approval Gregory's statement that, 'One does not come closer to God by changing one's place,'[169] and in an entry made in 1854 he quotes a passage on martyrdom which he ascribes to 'Basil or one of the Gregorys'.[170] Kierkegaard seems to have made use of Neander's *Denkwürdigkeiten*[171] and, in view of the fact that it was his major source for the Church Fathers, he most probably made use of Böhringer.[172] Other works dealing with Gregory of Nyssa in Kierkegaard's library are Arnold,[173] Hase,[174] and Guerike.[175] None of these is cited in Kierkegaard's

---

[160] *JP* i. 399, 531; ii. 1494; iii. 2667.
[161] Böhringer contains a chapter on Basil (*Kirche Christi*, i. 1. 152–274). Kierkegaard cites 190 (*JP* i. 399; ii. 2667) and 258 (*JP* i. 531).
[162] Neander, *Denkwürdigkeiten*, 164, 187, 209, 229, 232, 241.
[163] See n. 153.   [164] Arnold, *Unparteysche... Historie*, iv. 4. 37–9.
[165] Tennemann, *Geschichte der Philosophie*, vii. 200.
[166] Hase, *History of the Christian Church*, 117, 149.
[167] Guerike, *Manual*, 288, 330, 336.
[168] Schleiermacher, *Christian Faith*, 214.   [169] *JP* i. 264.
[170] *JP* iii. 2667. The reference is actually to Basil.
[171] According to Hong and Hong (*JP* i. 509 n. 154), *JP* i. 264 refers to Neander, i. 254 ff.
[172] Böhringer (*Kirche Christi*) contains a chapter on Gregory of Nyssa (i. 2. 275–356). But Kierkegaard does not directly refer to or cite Böhringer.
[173] Arnold, *Unparteysche... Historie*, iv. 4. 40, 42–4.
[174] Hase, *History of the Christian Church*, 117.
[175] Guerike, *Manual*, 330, 332, 336.

dealings with Gregory, nor do they make any reference to Gregory's apophaticism.

4. *Gregory of Nazianzus*

Kierkegaard was aware of Gregory of Nazianzus but does not seem to have studied his thought in any depth. In a journal entry made in 1851 he mentions Gregory's mother, Nonna,[176] and in an entry dated 1854 quotes a passage on martyrdom which, as already mentioned above, he ascribes to 'Basil or one of the Gregorys'.[177] Kierkegaard's reference to Gregory's mother would seem to indicate that he had read Böhringer's chapter on Gregory,[178] but as far as we can judge on the basis of the journals, this does not seem to have had any direct influence on him. Neander's *Denkwürdigkeiten* also frequently quotes passages from Gregory of Nazianzus[179] but is not cited by Kierkegaard. Mention of Gregory can also be found in Arnold,[180] Tennemann,[181] Hase,[182] Guerike,[183] Baader,[184] and Schleiermacher.[185] Once again, however, Kierkegaard does not seem to have made use of these works in his deliberations on Gregory of Nazianzus, nor do they contain any reference to negative theology.

5. *Dionysius the Areopagite*

As far as can be ascertained Kierkegaard makes no reference to Dionysius the Areopagite either in his published works or in his *Journals and Papers*.[186] However, Kierkegaard did own works which dealt with Dionysius. Minor references can be found in

---

[176] *JP* vi. 6741.

[177] *JP* iii. 2667.   [178] Böhringer, *Kirche Christi*, i. 2. 357–434.

[179] Neander, *Denkwürdigkeiten*, 117, 159, 162–3, 187, 263, 274, 284–5.

[180] Arnold, *Unparteysche . . . Historie*, iv. 4. 39–40, 41.

[181] Tennemann, *Geschichte der Philosophie*, vii. 138–9.

[182] Hase, *History of the Christian Church*, 115, 117.

[183] Guerike, *Manual*, 330–2, 336.

[184] Baader, *Über den christlichen Begriff der Unsterblichkeit* (Würzburg, 1835) (*ASKB* 405); contained in *Franz von Baader's Sämmtliche Werke* (16 vols., Leipzig, 1851–60), iv. 260–1. All our references are taken from this edition.

[185] Schleiermacher, *Christian Faith*, 744–5.

[186] According to M. M. Thulstrup, however, Dionysius the Areopagite is named in the journals (*Bibliotheca Kierkegaardiana*, i. 66). Unfortunately, Thulstrup does not cite the passage or passages where Dionysius is mentioned and I have been unable to locate any references to him.

Arnold,[187] Hase,[188] Görres,[189] Helfferich,[190] Hegel,[191] Schleiermacher,[192] and Baader.[193] More important is Marbach, who provides a brief description of Dionysius' apophatic theology.[194] Tennemann also deals with Dionysius' thought. He mentions briefly Dionysius' concept of the incomprehensibility of God and quotes Letter 5 and chapters 4 and 5 of the *Mystical Theology*, all of which emphasize the hiddenness of God.[195] On the basis of Kierkegaard's possession of several works dealing with Dionysius, it thus seems reasonable to assume that he had some knowledge of Dionysius' theology or was at least aware of Dionysius' existence.

6. Meister Eckhart

Kierkegaard seems to have been well acquainted with medieval theology. In his library he possessed Marbach's *Geschichte der Philosophie des Mittelalters*[196] and Tennemann's *Geschichte der Philosophie*, volume eight of which deals with the Middle Ages.[197] He also seems to have been interested in the medieval mystics. Works

---

[187] Arnold, *Unparteysche...Historie*, i. 2. 9.

[188] Hase, *Hutturus Redivivus*, 130, 180; *History of the Christian Church*, 132, 177.

[189] J. von Görres, *Die christliche Mystik*, i–iv (Regensburg, 1836–43) (*ASKB* 528–32), i. 233. This work is cited in *CA* 143 n. Kierkegaard also mentions Görres in *Pap.* V B 53:18 (from draft of *CA* 59, line 10; cited in *CA*, supplement, 187) as a member of 'the Schelling school'. Kierkegaard was clearly made uneasy by this work. In *CA* 143 n., he writes, 'I sincerely admit that I never had the courage to read the work completely and thoroughly, because there is such anxiety in it.' In the original draft for this passage he writes, 'this work is so uncanny that I have never dared to read it carefully' (*Pap.* V B 63; quoted in *CA*, supplement, 208).

[190] A. Helfferich, *Die christliche Mystik in ihrer Entwickelung und in ihren Denkmalen*, i–ii (Gotha, 1842) (*ASKB* 571–2), i. 133, 182, 185. We know that Kierkegaard used this volume for he cites it on two occasions in his Journals, namely *JP* ii. 1653 and iv. 3941, both of which refer to Hugo of St Victor.

[191] Hegel, *Lectures on the History of Philosophy*, iii. 59, 76.

[192] Schleiermacher, *Christian Faith*, 194.

[193] F. Baader, *Vorlesungen über religiöse Philosophie* (Munich, 1827) (*ASKB* 395); *Werke*, viii. 303–4.

[194] Marbach, *Geschichte der Philosophie*, 198–203. See esp. 199 for references to Dionysius' apophatic theology.

[195] Tennemann, *Geschichte der Philosophie*, vii. 168. Dionysius is also briefly mentioned in the course of a discussion of Nicolas of Cusa, ix. 133.

[196] Marbach, *Geschichte der Philosophie*. Kierkegaard refers to this work in *CA* 150–1 n. (Albert the Great) and *JP* ii. 3793 (Aristotelian categories).

[197] Kierkegaard cites this work with reference to the Middle Ages in *CA* 151 n. (Albert the Great, Simon Tornacensis) and *JP* v. 5595 (Bonaventure).

by or on Tauler,[198] Suso,[199] Thomas à Kempis,[200] Bernard of Clairvaux,[201] and Bonaventure[202] are cited in the auction catalogue of Kierkegaard's library and frequently mentioned in his works and journals. He also cites Teresa of Avila,[203] St Hildegard,[204] Hugo[205] and Richard of St Victor,[206] although he does not seem to have possessed their works. In addition to this, Kierkegaard possessed several survey works on mysticism, namely works by Joseph von Görres,[207] and Adolph Helfferich.[208] Kierkegaard also read Böhringer,[209] and Neander[210] on Bernard of Clairvaux.

In view of Kierkegaard's interest in and knowledge of medieval theology, it is thus somewhat surprising to discover that there is not a single reference in either his published works or his journals to the greatest of the medieval mystics and negative theologians, Meister Eckhart. This is particularly surprising in view of the fact that the auction catalogue reveals that Kierkegaard possessed H. L.

[198] In his library Kierkegaard possessed Tauler's *Predigten*, ed. E. Kuntze and J. H. R. Biesenthal, i–ii (Berlin, 1841–2) (*ASKB* 245–6). Böhringer also contains a chapter on Tauler (*Kirche Christi*, ii. 3. 1–296). In *JP* iv. 4598 Kierkegaard quotes a passage from Tauler, which according to Hong and Hong, *JP* iv. 721 n. 894, comes from M. Carriere, *Die philosophische Weltanschauung der Reformationszeit in ihren Beziehungen zur Gegenwart* (Stuttgart, 1847) (*ASKB* 458), 152–9. Kierkegaard also possessed *Nachfolgung des armen Lebens Christi*, ed. W. Casseder (Frankfurt am Main, 1821) (*ASKB* 282), a work falsely ascribed to Tauler. Kierkegaard cites this work in *CI* 291 (p. 254) and *JP* ii. 1844. See also *Pap.* VIII¹ A 575.

[199] Suso, H., genannt Amandus, *Leben und Schriften*, ed. M. Diepenbrock (2nd edn., Regensburg, 1837) (*ASKB* 809). Böhringer also contains a chapter on Suso (*Kirche Christi*, ii. 3. 296–441).

[200] Kierkegaard possessed: *De imitatione Christi* (Paris, 1702) (*ASKB* 272); *Om Christi Efterfølgelse*, i–iv, trans. J. A. L. Holm (3rd edn., Copenhagen, 1848) (*ASKB* 273); *Rosengaarden og Liliehaven*, trans. M. Boyesen (Copenhagen, 1849) (*ASKB* 274). Kierkegaard cites *Om Efterfølgelse Christi* in *JP* ii. 2016; iii. 2691; iv. 4783, 4784, 4785, 4786, 4787; vi. 6524.

[201] Kierkegaard owned the following works: Bernardi Clarevallensis, *Opera* (Basle, 1566); A. Neander, *Der heilige Bernhard und sein Zeitalter* (2nd edn., Hamburg, 1848); Böhringer, *Kirche Christi*, ii. 1. 436–719; Helfferich, *Die christliche Mystik*, i. 264. References to Bernard can be found in *JP* i. 201; ii. 1517, 1930; iii. 2722, 2899; iv. 4295, 5015; vi. 6703.

[202] Bonaventure, *Opusculorum*, i–ii (Lugd., 1647) (*ASKB* 435–6). Bonaventure is referred to in *SLW* 403 and *JP* v. 5595, where Kierkegaard cites Tennemann, *Geschichte der Philosophie*, viii. 2. 532.

[203] *JP* iii. 3120, 3435.   [204] *JP* iii. 2899.   [205] *JP* i. 7; ii. 1653, iv. 3941.

[206] *JP* iv. 5039.   [207] Görres, *Die christliche Mystik*.

[208] Helfferich, *Die christliche Mystik*.

[209] Böhringer, *Kirche Christi*, ii. 1. 436–719; cited in *JP* iii. 2899; iv. 4259.

[210] A. Neander, *Der heilige Bernhard*. See *JP* iii. 2722; iv. 5015; vi. 6703. Kierkegaard does not seem to have owned this book, for it does not appear in the auction catalogue of his library.

INTRODUCTION 33

Martensen's book on Eckhart.[211] This omission, as M. M. Thulstrup points out, 'was probably in protest against H. L. Martensen's comparison of his mystic to Hegelian speculation' and because the mystics were regarded as the forerunners of German idealism.[212] This would account for Kierkegaard's lack of discussion of the negative theology of such mystical theologians as Eckhart.[213]

Nevertheless, in view of the fact that Kierkegaard possessed several works which deal with Eckhart, it certainly seems highly likely that he had some knowledge of Eckhart's thought. Apart from Martensen's book, sections on Eckhart are to be found in Arnold,[214] Carriere,[215] Hase,[216] and Hegel.[217] The most important evidence of all that Kierkegaard had some knowledge of Meister Eckhart's thought, however, are Baader's frequent references to Eckhart.[218] We know that Kierkegaard possessed nearly all of Baader's works[219] and that he consulted them frequently.[220] In view of this, it seems highly likely that Kierkegaard had some knowledge of Eckhart's negative theology.

7. Nicolas of Cusa

Nicolas of Cusa seems to have been unknown to Kierkegaard. There is, as far as can be ascertained, not a single reference to Nicolas of

[211] H. Martensen, Mester Eckart. Et Bidrag til at oplyse Middelalderens Mystik (Copenhagen, 1840) (ASKB 649).

[212] 'Kierkegaard's Acquaintance with Various Interpretations of Christianity: Studies of Pietists, Mystics and Church Fathers', in Bibliotheca Kierkegaardiana, 1. 66.

[213] M. M. Thulstrup's statement, ibid. 70, that Kierkegaard's lack of discussion of 'the specifically mystical aspect' is due to the fact that 'It is as if the mystical were something holy for him' must, however, be questioned. In E/O ii. Kierkegaard, in the guise of Judge William, devotes several pages to a criticism of precisely that 'mystical aspect' that Thulstrup claims that he ignores. See E/O ii. 241–50.

[214] Arnold, Unparteysche... Historie, xiv. 2. 8.

[215] M. Carriere, Die philosophische Weltanschauung, 152–9.

[216] Hase, History of the Christian Church, 322.

[217] Hegel, Vorlesungen über die Philosophie der Religion, ed. P. Marheineke, i–ii (2nd edn., Berlin, 1840) (ASKB 564–5); Lectures on the Philosophy of Religion, trans. E. B. Speirs and J. Burdon Sanderson (London, 1895), i–iii; i. 217–18.

[218] Baader, Über den Blitz als Vater des Lichts (Nuremberg, 1815) (ASKB 391): Werke, ii. 44 n.; Fermenta Cognitionis (Berlin, 1822–4): Werke, ii. 410; Vorlesungen über religiöse Philosophie (Munich, 1827) (ASKB 395): Werke, i. 208 n., 273; Vorlesungen über speculative Dogmatik (Stuttgart, 1828) (ASKB 396): Werke, viii. 188; ix. 203; Über den Paulinischen Begriff des Versehenseins des Menschen (Würzburg, 1837) (ASKB 409–10, 413): Werke, iv. 359 n.; Religiöse Societäts-Philosophie (Würzburg, 1837) (ASKB 412): Werke, v. 93.

[219] See ASKB 391–418.

[220] See CI 262; CA 39–40, 59; PF 80; JP i. 420; ii. 1190; iv. 3990, 4863; v. 5066, 5200.

Cusa in either his published works or in his journals. However, Kierkegaard may have come across references to Nicolas in the works he possessed on the history of philosophy and theology. Tennemann's *Geschichte der Philosophie*, which we know Kierkegaard used extensively, contains a section on Nicolas which deals explicitly with his concept of learned ignorance and quotes several passages from the *De docta ignorantia*.[221] Carriere also has a section on Nicolas,[222] in which there is a brief discussion of Nicolas' concepts of *coincidentia oppositorum* and learned ignorance. Minor references to Nicolas can be found in Arnold[223] and Hase.[224]

The conclusion to which our analysis of Kierkegaard's knowledge of negative theology drives us, then, is that he seems to have been aware of the basic principles of negative theology. As we saw earlier, he occasionally mentions the *via negationis* and shows himself to be conscious of the method it employs. We have also seen that he appears to have been aware of most of the negative theologians and to have had some knowledge of their theology. He does not seem, however, to have been interested in the apophatic elements of their thought. The only possible exception to this is Clement, who may have influenced the development of Kierkegaard's theory of indirect communication.

Does this mean that it is invalid to interpret Kierkegaard as a negative theologian? If we were to attempt to argue that there is a direct relationship between Kierkegaard and the negative theologians or that he was directly influenced by them, this would indeed seem to be the case. However, an examination of Kierkegaard's works will reveal, I believe, that although Kierkegaard was not directly influenced by the negative theologians, his thought contains interesting parallels with certain aspects of negative theology. Indeed, it is my contention that it is not only possible to understand Kierkegaard as a negative theologian but to argue that he is *more apophatic* than the negative theologians. We now wish to justify this claim by carrying out a detailed examination of the apophatic motifs we believe to be present or implicit in Kierkegaard's thought.

[221] Tennemann, *Geschichte der Philosophie*, ix. 133–8.
[222] Carriere, *Die philosophische Weltanschauung*, 16–25.
[223] Arnold, *Unparteysche... Historie*, xv. 3. 2.
[224] Hase, *History of the Christian Church*, 345.

2

Dialectics

In this chapter I wish to examine to what extent apophatic motifs are present in the basic structure of Kierkegaard's thought, namely, in his dialectics. In the dialectical structure he gives his work and in the form of dialectics he employs to analyse existential and philosophical problems we shall see that apophatic motifs are to be found in the very foundations upon which his thought is based.

Kierkegaard's dialectics is exceedingly complex and there is a wide range of opinion amongst Kierkegaard scholars as to its precise nature. Most commentators make the point that Kierkegaard's dialectics is similar to Marxist/Feuerbachian 'transformational criticism' by which the direction and thrust of Hegel's thought is reversed. However, rather than turning Hegel 'upside down' as did Marx and Feuerbach, Kierkegaard turns him 'outside-in', as Alistair Hannay succinctly puts it.[1] That is, the Hegelian dialectic is transposed from the sphere of essence to that of individual human existence.[2]

Beyond the general agreement that Kierkegaard has transposed Hegelian dialectics from the essential to the existential, however,

[1] A. Hannay, *Kierkegaard* (London, 1982), ch. 2, 'Turning Hegel outside-in', 19–53; see esp. pp. 52–3. Apart from Hannay, other commentators who make this point are Schrey (*Søren Kierkegaard* (Darmstadt, 1971), p. ix), Adorno (*Kierkegaard: Konstruktion des Ästhetischen* (Frankfurt am Main, 1962), 60, 135) and Anz ('Philosophie und Glaube bei S. Kierkegaard: Über die Bedeutung der Existenzdialektik für die Theologie', in Schrey, *Søren Kierkegaard*, 213).

[2] Despite his opposition to Hegel, Kierkegaard is nevertheless profoundly influenced by him. As Anz points out, German idealism provided Kierkegaard with the intellectual framework within which to work (Anz, 'Philosophie und Glaube', in Schrey, *Søren Kierkegaard*, 10). Anz lists a whole series of categories which Kierkegaard has obtained from Hegel: existence, paradox, qualitative and quantitative dialectics, the reflection of anxiety, the moment, transition, leap, decision, synthesis, contradiction, recollection, idea, finite/infinite, possibility/actuality, self, spirit, personality, history (ibid., 10 n. 7). Dietrich Ritschl makes the interesting remark that Kierkegaard would never have attributed such importance to the criticism of and opposition to Hegel if he had not himself found his own questions and recognized similar objectives in Hegel's thought ('Kierkegaards Kritik an Hegels Logik', in Schrey, *Søren Kierkegaard*, 241).

opinion varies widely as to the nature and scope of Kierkegaardian dialectics.

Søren Holm attributes a vast spectrum of different meanings to 'dialectics', ranging from 'conceptually non-definable' to the 'particular constitution' of an entity.[3]

Dunning, who notes that 'the term "dialectical" . . . is justly notorious for its ambiguity',[4] employs the term in two ways in his interpretation of Kierkegaard. Firstly, it describes 'the dialectic between the two distinct poles of consciousness in every individual: inwardness, subjectivity, and selfhood are understood in contradistinction to externality, objectivity, and social relations'. Secondly, it designates 'the attempt to discern a holistic or systematic development within consciousness and experience'.[5] Dunning adds, however, that this 'does not, of course, exhaust the varieties of dialectics in Kierkegaard's thought'[6] and lists a variety of other forms of dialectics, namely, 'objective dialectics', 'existential dialectics',[7] and the dialectics of 'contradiction',[8] 'reciprocity', 'paradox',[9] and 'mediation'.[10]

Schröer[11] believes that the basic meaning of 'dialectics' is 'seeing both sides of an issue', and as evidence points to Kierkegaard's criticism of Luther for his inability to do this.[12] He then goes on to argue that this primary meaning is applied by Kierkegaard in four different ways, namely, to designate (a) philosophy in general; (b) indirect communication; (c) quantitative dialectics; and (d) qualitative dialectics. In addition to this, Schröer claims that Kierkegaard's dialectics can be categorized according to the paradoxes which underlie them.[13] He thus divides Kierkegaard's dialectics into anthropological dialectics, Christological dialectics, and the dialectics of sin-consciousness.[14] These he then further

---

[3] Søren Holm, *Søren Kierkegaards Geschichtsphilosophie* (Stuttgart, 1956). Indeed Holm doubts that he will ever be able to treat Kierkegaard's dialectics comprehensively (p. 6). In his book he attempts by means of a series of footnotes to show how varied the meanings of the terms 'dialectics' and 'the dialectical' are in Kierkegaard's works. See 28 (n. 10), 41 (n. 11), 67 (n. 2), 78 (n. 10), 80 (n. 19), 81 (nn. 23, 24), 82 (n. 27), 84 (n. 1), 85 (n. 5), 86 (n. 10), 93 (n. 5).

[4] Dunning, *Kierkegaard's Dialectic of Inwardness*, 6.

[5] Ibid.   [6] Ibid. 7.   [7] Ibid.   [8] Ibid. 8.   [9] Ibid.

[10] Ibid.

[11] H. Schröer, *Die Denkform der Paradoxalität als theologisches Problem* (Göttingen, 1960), 89.

[12] JP iii. 2541.   [13] Schröer, *Denkform*, 88.   [14] Ibid. 89–91.

qualifies by describing the first as supplementary dialectics and the latter two as complementary dialectics.[15]

Diem likewise understands Kierkegaard's dialectics to have initially one fundamental meaning. He writes that this 'general and formal sense' of dialectics is employed 'to denote the activity of that type of thought which reaches its goal by moving between question and answer or assertion and contradiction in dialogue'.[16] This primary meaning is then qualified, he argues, by the fact that 'this questioning-and-answering, assertion-and-contradiction, is always directed towards an *object*, the truth about which must be established'.[17]

Adorno believes dialectics to be the movement by which subjectivity proceeds out of its isolation in the attempt to regain meaning.[18] For Jolivet[19] Kierkegaard is proposing a dialectic of life. And Sylvia Walsh Utterback argues that 'Existential dialectic comes to expression in the awareness of a qualitative contradiction between one's present condition and one's existential *telos* and between the different qualities, capacities, or conditions that may be realized in human existence.'[20]

It seems clear, then, that there is a wide range of differing perspectives with regard to Kierkegaard's dialectics, a range which points both to the complexity and to the richness of his thought. How are we to make sense of this complexity? Is there a unifying principle according to which the different aspects of Kierkegaard's dialectics can be organized? There is indeed such a principle, namely, the underlying purpose of Kierkegaard's authorship. This purpose is to inculcate authentic existence in each individual human being.

To further this purpose it is necessary to combat two factors that undermine the human being's quest for authentic existence, namely, Hegelianism[21] and 'Christendom'. These are both expressions of a

---

[15] Ibid. 91.   [16] Diem, *Kierkegaard's Dialectic*, 9.

[17] Ibid. (original emphasis).

[18] Adorno, *Kierkegaard*, 56.   [19] Jolivet, *Introduction*, 115.

[20] S. W. Utterback, 'Kierkegaard's Inverse Dialectic', *Kierkegaardiana*, xi (Copenhagen, 1980), 35 (original emphasis).

[21] Klemke is right in claiming that Hegelianism is not the only rationalism Kierkegaard is at pains to combat, but it is surely going too far to argue that Kierkegaard regards Hegelian philosophy as 'comical, rather than a threat' (E. D. Klemke, *Studies in the Philosophy of Kierkegaard* (The Hague, 1976), 4). Although Klemke rightly points out that Grundtvig, Mynster, and Martensen are also attacked by Kierkegaard, it is Hegel (at least in the pseudonymous works) who is the main

tendency to conceive existence and existential problems in terms of knowledge. In the case of Hegel, this expresses itself in the attempt to understand existence in objective, rational terms. In the case of Christendom, it manifests itself in the treatment of Christianity as a doctrine requiring mental assent or dissent on the part of the existing individual. In Kierkegaard's opinion, these tendencies undermine the human being's quest for authentic existence because they present merely an abstract and idealized picture of existence. This idealized form of existence, however, is simply not applicable to the human being and the existential issues he faces. Far from aiding the human being in his quest for authentic existence, then, Hegelianism and Christendom positively hinder him. Indeed, in Kierkegaard's opinion Hegelianism and Christendom rob the human being of his self-understanding, his development as a self, and ultimately his God-relationship. It is to counter the debilitating objectifying tendencies of Hegelianism and Christendom, and to aid the human being in his quest for authentic existence that Kierkegaard develops his dialectics.[22]

target. This is because Kierkegaard regarded him as the main representative of the spiritual malaise he believed to be afflicting nineteenth-century Europe (cf. *CUP* 216, 317). In Klemke's defence it might be argued that Hegel's influence could not have been as great as is often held since Kierkegaard's literary activity began approximately ten years after the so-called 'collapse of idealism'. But idealism was very much alive in Denmark after the alleged 'collapse'. Furthermore, as Anz points out (*Kierkegaard und der deutsche Idealismus*, 55 n.), the philosopher is not a journalist. He does not pass over philosophical problems merely because they are no longer in fashion. The philosopher's task is to elaborate and articulate the reasons for the demise of a particular philosophical position. Only then can he construct a more adequate philosophy. Kierkegaard is in a similar position. He is, as Anz indicates (ibid. 50), concerned to correct the unforeseeable consequences of Hegelian philosophy. It also ought to be mentioned that Kierkegaard's attack on Martensen was motivated by the latter's attempt to introduce Hegelianism into theology. Now, it may well be that Martensen, as Sponheim points out, 'was by no means the simple disciple of Hegel he is often made out to be' (*Kierkegaard on Christ*, 65). But the point is how Kierkegaard regarded Martensen, and he clearly regarded him as one of the major proponents of Hegelianism in Denmark. This indicates that Hegel occupied a more important position in Kierkegaard's attack than Klemke would have us believe.

[22] Having said this, however, it should be pointed out that Kierkegaard's attention was not equally divided between Hegelianism and Christendom. Kierkegaard's attack on Hegelianism occurred above all in the early part of his authorship. Towards the end of his life, however, the balance shifted towards Christendom and his concern with Hegelianism receded into the background. Nevertheless, the issue in both cases remains the same, namely, the threat Hegelianism and Christendom pose to existential and religious truths. Furthermore, it is the tools that Kierkegaard developed in opposition to Hegelianism that enabled him to launch his attack upon Christendom.

We now wish to turn to a detailed discussion of Kierkegaard's dialectics. This discussion will fall into three parts. First, we shall analyse Kierkegaard's criticism of Hegelian dialectics. Secondly, we shall investigate how Kierkegaard develops a dialectics designed to overcome the shortcomings of Hegel's dialectics. Thirdly and finally, we shall consider Kierkegaard's dialectics of communication.[23] In the course of this discussion we will, of course, be attentive to any apophatic motifs that might emerge.

I. KIERKEGAARD'S ANTI-HEGELIANISM[24]

Kierkegaard classifies Hegel's dialectics in a number of different ways. He describes it as 'abstract thought', 'pure thought', 'objective thought', 'objective reflection', 'logic', 'quantitative dialectics', and 'mediation'. These types of thought, which for the sake of convenience we will group together under the heading of 'abstract thought',[25] are concerned with entities and categories as they are *sub*

[23] For a detailed analysis of the dialectical structure of Kierkegaard's thought considered from the perspective of the dialectic of inwardness, see Dunning, *Kierkegaard's Dialectic*.

[24] The issue here is not whether Kierkegaard's criticism of Hegel is justified but what impact his understanding of Hegel has upon the formulation of his own dialectics. A number of scholars have in fact pointed to the inadequacy of Kierkegaard's understanding of Hegel. Mark Taylor points out that Kierkegaard's categorization of Hegel as a philosopher of identity is a misinterpretation. Hegel in fact 'walks the fine line between the extremes of undifferentiated monism and abstract dualism or pluralism' (M. C. Taylor, *Journeys to Selfhood: Hegel and Kierkegaard* (Berkeley, Calif., 1980), 147). Lars Bejerholm notes that Kierkegaard regards Hegel and Hegelianism as more or less synonymous. This confusion leads Kierkegaard to criticize Hegel for subscribing to a theory of the correspondence of form and content, although Hegel himself attacks this position in his lectures on aesthetics. Bejerholm points out that it was actually the Danish Hegelian J. L. Heiberg who held this position (Lars Bejerholm, *'Meddelelsens Dialektik': Studier i Søren Kierkegaards teorier om språk, kommunikation och pseudonymitet* (Copenhagen, 1962), 307). A detailed historical analysis of Kierkegaard's knowledge of Hegel and his reaction to his thought can be found in Niels Thulstrup, *Kierkegaard's Relation to Hegel*, trans. G. L. Stengren (Princeton, NJ, 1980).

[25] These are not exact equivalents but reflect different aspects of the nature of thought. Kierkegaard himself does not elaborate on the relation between them but seems to use them more or less interchangeably. The main exception to this are certain uses of 'abstract thought'. This is often employed as a blanket term to designate Hegelian thought in general, but in CUP 278–9 Kierkegaard makes a clear distinction between abstract thought and pure thought. Here he argues that the existential combination of thought and being presents the human being with two possible media for thought, namely 'the medium of abstract thought, and the medium of reality'. Here, then, abstract thought would seem to be an alternative to existential or

specie aeterni,[26] i.e. they are concerned with the essence of entities, with establishing the 'ideas' that give entities their structure. As such, abstract thought performs a valuable service. It is vital in the establishment and clarification of concepts and categories. Such clarification is important because it is necessary to gain a clear understanding of a concept *in abstracto* before going on to examine it *in concreto*, i.e. how it manifests itself in existence.[27] Similarly, mediation is not in itself wrong, but only when it is incorrectly applied. It is a legitimate philosophical tool when applied to 'relative contrasts'.[28] In Kierkegaard's opinion, it is in this clarification of concepts and categories that Hegel's great contribution to philosophical thought lies.[29]

Hegel, however, is not content to restrict himself to this legitimate use of abstract thought. Rather than employing it as a means of gaining greater clarity with regard to existential issues, he severs the connection that abstract thought sustains with existence in order to move in the rarefied atmosphere of pure being and absolute truth. He carries out an 'exhaustive abstraction'[30] in which categories are considered not in relation to existence but as self-contained universal principles. On this basis Hegel is then able to work out the relation between the various categories and plot a course of necessary development. Having won a conception of what a category is in its pure and absolute form, Hegel then returns to the mundane world and attempts to interpret the categories as they are in existence in the light of this pure and absolute conception. It is at this point that Kierkegaard feels he must oppose Hegel. As Diem puts it, 'in those logical presuppositions in consequence of which formal logic suddenly develops into ontology, Kierkegaard sees the juncture at which the decisive battle must be fought out'.[31]

subjective thought. In addition to these two media, however, Kierkegaard mentions a third medium, namely that of pure thought. Unlike abstract thought, pure thought severs all relations with reality and is thus in Kierkegaard's opinion not a viable medium for an existing human being. Here, then, we seem to have a clear distinction between 'abstract thought' and 'pure thought'. Elsewhere, however, Kierkegaard condemns Hegel not because his thought is 'pure' but because it is 'abstract'. (For an analysis of the meanings of 'abstract' and 'abstraction' see Bejerholm, 'Abstraction', *Bibliotheca Kierkegaardiana*, 3 (Copenhagen, 1980), 122–5.) Clearly Kierkegaard was not interested in developing a coherent conception of the nature of thought, with the result that he is not always consistent in his terminology.

[26] Kierkegaard rewrites Spinoza's *sub specie aeternitatis* as *sub specie aeterni*.
[27] See *PF* 78 n.; *CA* 142; *SD* 90; *Pap.* V B 14, p. 73 (*PF* 202).   [28] *JP* ii. 1578.
[29] *JP* ii. 1605; cf. *CUP* 54, 99–100, 107, 275.   [30] *CUP* 276.
[31] Diem, *Kierkegaard's Dialectic*, 16.

In Kierkegaard's opinion, Hegel is guilty of a series of grave errors. He is in the first instance guilty of a logical error. Following Aristotle,[32] Kierkegaard argues that the principle of contradiction can only be cancelled by the use of this very principle. If a principle is employed to cancel itself, however, then it is clearly not cancelled. Kierkegaard writes: 'the thesis that the principle of contradiction is cancelled is based upon the principle of contradiction, since otherwise the opposite thesis, that it is not cancelled, is equally true.'[33]

Kierkegaard also believes Hegel's claim to have found a presuppositionless beginning for his system to be nonsense.[34] His reasons for arguing this are as follows. First, such a beginning can only be arrived at by means of reflection. If this is the case, then Hegel's system is not presuppositionless but presupposes reflection. Secondly, the problem arises of how to bring to a conclusion this initial act of reflection, which, as Kierkegaard points out, 'has the remarkable property of being infinite'.[35] If reflection has no capacity for stopping itself, then it is impossible by means of reflection to reach the point where one can begin with the construction of a philosophical system. Thirdly, the exhaustive abstraction which reflection is supposed to provide and upon which the system is to be constructed is simply not possible. 'This act of abstraction,' Kierkegaard points out, 'like the preceding act of reflection, is infinite.'[36] The individual is constantly engaged in this act of abstraction since, should he break it off, it ceases to be exhaustive. Consequently, if the thinker is to take exhaustive abstraction seriously, he can never arrive at a beginning.

Hegel also makes the mistake, Kierkegaard argues, of confusing the spheres in which abstract thought functions. Speculative philosophy belongs in the realm of pure being[37] because it functions according to the principle of pure being, namely, the identity of thought and being. In this sphere there is no discrepancy between the concept or idea of an entity and its reality. The being of an entity corresponds precisely to its concept and its concept is perfectly

---

[32] Aristotle, *Metaphysics*, 1005b–1006a, 1007b, 1008a; see *PF* 319 n. 47.

[33] *PF* 108–9.

[34] *CUP* 101–2; cf. *JP* iii. 3306. Kierkegaard was aided in the formulation of his position by his reading of Trendelenburg's *Logische Untersuchungen* (Berlin, 1840) (*ASKB* 843).

[35] *CUP* 102.   [36] *CUP* 104.

[37] *CUP* 85, 268, 272, 279, 467, 496, 505, 509, 533.

actualized in the (pure) being of the entity. In itself Kierkegaard concedes that Hegel's speculative construction of the realm of essence and the nature of the categories within it may well be correct. The problem is that in existence it is the principle of contradiction and not that of identity that is valid.

Hegel is utterly and absolutely right in asserting that viewed eternally, *sub specie aeterni*, in the language of abstraction, in pure thought and pure being, there is no either-or. How in the world could there be, when abstract thought has taken away the contradiction, so that Hegel and the Hegelians ought rather be asked to explain what they mean by the hocus-pocus of introducing contradiction, movement, transition, and so forth, into the domain of logic. If the champions of an either-or invade the sphere of pure thought and there seek to defend their cause, they are quite without justification. Like the giant who wrestled with Hercules, and who lost strength as soon as he was lifted from the ground, the either-or of contradiction is *ipso facto* nullified when it is lifted out of the sphere of the existential and introduced into the eternity of abstract thought. On the other hand, Hegel is equally wrong when, forgetting the abstraction of his thought, he plunges down into the realm of existence to annul the double *aut* with might and main. It is impossible to do this in existence, for in so doing the thinker abrogates existence as well. When I take existence away, i.e. when I abstract, there is no *aut-aut*; when I take this *aut-aut* away from existence I also take existence away, and hence I do not abrogate the *aut-aut* in existence.[38]

Hegel's application of abstract thought to existence, then, does not throw light upon the nature of existence but confuses the issue by confounding existence with essence.[39]

A further problem with Hegel's use of abstract thought is that not only does he fail to take into consideration the relation of the spheres

[38] *CUP* 270-1.

[39] See *CUP* 112, 176, 279, 294, 296. Bejerholm holds that Kierkegaard's criticism of Hegel's confusion of spheres implies that Kierkegaard himself possessed a definite knowledge of terms and notions. According to Bejerholm, Kierkegaard supposed 'that every linguistic term, every notion had one and only one eternal meaning' (*Meddelelsens Dialektik*, 306). Kierkegaard's division of being into two spheres, namely factual being or existence, and ideal being or essence shows, however, that a notion can have at least two meanings for Kierkegaard, i.e. an existential and an essential meaning. Although Kierkegaard concedes that the Hegelian approach may be valid in the realm of the eternal, he is not concerned with the one 'eternal' meaning of a category but with its meaning in existence. Our problem, then, is not, as Bejerholm would have us believe, 'to find the criterion actually used by Kierkegaard in his establishing of what a given term under all circumstances should denote' (ibid.), but is to understand and existentially appropriate the categories as they appear in existence.

of essence and existence to each other, but he also fails to consider his own relation to these spheres. A problem must be treated not only in a way which corresponds to the sphere in which the problem finds itself but also in a way which corresponds to the sphere in which the thinker dealing with the problem finds himself. As Kierkegaard puts it, the existing subject's 'thought must correspond to the structure of existence'.[40] Hegel fails to realize this, however. For him, personal engagement is a factor which disturbs the progress of pure thought and thus must be put aside.[41] Abstract thought is 'disinterested',[42] that is, it cultivates an attitude of neutrality towards the issues it investigates, even when these issues are of decisive importance to the abstract thinker's own existence. Abstract thought is thus 'thought without a thinker'.[43] It is only of theoretical interest, being merely the hypothetical construction of what existence might be in the sphere of essence.

But Kierkegaard's attack upon Hegel is not due merely to his belief that Hegel has failed to construct a philosophy capable of dealing adequately with existence. If the issue were merely one of rival philosophical theories, it would be difficult to follow the vehemence of Kierkegaard's reaction. More is at stake than this. Kierkegaard attacks Hegel because, in his opinion, Hegel's philosophy is *radically demoralizing*. It threatens the existential and religious welfare of the human being in four vital areas.

1. *The Negation of Existence as Actuality*

In existence essential categories are combined with elements which are not present in the realm of essence. Such categories are: infinitude, which is brought into conjunction with finitude; eternity, which is brought into conjunction with temporality; being, which is no longer pure but is determined as being in the process of becoming; and universality, which is conditioned by particularity. Taking over Hegel's terminology, Kierkegaard describes these conjunctions as a 'synthesis of the negative and the positive'.[44]

Hegel, however, eliminates these negative categories. For him negativity is merely a moment in the development of a concept. First, a concept is posited. This is its 'positive' form. If the concept is to

---

[40] *CUP* 74.   [41] *CUP* 268.
[42] *CUP* 23–4, 155, 173, 181, 268, 278–82, 302.
[43] *CUP* 296.   [44] *CUP* 74.

develop, however, it must pass over into its negative counterpart. This is because all finite determinations contain an inner dynamic which drives them out of themselves into their opposites. Hegel describes this process as the 'negation' of the initial positive concept. The next stage in the concept's development is the synthesis of the positive and negative forms of the initial concept. Hegel describes this as the negation of the negation, the end-product of which is the positing of a new and higher positive concept which incorporates both the positive and the negative forms of the initial concept. Out of the dialectic between positivity and negativity, then, a new positive concept emerges. The dialectical process then begins anew on the basis of the new and higher concept. In this way a concept develops into new and more sophisticated forms.

For Kierkegaard, however, Hegel's dialectics can only function at the expense of negating existence as actuality. There are three reasons for this. First, Hegel does not take seriously the negative categories that make up existence. The problem is that the principle at the heart of Hegel's dialectics is, as we have seen, the identity of thought and being. This means that negative concepts are at a deeper level fundamentally one with their positive counterparts. Consequently, any contradictions, oppositions, and discrepancies between negative and positive concepts are merely superficial and we can look forward to their ultimate elimination as their underlying identity becomes apparent. For Kierkegaard, however, negative categories such as finitude, temporality, particularity, etc. are not merely negative reflections of their positive counterparts but are independent realities. Consequently, they cannot be swallowed up in some higher concept but must be retained with the full force of their negativity. Should we proceed with the Hegelian programme in spite of this, we do so only at the expense of negating existence itself. This, however, is not a viable option for the human being, who is rooted in existence and subject to the contradictions and negativity which existence brings about.

Secondly, in order to think, abstract thought has to translate the object it wishes to think into a thinkable form. This thinkable form, as will become clear later, is possibility. In thinking, then, the human being is engaged in a process of transferring objects from actuality to possibility. The problem here is that possibility excludes precisely those elements which constitute existence, namely, finitude, temporality, becoming, particularity, etc.[45]

[45] Cf. *CUP* 267, 290.

Thirdly, thought is not able to cope with qualities that have not fully determined themselves but are still engaged in the process of becoming what they essentially are. The qualities are in movement, so to speak, and abstract thought can only deal with a quality by stopping this movement or, as Kierkegaard puts it, by translating a process into a result.

Speculative philosophy discounts existence; in its eyes the fact of existing amounts to having existed (the past), existence is a transitory factor resolved into the pure being of the eternal. Speculative philosophy as the abstract can never be contemporary with existence as existing but can only see it in retrospect.[46]

Kierkegaard's conclusion is that Hegel's incorporation of existence into a logical system is completely inadequate as a means of dealing with existence.[47] Thought 'is indifferent to existence in the sense of actuality'[48] and can only deal with it by negating it.[49] The existence Hegel treats in his speculative philosophy is thus merely 'conceptual existence'.[50] It is existence produced on paper,[51] which, of course, is no existence at all. If we are to treat existence in a meaningful way another, more adequate form of dialectics must be found.

2. *The Negation of Movement*

The category of movement plays an important role in the thought of both Kierkegaard and Hegel. Without movement there can be no development or progress either in thought or existence. An adequate conception of movement is therefore essential if we are to get to grips with philosophical and existential problems.

Hegel's concept of movement is based on the principle of the identity of thought and being. Movement, he argues, is the externalization of the idea inherent in the structure of an entity or concept.[52] It is thus 'quantitative' or 'immanent'. For Hegel this quantitative or immanent movement is responsible for the creation of new qualities.[53] There comes a point in the development of a quality where the distance from its initial state has become so great that the quality 'flops over' into a new quality. To put it more simply, we might say that the 'weight' of the quality has become so great

[46] *CUP* 506 (original emphasis).   [47] Cf. *CUP* 107.   [48] *CUP* 101.
[49] *CUP* 279, 281.   [50] Cf. *CUP* 293.   [51] *CUP* 376.
[52] *Hegel's Logic*, trans. W. Wallace (Oxford, 1975), §161.
[53] G. W. F. Hegel, *Wissenschaft der Logik*, i (Frankfurt am Main, 1969), 437.

through quantitative development or 'accumulation' that it tips the scales and becomes 'a new quality, a new something'.[54] The point at which this occurs is described by Hegel as a 'leap'.[55]

This approach is rejected by Kierkegaard. He castigates Hegel for 'the hocus-pocus of introducing contradiction, movement, transition, and so forth, into the domain of logic'.[56] Because logic functions according to the principle of identity, it cannot deal with movement. Logic annuls the existential division between thought and being and considers everything *sub specie aeterni*, i.e. from the eternal standpoint where reality and rationality are one. Where thinking and being are identical, however, there can be no discrepancy between possibility and actuality. Everything simply is and *necessarily* is. Without discrepancy between these two categories, however, there can be no movement.

In logic, no movement must *come about*, for logic is, and whatever is logical only *is*. This impotence of the logical consists in the transition of logic into becoming, where existence and actuality come forth. So when logic becomes deeply absorbed in the concretion of the categories, that which was from the beginning is ever the same. Every movement, if for the moment one wishes to use this expression, is an immanent movement, which in a profound sense is no movement at all.[57]

Hegel's employment of the category of movement in logic is thus a confusion. In the realm of logic there is no movement in the true sense of the word. All the logician does is bring out the various properties inherent in an entity. Movement itself, however, belongs in the sphere of existence, where it is not identity and continuity that determine development but contradiction and discontinuity. Hegel, then, can only incorporate movement into his system at the expense of negating its true nature.

3. The Negation of Ethics

Existence, Kierkegaard argues, must be understood first and foremost as the existence of the individual human being. This means that the problem of existence is not a philosophical problem but is something decisive for the personal existence of each individual. Put simply, the problem of existence is now the problem of how *I* am to

---

[54] Ibid.   [55] Ibid. 438.   [56] *CUP* 270, cf. 277.
[57] *CA* 12–13; cf. *R* 309.

live *my* life. Once we ask questions of this kind, we are speaking ethically.[58]

For Hegel, however, the problem of how the individual exists is unimportant. It is not the individual that is of significance but the thought that he thinks. This thought does not belong to the individual but is thought thinking itself through the medium of the thinker.[59] The crucial factor is the adequacy of thought. If this is adequate, then existence in it follows as a matter of course.

It is a fundamental confusion in recent philosophy to mistake the abstract consideration of a standpoint with existence, so that when a man has knowledge of this or that standpoint he supposes himself to exist in it; every existing individuality must precisely as existing be more or less one-sided. From the abstract point of view there is no decisive conflict between the standpoints, because abstraction precisely removes that in which the decision inheres: *the existing subject.*[60]

The consequence of Hegel's treatment of existence for ethics are as follows.

The first consequence is the negation of the dipolar nature of ethics. Because Hegel sees everything from the standpoint of identity there can be no real conflicts within his system. These are resolved by mediating the conflicting categories. This means, however, that what is decisive in ethics, namely decision, choice, and freedom, is annihilated. There is no question of freely choosing either one or the other of two conflicting categories, because both are fundamentally related and only conflict with each other on a superficial level.

If one admits mediation, then there is no absolute choice, and if there is no such thing, then there is no absolute Either/Or. This is the difficulty; yet I believe it is due partially to a confusion of the two spheres with each other, the spheres of thought and of freedom. For thought, the contradiction does not exist; it passes over into the other and thereupon together with the other into a higher unity. For freedom, the contradiction does exist, because it excludes it.[61]

With the negation of decision and choice, the key ethical categories of good and evil, truth and falsehood are also negated. They are simply mediated into a higher unity. Kierkegaard writes, 'Objectively there is no infinite decisiveness, and hence it is objectively in order to annul the difference between good and evil, together with

[58] *CUP* 279.   [59] *CUP* 296.   [60] *CUP* 262 (original emphasis), cf. 24.
[61] *E/O* ii. 173.

the principle of contradiction, and therewith also the infinite difference between the true and the false'.[62] The 'either-or' of ethics is thus replaced by Hegel with an amoral 'both-and'.[63]

The second consequence of the Hegelian position is that 'the ethical is confused with the world-historical'.[64] Because the primary issue is the self-development of the Absolute, ethics is considered in terms of its contribution to the world-historical movements and epochs in which the Absolute unfolds itself. This reduces ethical action to the attempt by each generation 'to discover its own world-historical moral idea, and to act out of a consciousness of this'.[65] This threatens genuine ethics on three fronts. Firstly, history 'does not show forth the ethical' but merely reveals 'something that corresponds to the abstraction which the race is'.[66] The conception of ethics provided by Hegel is thus not a reality but merely an abstraction from the experience of the human race. Secondly, the events which are of significance in world history do not necessarily, and sometimes clearly do not, manifest the ethical. Greatness on the stage of world history has no direct connection with ethics. Indeed, those qualities which are necessary for a human being to achieve greatness in the world may and often do conflict with ethical principles. Thirdly, even when leaving aside the amorality of world history, the very emphasis on historical events means that one concentrates on the *results* of certain actions and not on the ethical principles that may have motivated them. In Kierkegaard's opinion this 'paralyses all [ethical] activity, inasmuch as it abolishes not only the obviously egotistical but also the natural and enthusiastic assurance, at least in the moment of battle, that what one is working for is the one right thing'.[67] Similarly, ethical activity which has no observable results is simply ignored. True ethical behaviour, to will the good and yet to leave the result in God's hands, is unintelligible to the Hegelian approach.

The ultimate consequence of speculative philosophy, Kierkegaard concludes, is that ethics ceases to be the 'subjective-ethical'[68] and 'a correlative to individuality'[69] and becomes what we might call the 'objective-ethical'. The human being is no longer an actor but merely a spectator in the theatre of ethics.

The third consequence of Hegelianism is its utter incapacity to provide the existing individual with the means with which to structure

---

[62] *CUP* 181.   [63] Cf. *CUP* 358–9, 364, 366.   [64] *CUP* 129.
[65] Ibid.   [66] *CUP* 138.   [67] *JP* ii. 1232.   [68] *CUP* 129.
[69] *CUP* 138.

his existence. Put simply, abstract thought fails to help the individual to answer the fundamental ethical question: how am I to live my life?

For the philosopher, world history is ended, and he mediates. This accounts for the repugnant spectacle that belongs to the order of the day in our age—to see young people who are able to mediate Christianity and paganism, who are able to play games with the titanic forces of history, and who are unable to tell a simple human being what he has to do here in life, nor do they know what they themselves have to do.[70]

Should an existing individual be foolish enough to attempt to structure his own personal existence according to Hegelian philosophy, the result would be catastrophic. Because abstract thought requires that everything be transformed into a form which can be thought, the existential consequence for the existing individual would be to attempt to transform himself into such a form. It would therefore be necessary for him to translate himself into a 'result', in order to be able to abstract from himself. In other words, he would have to commit suicide.[71] Fortunately, the abstract thinker lacks the passion and seriousness that would bring him to such a fulfilment of his philosophy. He remains alive, merely making himself fantastic and ridiculous by intellectually deserting existence while existentially remaining in it.[72]

Abstract thought, then, is completely incapable of constructing an ethics relevant to human existence.

4. The Negation of the Distinction between Philosophy and Christianity

Hegel held that Christianity, although the highest expression of truth outside philosophy, had to be further articulated if it were to reach the level of absolute truth. This could only be done by stripping it of those distinctive elements which characterized it as a religion, the 'mythological' elements, and incorporating it into the rational structure of speculative philosophy.

For Kierkegaard, this is a parody of the true nature and significance of religion. Speculative philosophy does not articulate the truths present in Christianity, but 'deduces paganism logically from Christianity'.[73] Furthermore, this position spells the end of

---

[70] E/O ii. 171, cf. 172; CUP 275.   [71] CUP 273-4, cf. 295-6, 310.
[72] CUP 85, 268-9, 273.   [73] CUP 329.

theology.[74] As Anz points out, the logical conclusion of Hegel's position is the utter secularization of religion.[75]

For these reasons, and for those cited above, it becomes a matter of paramount importance for Kierkegaard to develop a dialectics which avoids the errors of Hegel's speculative philosophy.

II. EXISTENTIAL DIALECTICS[76]

Any attempt to comprehend existence, then, cannot take the principle of the identity of thought and being as its starting-point. Existence brings about a division of thought and being and thus makes a dialectic of the Hegelian kind impossible. If we are to do justice to existence, it must be treated on the basis of this division. This means that the principle of identity must be rejected and replaced by the principle of contradiction.

Instead of identity annulling the principle of contradiction, it is contradiction that annuls identity; or as Hegel so often says, lets it 'go to the bottom.'[77]

Existence involves a tremendous contradiction, from which the subjective thinker does not have to abstract, but in which it is his business to remain.[78]

This has far-reaching consequences for any attempt to comprehend existence. Since thought no longer corresponds to reality, there is no guarantee of knowing whether that which is thought is an actual expression of existence. This means that thought is penetrated by a radical uncertainty. Any replacement for Hegelian philosophy must take this uncertainty as its starting-point.

Danish philosophy—if there ever comes to be such a thing—will be different from German philosophy in that it definitely will not begin with nothing or without any presuppositions whatsoever or explain everything by mediating, because, on the contrary, it begins with the proposition that there are many things between heaven and earth that no philosophy has explained. By being incorporated in philosophy, this proposition will provide the necessary corrective and will also cast a humorous-edifying warmth over the whole.[79]

[74] Cf. 'The Book on Adler' (VII[2] B 235, p. 189), trans. as *On Authority and Revelation*, trans. W. Lowrie (New York, 1966), 145.
[75] Anz, *Kierkegaard und der deutsche Idealismus*, 54.
[76] For a description of the development of Kierkegaard's dialectical method, see Malantschuk, *Kierkegaard's Thought*, 105–78.
[77] CUP 377; cf. JP i. 703–4.   [78] CUP 313.   [79] JP iii. 3299.

In his existential dialectics Kierkegaard attempts to formulate such a philosophy.

In contrast to Hegelian dialectics, existential dialectics places a strict limitation upon the activity and competence of thought. It functions very much like a border guard, allowing thought to press forward to its legitimate boundaries, but stopping it from encroaching on existence itself. That is, thought may be legitimately employed in the clarification of existential issues but must stop short of absorbing these issues into itself and reducing them to its categories. This point is succinctly made in a reference to the relation between dialectics and faith.

For dialectics is in its truth a benevolent helper, which discovers and assists in finding where the absolute object of faith and worship is . . . Dialectics itself does not see the absolute, but it leads, as it were, the individual up to it, and says: 'Here it must be, that I guarantee; when you worship here, you worship God.' But worship itself is not dialectics.[80]

Existential dialectics, then, does not explain existence but helps the human being to become aware of crucial existential issues.

Furthermore, existential dialectics entails the reduction of the status of thought. In existence, thought finds that it exists alongside such categories as will, feeling, and imagination. Consequently, although thought plays an important role in the human being's existence, it does so only in conjunction with these non-intellectual elements.

Science organizes the moments of subjectivity within a knowledge of them, and this knowledge is assumed to be the highest stage, and all knowledge is an abstraction which annuls existence, a taking of the objects of knowledge out of existence. In existence, however, such a principle does not hold. If thought speaks deprecatingly of the imagination, imagination in its turn speaks deprecatingly of thought; and likewise with feeling. The task is not to exalt the one at the expense of the other, but to give them an equal status, to unify them in simultaneity; the medium in which they are unified is *existence*.[81]

Thought, then, is relegated by Kierkegaard to the status of one factor among many. Indeed Kierkegaard goes on to make clear that it is not by intellectual means that an existential union of thought and being is to be brought about but by *passion*.

There is an old saying that *oratio, tentatio, meditatio faciunt theologum*. Similarly there is required for a subjective thinker imagination and feeling, dialectics in existential inwardness, together with passion. But passion first

---

[80] *CUP* 438–9.   [81] *CUP* 311 (original emphasis).

and last; for it is impossible to think about existence in existence without passion.[82]

Thus the human being does not come to a comprehension of existence solely by intellectual means but by means of a combination of a variety of existential elements, only one of which is thought.

At this point we can see the apophaticism of Kierkegaard's thought beginning to emerge. An apophatic motif can be detected in Kierkegaard's strict limitation of the field of competence of dialectics. This means that everything that lies outside this field of competence is hidden. Furthermore, the linking of thought with non-intellectual elements such as passion and imagination considerably reduces the objectivity of thought. This also means that each individual's thought about existence is intensely personal. His conception of existence and his attempt to realize this conception in his own existence is achieved by combining the unique elements which comprise his being. Thus we can see the apophaticism implicit in Kierkegaard's thought. Here it can be detected in the radical individuality of thought. Thought is not objectively accessible but is bound up with the subjectivity of each existing individual.

A second characteristic of existential dialectics is that, in contrast to Hegel, it takes the structure of existence seriously and proceeds on the basis of the division of thought and being to which existence is subject. Thus existential dialectics employs what Kierkegaard calls 'the absolute disjunction'. This aims at keeping distinct qualities apart and preventing them from dissolving into a pantheistic whole. As Kierkegaard puts it,

The subjective thinker has the absolute disjunction ready to hand; therefore, as an essential existential moment he holds it fast with a thinker's passion, but he holds it as a last decisive resort, to prevent everything from being reduced to merely quantitative differences.[83]

Because it is concerned with holding distinct qualities apart, Kierkegaard often describes existential dialectics as 'qualitative dialectics' in contrast to Hegel's 'quantitative dialectics'.[84] He writes,

Everything turns upon making the distinction absolute between quantitative dialectic and qualitative dialectic. All logic is quantitative dialectic or modal dialectic, for everything is and the whole is one and the same. Qualitative dialectic belongs in existence.[85]

---

[82] *CUP* 312–13.   [83] *CUP* 313.   [84] *CUP* 120, 126, 536.
[85] *JP* i. 759.

Qualitative dialectics allows each category to be given its proper place—the relative is understood as the relative and the absolute as the absolute, and not confused by the mediation of categories which should be held apart.

It is necessary always to hold the different spheres apart by the use of the qualitative dialectic, sharply distinguishing them lest everything come to be all of a piece.[86]

No, everything has its dialectic, not indeed such a dialectic as makes it sophistically relative (this is mediation), but a dialectic by which the absolute becomes manifest as the absolute by virtue of the dialectical.[87]

Existential dialectics also expresses the negativity of existence or, as Kierkegaard puts it, 'The negativity that pervades existence, or rather, the negativity of the existing subject . . . should be essentially reflected in his thinking in an adequate form.'[88] This is achieved by 'constantly keep[ing] the wound of the negative open'.[89] That is, existential dialectics does not proceed by negating the negative but by holding the positive in conjunction with the negative. As Kierkegaard puts it,

When it is the case that he [the subjective existing thinker] actually reflects existentially the structure of existence in his own existence, he will always be precisely as negative as he is positive; for his positiveness consists in the continuous realization of the inwardness through which he becomes conscious of the negative.[90]

Only in this way can thought do justice to existence and the division of thought and being to which it is subject.

The significance of this second principle of existential dialectics for our investigation of Kierkegaard's apophaticism is twofold.

First, the incorporation of negativity into dialectics means that it is impossible directly to appropriate positive concepts such as eternity, infinitude, and being. These are conditioned by the negativity of existence, the existential contradiction between thought and being, and accompanying negative phenomena such as contingency, finitude, temporality, etc. Thus in existence, being, for example, is no longer being but 'becoming'. We might express the point Kierkegaard is making by saying that positive concepts are no longer

---

[86] *CUP* 390, cf. 347–8, 463.   [87] *CUP* 468.   [88] *CUP* 75.
[89] *CUP* 78.
[90] *CUP* 78. Should the negative be eliminated, the positiveness that results is 'sheer falsity' and 'illusory' (*CUP* 75).

static but have been set in motion. The consequence of this is that in the sphere of existence the individual can never gain a firm hold on positive concepts.

Secondly, the human being can never arrive at a result as long as he is in existence.[91] This is because the certainty upon which results are constructed is simply not possible in a sphere where everything is in a process of becoming and nothing is static. As Kierkegaard puts it, 'Constantly to be in process of becoming is the elusiveness that pertains to the infinite in existence. . . . The incessant becoming generates the uncertainty of the earthly life, where everything is uncertain'.[92] 'Certainty', Kierkegaard holds, 'can be had only in the infinite, where [the human being] cannot as an existing subject remain, but only repeatedly arrive.'[93] The most he can do is to strive for certainty or, as Kierkegaard puts it, 'Since he is always just as negative as he is positive, he is always striving.'[94]

Existential dialectics is, however, not only concerned with doing justice to the negativity of existence but also with overcoming this negativity by bringing about a reconciliation between thought and being. It does this, however, *within* existence and the strictures which existence places upon the human being. Kierkegaard describes the means by which this is carried out as 'subjective reflection'. Subjective reflection, unlike its objective counterpart, proceeds not away from but towards existence, namely the existence of the individual human being. It is called 'subjective' because it turns towards the 'subjectivity',[95] that is, the innermost personal being, of the single individual. It is concerned not with establishing a speculative system but with applying the categories of abstract thought to the concrete existence of the individual human being. Kierkegaard writes,

While abstract thought seeks to understand the concrete abstractly, the subjective thinker has conversely to understand the abstract concretely. Abstract thought turns from concrete men to consider man in general; the subjective thinker seeks to understand the abstract determination of being human in terms of this particular human being.[96]

Thus whereas objective reflection only moves in one direction, namely away from existence to the abstract and essential, subjective thought moves in two directions. First, it makes the movement of

---

[91] *CUP* 75, 78–9.   [92] *CUP* 79.   [93] *CUP* 75.   [94] *CUP* 78.
[95] See Ch. 4 for an analysis of this term.   [96] *CUP* 315.

objective reflection. That is, abstract thought is employed to obtain a conception of existence and of the categories which make it up. Secondly, it bends objective reflection back on to itself and applies it to existence. A circular movement is created in which thought first moves away from existence but is then turned back and applied to its point of origin. A dialectical movement is thus established between existence, the abstract conception of existence, and the existential application of this conception.

The significance of this is twofold. First, subjective reflection provides the existing individual with the means with which to understand his own personal existence. By means of the first movement, namely that of abstract thought, the individual acquires the concepts with which to understand himself. Thus, in the case of the passage quoted above, abstract thought provides the existing individual with a concept of humanity. This concept can then be employed by the individual to interpret and comprehend his own individual humanity. By making the second movement of subjective reflection, that is, by applying the abstract concept of humanity to himself, the individual achieves an understanding of his own humanity. In this sense, then, subjective reflection is a reformulation of the Socratic dictum 'know thyself'. It is the process by which the individual comes to achieve a greater understanding of himself.[97]

Secondly, subjective reflection has an 'ethical' function. That is, it not only provides the human being with the wherewithal with which to interpret his own existence, but also provides him with the means with which to develop and improve this existence. For Kierkegaard the categories of objective reflection are not only forms of thought but are also possibilities. As will be shown in the next chapter, Kierkegaard holds that the process of abstraction employed by abstract thought results in an object or aspect of reality being transferred *ab esse ad posse*. This is necessary in order to transform an external reality into a thinkable form. But these conceptual possibilities form not only the basis for thought, but are also possibilities for action. If the individual discovers that his existence does not correspond to his abstract conception of what existence ideally is, he is compelled to 'act' to restructure his existence so that it corresponds to this conception.

The question now arises as to how this dialectical process of subjective reflection results in the overcoming of the contradiction

[97] *CUP* 314–16.

between thought and being that existence brings about. This division is overcome by the existing individual positing an identity between them *in his own personal existence*. That is, through his application of the categories of objective reflection (thought) to his own existence (being), an identity can be created. By attempting to live according to his conception of what existence truly is, the existing individual brings about an identity between thought and being.[98]

This does not explain, however, how the contradiction between such conflicting categories as eternity/temporality and finite/infinite is overcome. How does a particular conception of existence enable the existing individual to synthesize the conflicting categories which comprise his being and to overcome the negativity of existence? To answer these questions we must examine briefly Kierkegaard's conception of the self.

According to Kierkegaard the self is, first, a 'synthesis' or 'relation'. That is, it is an entity which comprises two elements which exist in relation to each other, namely, body and mind,[99] the temporal and the eternal,[100] infinitude and finitude,[101] possibility and necessity.[102] These two elements are simply given to the self. They are the basic components which provide the structure or, as Helmut Fahrenbach puts it, the *Was-sein*,[103] of the self.

Secondly, the self is a 'relation which *relates itself to itself*'.[104] This statement qualifies the initial definition of the self as a relation and makes clear that the self is not an entity which is subordinate to the dipolar elements which go to make it up. A synthesis which united these elements in a manner which made them dominant over the self would only be a 'negative unity'.[105] The self, however, if it is truly to be a self, must be a 'positive third',[106] that is, it must be the dominant element in the synthesis or 'controlling factor', as Hannay puts it.[107] 'Relating itself to itself' thus means that the self is concerned with the relation between the elements that give it its structure but in a way that sets it above its structure. The self is to take the

---

[98] This existential identity will be dealt with in more detail in Chs. 4 and 5. Here we wish to concentrate upon the conceptual aspect of Kierkegaard's dialectics.

[99] *CA* 43, 81, 85, 88, 90, 122; *SD* 43.   [100] *CA* 85, 88.

[101] *SD* 13, 29–30, 35.

[102] *SD* 29, 40.

[103] H. Fahrenbach, *Kierkegaards existenzdialektische Ethik* (Frankfurt am Main, 1968), 11.

[104] *SD* 13 (emphasis added).   [105] Ibid.   [106] Ibid.

[107] Hannay, *Kierkegaard*, 191.

given components of its structure and to actualize them in relation to itself in a synthesis. Only by this means does the self become a *real* self. What is crucial for the self, then, is its *Wie-sein*, as Fahrenbach puts it,[108] that is, the manner in which it takes its *Was-sein* and actualizes it and itself in the synthesis.

The point of contact between the overcoming of the existential division of thought and being and the resolution of the contradiction between eternity and temporality, infinitude and finitude would seem to be that it is subjective reflection which is the key to both. Subjective reflection provides the human being with a concept of existence which the latter then attempts to realize in his own personal existence. Among the various concepts that abstract thought produces may well be a number that posit a relation between the eternal and the temporal, i.e. a concept of how eternity and temporality should be synthesized. The human being then appropriates this concept, thus effecting a synthesis between the contradictory elements that comprise his self. If our interpretation is correct, there exists in Kierkegaard's thought what we might call an 'anthropological dialectic', in which a concept developed by subjective reflection provides the human being with the basis for structuring the synthesis that constitutes the self.

However, even when the individual has established an identity between thought and being, the existential division is not eliminated. This is because the identity brought about by the existing individual is only of a temporary nature: 'It is only momentarily that the particular individual is able to realize existentially a unity of the infinite and the finite which transcends existence. This unity is realized in the moment of passion.'[109] The significance of this is that human existence is transformed into *striving*.[110] Although the human being may bring about an identity between thought and being in the moment of passion, he is never able to achieve a full identity as long as he remains in existence. Consequently there are no definitive answers in existence, only new questions. Life itself is transformed into a striving towards answers to these questions. The answers themselves, however, always remain elusive. In this elusiveness and in the impossibility of achieving complete identity of thought and being in existence, the apophatic strand in Kierkegaard's thought again becomes apparent.

[108] Fahrenbach, *Kierkegaards existenzdialektische Ethik*, 11.   [109] *CUP* 176.
[110] *CUP* 78–9, 84, 97–9, 109–10, 182; *Pap.* IV B 35.

III. THE DIALECTICS OF COMMUNICATION

We have seen, then, that Kierkegaard develops a form of dialectics designed to give existence a more prominent role. The purpose of this dialectics is, as we saw earlier, to rectify the debilitating objectifying tendencies of Hegelianism and Christendom, which undermine the human being's quest for authentic existence. To counter this Kierkegaard develops a dialectics which takes the existential contradiction between thought and being as its starting-point and which takes seriously the negativity that conditions existence.

If we wish to communicate the insights gained by our use of the existential dialectic, we must develop a mode of communication which remains true to the principles of existential dialectics and to the existential division between thought and being. In this section we wish to examine how Kierkegaard tackles this problem, dealing first with the inadequacies of objective communication before turning to a discussion of Kierkegaard's theory of indirect communication. In the course of our examination we shall once again draw attention to any apophatic motifs that are present in Kierkegaard's thought.

1. *Objective Communication*

We saw earlier how abstract thought was concerned with establishing the objective truth. Corresponding to this form of reflection there exists an objective form of communication.

Once the abstract thinker has ascertained the objective truth, the question arises as to how he is best to communicate this to his fellows. In Kierkegaard's opinion this presents no problem to the abstract thinker. Because the information he wishes to impart is objective, it can be communicated simply as it is. Consequently, the form of communication is *direct*.[111] Objective communication, Kierkegaard asserts, is concerned either with 'present[ing] something to the attention of one who knows, that he may judge it, or to the attention of one who does not know, that he may learn something'.[112] The recipient of this information can examine it and either accept it or reject it. This whole process of communication and reception of information is carried out on a level where there is no

---

[111] *CUP* 70.   [112] *CUP* 247.

(apparent) hindrance to communication and comprehension of this communication. 'It imparts itself', Kierkegaard says, 'without further ado.'[113]

This form of communication is fundamentally inadequate, however, and Kierkegaard cites a number of objections that can be raised against it. It is, he argues, epistemologically inadequate. This is because it fails to consider the difficulties involved in any transfer of information. This inadequacy is due to two factors.

First, even in the apparently free and easy flow of information on an objective level, there arises the possibility of misunderstanding. Although the communicator may communicate in a direct and intelligible form, it is by no means certain that the recipient of this communication understands its verbal formulation in the sense intended by the communicator. In other words, the same proposition may have a different content for two different individuals.[114]

Secondly, language works according to what Kierkegaard calls a 'foreshortened perspective'.[115] That is, in order to express anything, language has to transform realities into symbols. Only by means of these symbols is it possible to describe and communicate anything about reality. The problem is that these symbols are not capable of fully and truly expressing the richness and complexity of the realities they purport to describe. As Herbert Garelick points out, 'No matter what wordiness one may use in embroidering the statement: "For five years I have been suffering," it will always be infinitely easier for one to say than *be*.'[116] There is thus a discrepancy between language and the realities it seeks to express. Consequently, purely from the epistemological perspective objective communication is confronted by considerable difficulties.

Furthermore, objective communication fails to recognize that the subjectivity and inwardness of the communicator, i.e. his own personal relation to the truth, cannot be communicated objectively. To do so would mean transforming something intrinsically inward into something outward. As Kierkegaard puts it, 'Inwardness cannot be directly communicated, for its direct expression is precisely externality, its direction being outward, not inward.'[117]

[113] *CUP* 70.   [114] *CUP* 131.   [115] *CUP* 414.

[116] H. M. Garelick, *The Anti-Christianity of Kierkegaard* (The Hague, 1965), 12.

[117] *CUP* 232. Kierkegaard gives three examples of the absurdity of attempting to communicate an existential truth directly. These existential truths are 'having disciples is an act of treason to God and man' (*CUP* 70), 'truth is inwardness' (*CUP* 71), and 'the way is the truth' (*CUP* 72). The communicator of such truths would be

Another objection that Kierkegaard raises is that 'objective thought translates everything into results, and helps all mankind to cheat, by copying these off and reciting them by rote.'[118] Two criticisms are contained in this objection. First, the obsession of objective thought with results has the consequence that commitment and appropriation on the part of the recipient are negated. The need for committing oneself to the truth imparted is cancelled out because it is objectively certain and must therefore be simply accepted as it is. Secondly, objective thought fails to realize that results cannot be achieved as long as the human being is in existence. The results of objective reflection are won by taking a certain segment of existence as its norm, failing to perceive that this segment is part of a moving and developing whole. The results communicated by means of objective communication are therefore no such thing. They are merely expressions of the state of a particular thing at a particular point in time, and as such fail to impart the definitive, objective information they profess to contain.

Kierkegaard also objects to objective communication on the grounds that it overrides the autonomy of the recipient. As we have already mentioned, objective communication holds the problem of appropriation to be solved by the objectivity of the material communicated. The mere fact of its objectivity, i.e. that it is or contains an objectively and universally valid principle, means that appropriation presents no problems and follows as a matter of course on communication of the information. This means, however, that a relationship of inequality is established between human beings. One, the teacher, has something to impart to another, the learner. The learner, by virtue of the fact that he does not possess that which the teacher wishes to impart, is in an inferior position to the teacher. He does not have a relationship to the truth in his own right but only by virtue of his relationship to the teacher. Now this is all well and good in the case of the communication of information concerning such subjects as mathematics and woodwork. Such subjects can, indeed must, be communicated directly by the teacher to the pupil. In such a situation the pupil is dependent upon the teacher. If, however, the information to be communicated is

guilty of a blatant contradiction if he were to communicate these in such a way that he acquired disciples, expressed inwardness outwardly, and translated the way into a result.

[118] *CUP* 68.

existential in nature, such an approach would be gravely mistaken. Let us suppose that someone wishes to communicate the truth that the highest form of existence is to be oneself. He cannot teach this in a direct manner because 'being oneself' is something unique to each individual. Should Mr Smith attempt to teach Mr Jones directly what it is to 'be oneself', he would end up teaching Mr Jones not how to be Mr Jones but how to be Mr Smith; i.e. the teacher would be advocating the emulation of his, the teacher's, self rather than that the learner develop his, the learner's, self. As Kierkegaard puts it, 'A direct relationship between one spiritual being and another, with respect to the essential truth, is unthinkable. If such a relationship is assumed, it means that one of the parties has ceased to be spirit.'[119] Similarly, if an individual should attempt by means of direct communication to inculcate a God-relationship in another person, he succeeds only in establishing a God-relationship through his own person.[120] Such a God-relationship is, however, not genuine. Indeed, objective communication 'is an attempt to defraud God, possibly depriving him of the worship of another human being in truth'.[121]

A further problem with objective communication is that it fails to take the negativity of existence into account. Because existence is in a process of becoming, it is 'elusive'.[122] That is, because existence is a synthesis of the eternal and the temporal, the infinite and the finite, the positivity of a direct and objective form of communication is not possible. Eternity's presence in time and the infinite's presence in the finite create a contradiction that makes it impossible to achieve certainty with regard to anything existent. As long as the single individual is in existence, this 'negativity' cannot be overcome. If we are to make any meaningful statements about existence, it is necessary that this fundamental principle of human existence be reflected in the mode of communication. If negativity is not incorporated into the form of communication, then the communicator 'transform[s] a learner's existence into something different from what a human existence in general has any right to be'.[123] This is precisely the error that objective communication commits.

Finally, objective communication misinterprets Christianity by

---

[119] *CUP* 221.   [120] *CUP* 63, 69.   [121] *CUP* 69, cf. 92.
[122] *CUP* 76.   [123] *CUP* 78.

treating it as a doctrine or set of propositions. In doing so it creates the misguided belief that the individual has done enough when he has acquired objective knowledge of Christianity. Kierkegaard complains, 'Because everybody knows it, the Christian truth has gradually become a triviality, of which it is difficult to secure a primitive impression.'[124] Everybody knows what Christianity is and everybody, by virtue of this knowledge, regards himself as a Christian. If a so-called Christian is to become a genuine Christian a mode of communication must be found which educates him to perceive Christianity not as a doctrine but as an 'existential communication'[125] that must be acted upon.

This education Kierkegaard attempts to provide in his development of indirect communication.[126]

2. Indirect Communication

On the basis of Kierkegaard's criticism of objective forms of communication the impression may arise that no communication is possible between individuals on matters of existential and religious significance. This, however, is not the point Kierkegaard wishes to make. His concern is not to eliminate communication altogether but to establish a form of communication which allows the individual to appropriate truth in a manner decisive for his existence. Kierkegaard is concerned with inculcating 'subjectivity' in the existing individual, that is, he is concerned with aiding another human being to become a genuine self. His method of communication is therefore not aimed at imparting information but at 'edifying', i.e. at building up the subjectivity of the recipient.

As we saw earlier, this process of inculcating subjectivity in the individual cannot be carried out directly or objectively because this would override the autonomy and freedom to choose that is essential for a genuine appropriation of the truth. Furthermore, existential truth is concerned with the very being of the human individual. This, however, is something intrinsically incommunicable. If it is communicated, it is transferred into an outward form, which results in its negation. The individual who wishes to communicate

---

[124] *CUP* 245 n.   [125] *CUP* 339, 342, 499, 501, 513.
[126] Such was the importance of the question of communication for Kierkegaard that he actually considered giving a course of twelve lectures on the dialectics of communication (*JP* i. 648–57).

subjectivity thus has a problem, namely, how is he to communicate this truth without robbing it of precisely that which determines it as truth?[127]

Kierkegaard attempts to solve this problem by developing what he calls a 'new military science'.[128] This is a form of communication which aims not at imparting information but at 'emancipating the recipient'.[129] That is, the intention is not to provide the recipient with a series of objective propositions or facts but to enable him to adopt a certain attitude or stance towards himself and his life.

In developing a method of communication suitable for existential truths, Kierkegaard takes Socrates' dialectical method as his starting-point. This method consists of a dialogic technique in which Socrates converses with a partner and attempts to guide him towards an independent discovery of the truth. Kierkegaard takes up this method and gives it a new application. However, rather than giving the internal structure of his works a dialogic form in the manner of Plato, he constructs them in such a way that they come to form a *dialogue with the reader*. As Diem points out, 'In truth he [Kierkegaard] did not renounce the dialogue form, but made one single sustained dialogue of the entire work of his pseudonymous characters. The reader takes the place of the conversational partner.'[130] Kierkegaard develops this dialogic technique in two closely related ways.

(a) Pseudonymity

Pseudonymity has two functions for Kierkegaard, both of which express his Socratic intention of bringing the reader to the point of independently discovering the truth. The first is to avoid the recipient's 'having to drag the weight of my personal reality instead of having the doubly reflected, light ideality of a poetically actual author to dance with'.[131] Kierkegaard hopes to withdraw himself from the gaze of his reader, thereby allowing the latter to participate in a dialogue with the characters in his works free of prejudicial interference or guidance from the author. As Mark Taylor succinctly puts it, 'Kierkegaard's pseudonymity is the curtain separating him from the drama he stages. His multiple literary devices seek to focus

---

127 *CUP* 68 n.   128 *PV* 38.   129 *CUP* 69.
130 Diem, *Kierkegaard's Dialectic*, 41.   131 *CUP* 553.

the reader's attention on the play his personae enact rather than on the complex behind-the-scenes manœuvres necessary to mount the production.'[132]

The second function of pseudonymity is to present various existential possibilities to the reader. As Kierkegaard points out in *Armed Neutrality*, 'A pseudonym is excellent for accentuating a point, a stance, a position. It creates a poetic person.'[133] Each of these poetic persons 'has his definite life-view'[134] which the reader has to weigh up as a possibility for his own personal existence. By entering into a dialogue with the different pseudonyms, questions are asked of the reader, compelling him to take a stance on crucial existential and religious issues. As Jolivet points out, 'What Kierkegaard writes is not written in order to reveal himself to other men, but to reveal other men to themselves.'[135]

At this point we can begin to see the apophatic strand in Kierkegaard's thought rising to the surface. It is present in the fact that the purpose of Kierkegaard's employment of pseudonymity is to *conceal* the communicator from the recipient of his communication.

---

[132] Taylor, *Journeys to Selfhood*, 102.

[133] Pap. XI 510, in *Armed Neutrality and An Open Letter*, trans. and ed. H. V. Hong and E. H. Hong, 88.

[134] *CUP* 552.

[135] Jolivet, *Introduction*, 110. The question of Kierkegaard's pseudonymity is far more complex than I have portrayed it here. Indeed, Bejerholm argues that the apparently coherent structure of the pseudonymous works was imposed by Kierkegaard as an afterthought. In his opinion, Kierkegaard's use of pseudonyms arises from the fact that *Either/Or* 'was concerned with delicate matters; readers in Copenhagen could not be expected to look favourably upon an author who had just recently caused a great scandal by breaking his engagement. Kierkegaard uses pseudonyms because he must hide his identity' (*Meddelelsens Dialektik*, 316). It is only after Kierkegaard's reputation has suffered in literary circles through his having written nothing but religious works between 1846 and 1848 that he attempts to work out the relationship between his pseudonymous and religious works. He does this by proceeding 'to "prove" that the "aesthetic" part of his authorship has a special function: it is the religious author Kierkegaard's way of "betraying" readers into the "truth", of catching the aesthetic reader and leading him to the religious books' (ibid. 317). There are many objections which can be raised against this approach. Sponheim points out (*Kierkegaard on Christ*, 32) that Bejerholm's explanation does not account for Kierkegaard's practice of accompanying his pseudonymous works with Edifying Discourses written in his own name. Furthermore, Bejerholm's approach sheds no light on the existential significance of indirect communication. The interesting question is not whether there are elements in Kierkegaard's personal development that may have led to his adoption of such a technique but whether it is a viable means of communication. This is something that must be considered on its own merits and not by attempting to map the various pseudonyms on to the various traits of Kierkegaard's personality.

Author and reader are intentionally hidden from each other. This, however, is not the only area in which apophaticism is present in Kierkegaard's use of pseudonymity. A second apophatic motif can be observed in the fact that the principle upon which pseudonymity is based is the fundamental hiddenness of existential truth. The whole pseudonymous technique is designed to take the recipient from his position of distance from the truth and bring him closer to the truth. This involves beginning at the point where the recipient is and then bringing him to the point where he should be.[136] For Kierkegaard this means beginning with aesthetics[137] since this is the sphere in which most human beings live their lives. Apophatic motifs can be detected here in two respects.

First, Kierkegaard's pseudonymous method involves 'incognito and deceit'.[138] 'Incognito' is involved because Kierkegaard has deliberately hidden his own identity and his role as communicator behind a battery of pseudonyms. 'Deceit' is involved because Kierkegaard is attempting to 'trick' his reader into the truth by meeting the reader on the reader's terms. The truth itself is 'teleologically suspended' in order that the basis may be created for the genuine acceptance of this truth.[139] The truth Kierkegaard wishes to impart, then, is hidden from the recipient and must be imparted to him in a surreptitious way.

Secondly, the recipient of the truth is, at least in the initial stage of communication, infinitely distanced from the truth. The communicator attempts to bring the aesthetic recipient closer to the truth by employing aesthetic categories in a way that drives the latter away from the aesthetic towards the religious. In a sense, the communicator is concerned to make the truth more hidden, i.e. he is concerned to make clear that the truth does not reside in the sphere in which the aesthetic recipient has his life.

(b) Doubly Reflected Communication

The second way in which Kierkegaard develops his dialogic method of communication is to restructure the truths he wishes to impart in a way which makes it impossible to appropriate them directly. The basic principle of this form of communication is 'double reflection'. In contrast to objective communication, this indirect form of

---

[136] *PV* 27–31.   [137] *PV* 33, 41, 45, 94, 148–9; cf. *CUP* 224; *Pap.* VIII A 548.
[138] *PV* 45; cf. *TC* 128–30; *Pap.* X² A 196.   [139] *PV* 91.

communication reflects not only upon the truth to be communicated but also upon the relation to the truth of, first, the communicator and, secondly, the recipient.

The first movement the communicator must make is to establish his own relation to the truth he wishes to communicate. Kierkegaard writes,

The form of a communication must be distinguished from its expression. When the thought has found its suitable expression in the word, which is realized by means of a first reflection, there follows a second reflection, concerned with the relation between the communication and the author of it, and reflecting the author's own existential relationship to the Idea.[140]

Since the issue here is the *communicator's* relation to the truth, this might at first sight appear to contradict our earlier assertion that for Kierkegaard the crucial issue in communication is the *recipient's* relation to the truth. Kierkegaard's point, however, is that it is only by reflecting upon his own relation to the truth he wishes to communicate that the communicator can come to understand how this truth should be communicated to the recipient. The reason for this is that the recipient has to make the same movement as the communicator, namely, subjective appropriation of the truth and its application to his own existence.

Having established his own relation to the truth, the communicator must then apply his energies to attempting to encourage the recipient to emulate him. This emulation should not be brought about by the communicator's setting up of himself as a paradigm for the recipient, however. Such an approach would result in the interposition of the communicator between the truth and the recipient, with the consequence that the recipient would sustain a relation to the truth *through* the communicator. As we saw in our analysis of objective communication, this would result in the negation of the recipient's autonomy and *eo ipso* the negation of a genuine relation to the truth.

Consequently, the communicator and the recipient must be held strictly apart.[141] This is achieved by the individual's hiding both himself and his communication behind a form which contradicts the truth to be communicated. Thus Kierkegaard speaks approvingly of Socrates' ugliness since,

[140] *CUP* 71, cf. 68 n.   [141] *CUP* 73.

Through the repellent effect exerted by the contrast, which on a higher plane
was also the role played by his irony, the learner would be compelled to
understand that he had essentially to do with himself, and that the
inwardness of the truth is not the comradely inwardness with which two
bosom friends walk arm in arm, but the separation with which each for
himself exists in the truth.[142]

'Positive', direct forms of communication, then, must be avoided.
The communicator must transform his message into an enigmatic
synthesis of the positive and the negative. As Kierkegaard puts it in
Training in Christianity, 'This art consists in reducing oneself, the
communicator, to nobody, something purely objective, and then
incessantly composing qualitative opposites into unity.'[143] This
entails 'bring[ing] defence and attack together in such a unity that
no one can say directly whether one is attacking or defending'.[144]
This mixture of positive and negative 'transforms a supposed
communication into an illusion'.[145] Consequently, the recipient
cannot relate directly to its content.

There must also be something in the form of the communication,
however, which attracts the attention of the intended recipient. If he
were only repulsed, there would be no reason or opportunity for him
to attempt to appropriate the truth the communicator wishes to
impart. The communicator must thus attract the attention of the
intended recipient of his communication but in such a way that the
recipient himself must make the effort to appropriate this
communication. This is achieved by communicating via riddles.

If a man were to stand on one leg, or pose in a queer dancing attitude
swinging his hat, and in this attitude propound something true, his few
auditors would divide themselves into two groups; and many listeners he
would not have, since most men would give him up at once. The one class
would say: 'How can what he says be true, when he gesticulates in that
fashion?' The other class would say: 'Well, whether he cuts capers or stands
on his head, even if he were to throw handsprings, what he says is true and I
propose to appropriate it, letting him go.'[146]

To appropriate such a communication the recipient must discover
for himself the 'idea' expressed in the ambiguity of the
communication. He himself must now untie the 'dialectical knot'[147]
of the communication. This requires decision and commitment on

---

[142] *CUP* 222, cf. 217, 235.   [143] *TC* 132.   [144] *TC* 133.
[145] *CUP* 70n.   [146] *CUP* 235–6.   [147] *TC* 133.

the part of the recipient. He is forced to make the same movement as the communicator in appropriating the truth, namely, the reproduction of the inwardness of the communicator in his own existence. This is achieved not by a mere imitation of the communicator's inwardness but by his own inward appropriation in which 'the thing said belongs to the recipient as if it were his own— and now it is his own'.[148]

Apophatic elements can be detected here in Kierkegaard's emphasis that the truth must be communicated in a manner which does not openly and directly declare it to be the truth. There is no correspondence between form and content or, to employ the Hegelian terminology favoured by Kierkegaard, the inward and outward. The recipient receives a hidden truth. It lies concealed beneath an appearance which contradicts the truth it allegedly communicates.

Other apophatic motifs emerge in Kierkegaard's emphasis that communication should have a form which avoids the transmission of results. Results hinder the self-development of the recipient. The teacher must therefore not communicate by means of an objective pouring out of inwardness. Such inwardness is not genuine inwardness but merely an externalization of feeling.[149] Similarly, the recipient who is devoted to the communicator and who publishes his praises in the strongest possible terms does not prove his inwardness but merely his dependence upon the communicator.[150] Inwardness, both on the part of the communicator and on the part of the recipient, is something essentially hidden. As Kierkegaard puts it, 'the devout and silent accord, in which the learner by himself assimilates what he has learned, keeping the teacher at a distance because he turns his attention within himself, this is precisely inwardness'.[151]

Another indication of the apophatic nature of Kierkegaard's thought is his desire to *decrease* the amount of knowledge the recipient has at his disposal. In Kierkegaard's opinion, one of the causes of the dire state of religious life in nineteenth century Denmark was a surfeit of knowledge.[152] Knowledge was held to be the key to understanding existential and religious issues. If difficulties arose with the comprehension and/or implementation of existential and religious issues, this was merely because the

---

[148] *CUP* 232.   [149] *CUP* 217.   [150] Ibid.   [151] Ibid.
[152] *CUP* 228, 245.

individual had not yet acquired the requisite knowledge. Kierkegaard, however, saw the problem as being one not of a lack of knowledge but of a lack of commitment and inwardness.[153] If the individual is to return to understanding truth in 'existential transparency',[154] it is necessary that some knowledge be taken away.[155] Only in this way can the individual regain an impression of the existential and religious realities of existence. This denial of the importance of knowledge and the attempt to reduce its availability to the existing individual is, we contend, another indication of the underlying apophatic structure of Kierkegaard's dialectics of communication.

Further evidence of the apophatic nature of Kierkegaard's thought is provided by his emphasis that the truth is always hidden until the recipient follows the communicator in appropriating the communication by means of double reflection. As Kierkegaard puts it, 'The fact that the knowledge in question does not lend itself to direct utterance, because its essential feature consists of the appropriation, makes it a secret for everyone who is not in the same way doubly reflected within himself.'[156]

Finally, apophaticism is present in the fact that Kierkegaard deliberately abstains from providing his reader with any answers to the existential questions he poses. He wishes to prompt the reader to answer these questions himself. Consequently, there are many gaps and loose ends in Kierkegaard's philosophy. He leaves it up to each individual reader to fill these gaps and tie these loose ends for himself. The result of this is that a reading of Kierkegaard's works is never simply just a reading but is a process of self-interpretation and self-discovery. Apophaticism is present here in Kierkegaard's deliberate concealment of solutions to existential and religious questions. These are only revealed through each individual's act of commitment and inwardness.

In conclusion, then, it seems clear that apophatic motifs can be detected in Kierkegaard's dialectics. We have seen how his criticism of Hegel was based on the conviction that the Hegelian dialectical method fails to deal with the negativity brought about by the existential division of thought and being. We have seen how Kierkegaard attempts to construct a dialectics which overcomes this

---

[153] *CUP* 223, 232, 542.   [154] Cf. *CUP* 228.   [155] *CUP* 245 n.
[156] *CUP* 73.

shortcoming by taking as its starting-point the elusiveness of existence and its inaccessibility to thought. Finally, we have seen how Kierkegaard develops a method of communication which expresses the principle that the object of communication, namely, existential and religious truth, is always hidden until the recipient appropriates it for himself. We can conclude, then, that apophaticism is an intrinsic element in Kierkegaard's dialectics.

3

Epistemology

EPISTEMOLOGY in the traditional sense of the term is not amongst Kierkegaard's primary interests. Kierkegaard is not interested in constructing a theory of knowledge that accounts for the way we perceive and know reality but is interested in epistemology only in so far as it bears on existential and religious issues. Nevertheless, in the course of his development of these existential and religious issues Kierkegaard is forced to confront epistemological problems.[1] This is because there are several epistemological issues which, if left unchallenged, could undermine both the Christian faith and the integrity of the human being. We shall begin our discussion by looking at these issues and the threat they pose.

1. It is important for Kierkegaard's discussion of what it means to be a Christian to show that neither Christianity nor faith are undermined by epistemological considerations. He thus attempts to

---

[1] A number of scholars have pointed to the existence of an epistemology in Kierkegaard's thought. Indeed, Elrod argues that 'Kierkegaard's dispute with the Western tradition centres on the issue of epistemology' (J. W. Elrod, *Being and Existence in Kierkegaard's Pseudonymous Works* (Princeton, NJ, 1975), 200). Abrahim Khan writes that Kierkegaard did not deliberately eschew epistemology but 'was perceptive and astute in realizing that the kind of epistemology that in our day is sponsored by logical positivism is too narrow and shallow to recognize that there is an aspect of the passional life, an inwardness, which is integral to human knowledge' (A. H. Khan, *Salighed as Happiness? Kierkegaard on the Concept Salighed* (Waterloo, Ont., 1985), 103). Patrick Gardiner also sees epistemological interests playing a role in Kierkegaard's thought. In his opinion, 'traces of an empiricist epistemology, discernible on occasion in the *Fragments*, surface again from time to time in the anti-Hegelian polemics of the *Postscript*' (P. Gardiner, *Kierkegaard* (Oxford, 1988), 88). Louis Pojman writes that Kierkegaard develops a 'Christian epistemology' which attempts to show that 'Christianity is the only reasonable world view for a rational person to accept and integrate into his existence' (Pojman, *Logic of Subjectivity*, p. x). Similarly, Robert Perkins ('Kierkegaard: a Kind of Epistemologist', *History of European Ideas*, 12/1 (1990), 8) claims that 'much of Kierkegaard's argument has epistemological import'. He goes on to argue that Kierkegaard's epistemology is 'epistemological in a different sense from the way the word is usually used in modern times, i.e. Kierkegaard is reshaping epistemology', and concludes that Kierkegaard is a 'moral epistemologist'.

show that the uncertainty to which the Incarnation is subject is not unique but is something common to *all* forms of knowledge.

2. Kierkegaard's discussion of epistemology is part of his ongoing dispute with Hegel. As Hannay rightly points out, 'Kierkegaard is arguing against the Hegelian doctrine that historical events occur with a retrospectively discernible necessity.'[2] Consequently, it is important for Kierkegaard to show that historical events are rooted in possibility, even after they have taken place and belong to the past.

3. Kierkegaard wishes to reject the contemporary reduction of knowledge to propositional knowledge. Although this may be appropriate in the scientific realm,[3] it is wholly inappropriate when the issue is what it means to be a human being. As Kierkegaard puts it, 'All this positive knowledge fails to express the situation of the knowing subject in existence.'[4] There are two reasons for this. First, if knowledge is considered exclusively in terms of pro-positional knowledge, a discrepancy opens up between what one thinks and knows and how one behaves. As Kierkegaard writes with regard to historical knowledge, 'In historical knowledge, the subject learns a great deal about the world, but nothing about himself.'[5] It is this that prompts Kierkegaard to develop his controversial thesis that truth is subjectivity. Secondly, it eliminates passion, decision, and commitment, but, as we shall see later, it is precisely these categories that are decisive both for the human being's acceptance of epistemological truths and for his establishment of a valid mode of existence.

To combat these various tendencies and to develop an epistemology that protects both the Christian faith and the integrity of the human being, it is therefore important for Kierkegaard to show two things. First, he must show that knowledge is not capable of bearing the weight that is often placed upon it. That is, he must show that all knowledge is intrinsically uncertain and that we therefore cannot look to knowledge to deal with existential and religious issues.

Secondly, Kierkegaard must show that even in everyday realities the knower and the known are inextricably bound up with each other. That is, knowledge is never simply given but is organized and processed by the knower. It is this interaction of the knower with the

² Hannay, *Kierkegaard*, 101.   ³ See *JP* iii. 2809–20.   ⁴ *CUP* 75.
⁵ Ibid.

object known that constitutes knowledge. This principle provides Kierkegaard with the foundation for shifting the emphasis from traditional epistemology to ethical and religious knowledge. We now turn to a consideration of Kierkegaard's attempt to undermine the certainty of knowledge.

I. KIERKEGAARD'S SCEPTICISM

It is helpful for our interpretation if we distinguish between two forms of scepticism in Kierkegaard's thought. First, there is what we might term 'anthropological scepticism'. This term is intended to describe the scepticism that arises from the position of the *knower*. That is, the position of the human being in the act of knowledge makes it impossible for the knowledge he acquires to attain to objectivity. Secondly, there is what we have chosen to call 'ontological scepticism'. This term is intended to describe the scepticism that arises from the nature of the *object known*.

1. *Anthropological Scepticism*

This form of scepticism is due to a fundamental incompatibility or mismatch between the two poles of the cognitive act. According to Kierkegaard, all knowledge consists of an interaction between the object known, or rather the 'sense data' produced by this object, and the knower. The problem is that there is no direct correlation between sense data and knowledge. Sense data are simply brute facts which are not open to question. As Kierkegaard puts it, 'immediate sensation and immediate cognition cannot deceive.'[6] In their raw form as brute facts, however, these sense data do not of themselves constitute knowledge. To qualify as knowledge they must be *organized* or, as Kierkegaard puts it, the human being must possess a category by means of which he can interpret the sense data he receives. He writes:

To be able to use one's category is a *conditio sine qua non* if observation in a deeper sense is to have significance. When the phenomenon is present to a certain degree, most people become aware of it but are unable to explain it because they lack the category, and if they had it, they would have a key that

6 *PF* 81, cf. 82.

opens up whatever trace of the phenomenon there is, for the phenomena within the category obey it as the spirits of the ring obey the ring.[7]

The development and use of this category, Kierkegaard holds, is a creative act. That is, the organization of our sense data involves a creative act of interpretation in which the knower constructs a coherent and intelligible whole from the sense data at his disposal. As Kierkegaard puts it, 'It depends, then, not only on what a man sees, but what a man sees depends on how he sees it; for all observation is not only a receiving, a discovery, but also a creation, and in so far as it is that, the crucial thing is what the observer himself is.'[8] It is with the introduction of this creative element that epistemological difficulties begin to emerge. The problem is that in organizing our sense data into a coherent whole we are incorporating an element into the act of knowledge which is not present in the sense data themselves, or as Kierkegaard puts it, 'As soon as I frame a law from experience, I insert something more into it than there is in the experience.'[9] This alien element is 'reflection'.

Reflection is an alien element because it is not contained in the sense data themselves. Consequently, in using our reflection to organize our sense data, we are imposing an alien framework upon them, a framework which is not contained in or posited by the sense data but is provided by the knower.

It is this introduction of reflection into the cognitive act that undermines the certainty of knowledge. This is because reflection may incorrectly organize the sense data at its disposal or simply go beyond what is contained in the sense data. Put more simply, it is not in the sense data that the possibility of error lies but in our organization of these data and the conclusions we draw from them. The result of this is that 'the certainty of sense perception, to say nothing of historical certainty, is only an approximation'.[10] That is, our organization of sense data may give us an approximation to the truth, but because it involves the incorporation of an alien element not included in or derived from the sense data themselves, there is always the possibility of a mismatch between the sense data and the conclusion we draw. This possibility is enough

[7] *CA* 127 n.
[8] *Edifying Discourses*, trans. D. F. and L. M. Swenson (Minneapolis, 1943–6), i. 67.
[9] *JP* i. 1072.   [10] *CUP* 38.

to undermine the whole epistemological enterprise. Indeed, Kierkegaard goes on to write that 'the apparent trustworthiness of sense is an illusion'.[11]

The problem faced in constructing a theory of knowledge, then, is that of developing a method which avoids doing violence to the sense data and yet allows the knower to draw valid conclusions on the basis of these sense data. Kierkegaard discusses two approaches to this problem, namely, empiricism and scepticism, before going on to offer his own solution.

(a) The Empirical Approach

The empiricist attempts to construct a basis for knowledge by seeking to increase the amount of sense data available to the knower. If the information the knower has at his disposal is truly exhaustive, the empiricist argues, then he cannot fail but to draw the correct epistemological conclusions. By virtue of the comprehensiveness of the sense data the possibility of error is ruled out and the knower attains knowledge.

For Kierkegaard, however, the empiricist position is invalid. In his opinion, the comprehensiveness necessary for knowledge is simply not possible. No matter how exhaustive an analysis may be, it will never be able to encompass the full reality of an object. The knower will always discover that some aspect of the perceived object escapes his grasp or that, on acquiring a new piece of information, it becomes necessary to acquire still more. As a result, far from reaching absolute certainty, the perceiver becomes trapped in an infinite 'approximation-process' in which he is constantly approaching the truth but never actually arrives at it. As Kierkegaard remarks in a journal entry, 'Empirical knowledge is a perpetually self-repeating false sorites, both in the progressive and the regressive sense.'[12]

---

[11] *CUP* 280. Patrick Gardiner points to the similarity between Kierkegaard's epistemology and that of David Hume: 'Both tend to restrict the attribution of cognitive certainty to necessary truths of reason and to propositions reporting immediate sensory data: likewise, both again imply that causal inferences concerning matters of empirical fact are lacking in rational, in the sense of demonstrative, justification' (*Kierkegaard*, 76). But as we shall go on to see, Kierkegaard works out the consequences of this scepticism in a radically different way from that of Hume.

[12] *JP* ii. 2254.

(b) The Sceptical Approach

The sceptic deals with the problem of knowledge in a very different manner from that of the empiricist. In his opinion, the correct procedure is not to attempt to acquire more reliable information but to refuse to recognize anything as knowledge. By an act of will he refrains from drawing any conclusions on the basis of the sense data at his disposal. By this means he avoids the danger of error inherent in every act of cognition.

The Greek sceptic did not deny the correctness of sensation and of immediate cognition, but, said he, error has an utterly different basis—it comes from the conclusion I draw. If I can only avoid drawing conclusions, I shall never be deceived. If, for example, sensation shows me in the distance a round object that close at hand is seen to be square or shows me a stick that looks broken in the water although it is straight when taken out, sensation has not deceived me, but I am deceived only when I conclude something about that stick and that object. This is why the sceptic keeps himself continually *in suspenso*, and this state was what he *willed*.[13]

Kierkegaard has a good deal more sympathy for this argument than he does for the empiricist position. As he sees it, the significance of the sceptical position is that it correctly perceives that the problem of knowledge is based not upon the amount of information at one's disposal but upon the relation of the knower to this information. As it stands, however, the sceptical position is not a solution, but merely indicates the problem without offering any solutions.

On the basis of our discussion so far, it would seem that Kierkegaard favours a sceptical position towards knowledge. As we have seen, he believes that the inability of the human being to know something immediately and the necessary intrusion of reflection into the act of knowing leave all forms of cognition open to error. Attempts to reduce the possibility of error by increasing the quantity and quality of sense data are also doomed to failure; we can never reach the level that constitutes *certain* knowledge, and for Kierkegaard the slightest doubt or omission is sufficient to undermine knowledge completely.

Unlike the Greek sceptics, however, Kierkegaard does not wish to remain in a sceptical position. Before we go on to see how Kierkegaard escapes from the sceptical impasse, however, we must

---

[13] *PF* 82–3 (original emphasis).

first examine the second form of scepticism present in his thought, namely, 'ontological scepticism'.

2. *Ontological Scepticism*

Whereas anthropological scepticism arises from the position of the human being and the discrepancy that exists between sense data and the conclusions we base upon them, ontological scepticism arises from the structure of the object that is known. Although much of what Kierkegaard says in this respect is applicable to all forms of knowledge, he concentrates his attention primarily upon the problem of how we know a historical event. Indeed, Kierkegaard's previous epistemological deliberations, including his anthropological scepticism, merely constitute prolegomena to his treatment of historical knowledge. His aim, as mentioned earlier in this chapter, is to show that our knowledge of all historical events is undermined by a fundamental uncertainty. If this can be shown, then rejection of the Incarnation on the basis of its historical uncertainty is undermined, for in denying the possibility of the Incarnation the religious sceptic would also be forced to deny the possibility of historical knowledge *per se*.

Kierkegaard begins by countering the argument that the past is certain and necessary simply because it is past. Initially, however, he appears to concede this point. The past is past and thus 'it is certain and trustworthy that it occurred'.[14] Having said this, he then goes on to assert that despite the apparent certainty accruing to a past event, the very fact that it has taken place is the cause of uncertainty. He writes: 'But that it occurred is, in turn, precisely its uncertainty, which will perpetually prevent the apprehension from taking the past as if it had been that way from eternity.'[15] There are four reasons for this. First, the transition by which something comes into existence occurs not by necessity but by freedom.[16] Kierkegaard writes that, 'All coming into existence occurs in freedom, not by way of necessity,'[17] and freedom, he asserts, is a 'leap'.[18] To understand what Kierkegaard means by this it is necessary to look briefly at the distinction he makes between a 'ground' and a 'cause'.

According to Kierkegaard, 'Nothing coming into existence comes into existence by way of a ground, but everything by way of a

[14] *PF* 79.   [15] Ibid.   [16] *PF* 75, 77–8.   [17] *PF* 75.
[18] *CA* 85.

cause.'[19] The term 'ground' here seems to designate a base from which logical and immanent progression and development can take place. To say that an existent thing does not come into being through a ground is to say that it is not the result of a logical progression whereby one concept develops immanently out of another.[20]

The concept of 'cause', on the other hand, is not an immanent but a transcendent concept. That is, it is not deducible from what has gone before but is a breach of continuity which posits something qualitatively new. In the case of a historical event, this means that it is reducible neither to the elements which make it up nor to the factors which have influenced it. 'Ground and cause', then, as Hannay points out, 'belong to mutually exclusive categories, as therefore do their cognates, necessity and change.'[21]

In speaking of coming into existence as a leap of freedom, then, Kierkegaard is arguing that no existent thing is reducible to the elements which comprise it or to the events that precede and influence it. No matter to what extent preceding factors influence an entity's coming into existence, the point at which the transition actually takes place is a free act.

This inability to grasp the point at which something comes into existence means that historical events become radically uncertain. The fact that something has come into existence, i.e. the fact that it has become an actuality, is a certainty. This fact is open to perception. But what one perceives is the mere externality of the object that has come into existence. One does not perceive its very foundation, the decisive act of freedom that brought it into existence. Kierkegaard writes:

Because the historical intrinsically has the *illusiveness* of coming into existence, it cannot be sensed directly and immediately. The immediate impression of a natural phenomenon or of an event is not the impression of the historical, for the *coming into existence* cannot be sensed immediately—but only the presence. . . . In relation to the immediate, coming into existence is an illusiveness whereby that which is most firm is made dubious. For example, when the perceiver sees a star, the star

[19] PF 75.
[20] Nor, Kierkegaard argues, can an existent be traced back through a series of causes to an ultimate ground. This is because 'every cause ends in a freely acting cause' (PF 75) and '*definitively* point[s] back to a freely acting cause' (PF 75. Original emphasis).
[21] Hannay, *Kierkegaard*, 101.

becomes dubious for him the moment he seeks to become aware that it has come into existence. It is just as if reflection removed the star from his senses.[22]

Consequently, the historian's work is thwarted. He can examine the background to an event but the 'leap' which finally brings the event into existence is inaccessible. Historical knowledge, then, is intrinsically uncertain because the factor which would provide certainty is hidden. The best that the historian can achieve is an approximation.

The second reason for the uncertainty of historical knowledge is that an existent reality always retains the imprint of the non-being from which it emerged. The fact that everything has its origin in non-being and retains 'the nothingness of non-being',[23] even after having come into existence, is another source of uncertainty for the historian.[24] Kierkegaard writes, 'The illusiveness of the occurrence is that it has occurred, and therein lies the transition from nothing, from non-being, and from the multiple possible "how".'[25]

The third reason for the intrinsic uncertainty of historical knowledge is that a reality, despite becoming actual, always retains elements of the possibility which it lost on coming into existence. This retention of possibility is the natural consequence of the fact that a reality comes into existence not by necessity but by freedom. Although possibility is *annihilated* by actuality'[26] and this actuality cannot be changed, this does not mean that a reality has come about by necessity.[27] The fact still remains that it came into existence by the free actualization of possibility[28] and therefore *could have occurred differently*. Kierkegaard's point is best illustrated by an analogy.

At the start of a football match there exists an almost infinite number of possibilities as to how the game could develop and what its result might be. During the game some possibilities are actualized whereas others are excluded and the result is always uncertain. When the final whistle is blown and the game is over, however, the result *is* certain. It is finished and belongs to the past. This does not mean, however, that the game could not have ended differently. The

---

[22] *PF* 81 (original emphasis).   [23] Ibid.

[24] Kierkegaard does not deal with this form of uncertainty in detail but makes only two passing references to it in *PF* 81–2.

[25] *PF* 82.   [26] *PF* 74 (original emphasis).   [27] *PF* 76–7, 80.

[28] *PF* 77.

result is not the outcome of a necessary development but is the consequence of the free actualization of the possibilities that arose during the game. When we look back on the game we are still able to recognize certain phases and incidents which could have occurred differently and have led to a different result. The result may thus be certain but it still in a sense retains the imprint of possibility through our awareness that it *could have been different*.

The transition of coming into existence occurs in a similar fashion. At the point of the transition the object stands ready for the kick-off, as it were, confronted by the innumerable possibilities afforded to it by its essence, very much like the possibilities allowed to the footballer by the rules of the game. At this point the form of the actualization of the object, its 'result', so to speak, is uncertain. Only when it has come into existence, only when the transition from essence to existence has occurred, is it certain what the object has become. Again, as was the case with the football match, the object retains an imprint of the possibility from which it has emerged. If we turn our minds away from the actualized object back to the point at which it came into existence we see that the object *could have been actualized differently*. This means that the object could have taken on a different form from that of the apparently certain and fixed form it now possesses. The consciousness that it could have been otherwise is a source of uncertainty for the historian when he attempts to investigate what gave rise to an object or an event.

Fourthly, historical knowledge is uncertain because it is impossible for the human being to occupy the position in which historical knowledge would acquire certainty. There is a discrepancy between the position of historical knowledge, namely, the past, and that of the existing human being, namely, the present. Because of this discrepancy the human being is only able to achieve an approximation to a historical reality and can never attain certainty. As Kierkegaard puts it, 'The reason for this is in part the impossibility of being able to identify oneself absolutely with the objective, and in part it is the consideration that everything historical, in the fact of being known, is *eo ipso* past and has the ideality of recollection.'[29]

In summary, if the human being is truly to acquire knowledge of an object or an event he must go beyond mere appearance to the point of transition from non-existence to existence, from possibility

---

[29] *CUP* 509.

to actuality. The result of this is that the individual becomes uncertain in his relationship to the perceived object, first, because this transition is something that lies beyond human comprehension and, secondly, because the individual becomes aware of the manifold possibilities that accrue to an object and which live on into the period of actualization in the form of ghostly 'what if's'.

The underlying apophatic structure of Kierkegaard's thought has, we contend, again become apparent in our analysis of his epistemology. As we have seen, Kierkegaard takes as his starting-point the sceptical principle that it is impossible to reach certainty with regard to knowledge. For the sceptic this uncertainty throws the possibility of knowledge *per se* into doubt. This position is radicalized by Kierkegaard in his extension of the sceptical principle to ontology. In showing what a disturbing effect the transition of coming into existence has upon our ability to know, Kierkegaard provides scepticism with an ontological basis. An apophatic motif is present here in that by means of his 'ontological scepticism' Kierkegaard drives the gap between sense data and the conclusion one wishes to base upon these data so far apart that knowledge becomes impossible. Every act of perception, every attempt to attain knowledge becomes radically uncertain because doubt, by virtue of the mysterious and incomprehensible transition of coming into existence, is an intrinsic part of the structure of all that is perceived and known.

In knowing something, then, the human being is in a very difficult position. He seems to be faced by two problems. First, as we saw in our discussion of anthropological scepticism, the intrusion of the alien element of reflection into every act of perception results in epistemological uncertainty. Secondly, there is a fundamental uncertainty present in knowledge of the past. Kierkegaard does not wish to remain in the sceptical position to which his analysis of knowledge has brought him, however. To provide a solution to the epistemological impasse at which he has arrived, Kierkegaard shifts the debate from the objective to the subjective sphere. It is in the subjectivity of the human self that epistemological problems are to be solved. Kierkegaard develops this solution in two different, albeit closely related ways. In the following sections we will examine his concept of ethical knowledge before going on to consider his concept of belief.

II. ETHICAL KNOWLEDGE[30]

We have seen, then, that reality is pervaded by a fundamental uncertainty. If we are to avoid allowing this to drive us into a sceptical position, we must find a way of coming to terms with and overcoming this uncertainty. Kierkegaard's first solution to this problem, which will be the subject of this section, is that we cope with scepticism by *acting*. That is, we overcome uncertainty by making a decision to construct our lives upon an acceptance of the disputed proposition, despite its uncertainty. It is this decision to *act*, to realize a disputed principle in one's own existence, that constitutes *ethical* knowledge.

Kierkegaard describes this 'action' in two different but closely related ways. First, he speaks of the individual allowing the ideal to become 'transparent' in his own personal existence.[31] Secondly, he describes this process as 'reduplication', which he defines in the following manner: 'To reduplicate is to "exist" in what one understands.'[32]

How, then, does this action come about and why does it allow the human being to overcome the scepticism present in all knowledge? To answer these questions we must first recall what was said about objective and subjective reflection in Chapter 2. There we saw that it is objective reflection's function to abstract from concrete reality in order to provide the human being with the concepts which make thinking possible. Subjective reflection, on the other hand, is concerned with taking these abstract concepts and both applying them to and realizing them in the concrete existence of the individual human being. It is this relationship between objective and subjective reflection that forms the background to Kierkegaard's first solution to the epistemological impasse.

When dealing with the ethical dimension of objective and subjective reflection, however, Kierkegaard prefers to employ the

---

[30] The terms 'ethical' and 'ethics' here should not be confused with the ethical sphere of existence. The term 'ethical' in this context is a synonym for 'existential'. It refers to the need for the individual to actualize a possibility in his own personal existence. The term 'ethics' is applied to the science of transforming possibility into reality or as Kierkegaard puts it in the *Concept of Anxiety*, 'Ethics proposes to bring ideality into actuality' (*CA* 16).

[31] *CUP* 228; *JP* i. 1043; cf. *E/O* i. 54, 169; ii. 160, 179, 190, 248, 253–4, 258; *SLW* 428, 483; *JP* i. 995, 1044, 1050; iv. 4434, 4564.

[32] *TC* 133. See Ch. 4 for further discussion of this and related terms.

terms 'possibility'[33] and 'actuality' or, as he alternatively puts it, 'posse' and 'esse'. It is upon this dialectical relationship between objective and subjective reflection and between possibility and actuality that the first of Kierkegaard's solutions to scepticism is based. In knowing anything other than oneself, Kierkegaard argues, the knower lifts the given reality of the perceived object out of the 'esse' of reality and translates it into the 'posse' of thought. This, he says, is the aesthetic and intellectual principle. He writes, 'The aesthetic and intellectual principle is that no reality is thought or understood until its *esse* has been resolved into its *posse*.'[34] This aesthetic and intellectual principle also applies to the individual's knowledge of other people's actions.

When I think about something that another has done, and so conceive a reality, I lift this given reality out of the real and set it into the possible; for a conceived reality is a possibility, and is higher than reality from the standpoint of thought, but not from the standpoint of reality.[35]

Only in this way can the existing individual come to 'know' anything, because only in this way is reality translated into a form capable of being thought. Thus for Kierkegaard 'all knowledge about reality is possibility.'[36]

If we remain at this stage, however, we exist merely in the realm of the poetic and the ideal. If the human being is to exist in the realm of reality he must not only make the movement *ab esse ad posse* but also *ab posse ad esse*. This, Kierkegaard writes, is the 'ethical principle': 'The ethical principle is that no possibility is understood until each *posse* has really become an *esse*.'[37] Possibility becomes reality by the individual's acting upon it. That is, possibility confronts him with a form of life which he can reject or accept. If he rejects it, it continues to exist as a possibility or sustain a ghostly existence as an excluded possibility. If he accepts it, however, it becomes a reality, for it is now the principle upon which he constructs his concrete, personal existence. Indeed, Kierkegaard even goes so far as to write that 'the individual's own ethical reality is the only reality'.[38]

---

[33] As Hannay points out, 'Kierkegaard's category of the possible is a capacious one' (*Kierkegaard*, 154). We cannot go into Kierkegaard's different uses of this term here. The fullest analysis of which I am aware is G. J. Stack, *Kierkegaard's Existential Ethics* (Tuscaloosa, Ala., 1977), ch. 2, 'Existence and Possibility', 44–84.
[34] *CUP* 288. [35] *CUP* 285, cf. 288. [36] *CUP* 280.
[37] *CUP* 288.
[38] *CUP* 509.

This reality need not be an external reality, however. For Kierkegaard the important thing is not an external action but the actualization of possibility as a mode of existence. Consequently, a possibility becomes real even if it should for some reason not manifest itself in specific concrete actions. As Kierkegaard puts it: 'The real action is not the external act, but an internal decision in which the individual puts an end to the mere possibility and identifies himself with the content of his thought in order to exist in it.'[39]

Kierkegaard's first solution to the dilemma posed by scepticism, then, is to make the subjectivity of the human being the sphere in which knowledge is constructed. We only truly know something when we accept it as real and construct our own personal lives in accordance with it.

Can apophatic motifs be detected in Kierkegaard's conception of ethical knowledge? In my opinion, such motifs can be detected in two areas. First, an apophatic motif is visible in the fact that the means by which the transition from possibility to actuality takes place is the leap.

The transition from possibility to actuality is, as Aristotle rightly says, a $\kappa\iota\nu\eta\sigma\iota\varsigma$, a movement. This cannot be expressed or understood in the language of abstraction; for in the sphere of the abstract, movement cannot have assigned to it either time or space which presuppose movement or are presupposed by it. Here then there is a pause, and a leap.[40]

Apophaticism appears here in the fact that the leap is not open to intellectual analysis. It is 'a $\mu\varepsilon\tau\dot{\alpha}\beta\alpha\sigma\iota\varsigma$ $\varepsilon\dot{\iota}\varsigma$ $\ddot{\alpha}\lambda\lambda o$ $\gamma\dot{\varepsilon}\nu o\varsigma$, a leap, whereby I burst the whole progression of reason and define a qualitative newness.'[41] It is an enigmatic transition that is not reducible to logical immanence,[42] but 'is subject to a qualitative dialectic, and permits no approximating transition'.[43] Beyond this we cannot go. As Kierkegaard remarks with reference to the leap involved in the transition from innocence to sin, the best we can achieve is to explain the development up to the point immediately prior to making the leap.[44] The leap itself, however, is shrouded in mystery. In this fundamental elusiveness of the transition from possibility to actuality, the apophatic strand in Kierkegaard's thought once again becomes apparent.

[39] CUP 302; cf. 289, 304, 347, 509; JC 124; CA 16–20; FT 41; TC 185–7; E/O ii. 210, 258.
[40] CUP 306.   [41] JP iii. 2358.   [42] CA 30.   [43] CUP 94.
[44] CA 21–2, 39.

A second area which indicates the apophatic nature of Kierkegaard's epistemology is the manner in which he elevates 'ethical knowledge' above more objective types of knowledge. This stems primarily, of course, from his religious interests. His purpose, as was stated earlier, is not to develop an epistemology for its own sake but to lay the foundations for faith. Having said this, however, there is also an epistemological reason for the importance of ethical knowledge. If knowledge of external things is intrinsically hidden, then the only sphere in which the human being can acquire certain knowledge is himself. As Kierkegaard puts it, the individual's own reality 'is the only reality which does not become a mere possibility through being known'.[45] Consequently, he can write:

> The ethical alone is certain; to concentrate upon the ethical yields the only knowledge which may not possibly in the last moment transform itself into an hypothesis; to exist in the ethical constitutes the only secure knowledge, the knowledge being rendered secure by something else.[46]

Apophatic motifs are present here in the restriction of secure or certain knowledge to the reality of the single individual. The only knowledge which is not open to doubt and of which the individual can be absolutely certain is that concerning his own reality. Knowledge thus comes to be restricted to the domain of the private and the personal, whereas objective knowledge is undermined by the uncertainty present in all knowledge, as we saw above.

III. BELIEF

Kierkegaard's second solution to the sceptical impasse to which his epistemological reflections have brought him is the concept of 'belief'. He begins his development of this concept by arguing that the individual must first become 'a prophet in reverse'.[47] This phrase 'expresses the fact that the certainty of the past is based upon an uncertainty, an uncertainty that exists for the past in precisely the same sense that it exists for the future, being rooted in the possibility . . . out of which it could not *emerge* with necessity'.[48] To be a

---

[45] *CUP* 284, cf. 295.   [46] *CUP* 136.

[47] *PF* 80. Kierkegaard borrows this phrase from Carl Daub's 'Die Form der christlichen Dogmen- und Kirchen-Historie', in *Die Zeitschrift für spekulative Theologie*, i (1836), 1.

[48] Ibid. (original emphasis). Swenson's translation, 99. This translation is clearer at this point than that of Hong and Hong.

'prophet in reverse' demands two things. First, one must adopt a new disposition towards knowledge. Although the intellect plays an important role, the dominant attitude should be 'wonder'. Conscious of the mystery of the transition of coming into existence, the individual should contemplate reality with awe and reverence.

The historian once again stands beside the past, stirred by the passion that is the passionate sense for coming into existence, that is, wonder. If the philosopher wonders over nothing whatsoever . . . then he *eo ipso* has nothing to do with the historical, for wherever coming into existence is involved (which is indeed involved in the past), there the uncertainty (which is the uncertainty of coming into existence) of the most certain coming into existence can express itself only in this passion worthy of and necessary to the philosopher.[49]

Secondly, if this uncertainty is to be overcome and the individual is to progress from wonder to knowledge, a faculty is needed which corresponds to uncertainty and which, on the basis of this correspondence, overcomes it.

It is clear, then, that the organ for the historical must be formed in likeness to this [i.e. the historical], must have within itself the corresponding something by which in its certitude it continually annuls the incertitude that corresponds to the uncertainty of coming into existence.[50]

The organ Kierkegaard sees as fulfilling this requirement is *Tro*: 'This is precisely the nature of *Tro*, for continually present as the nullified in the certitude of *Tro* is the incertitude that in every way corresponds to the uncertainty of coming into existence.'[51] *Tro* is a difficult word to translate because the English language employs two words to convey the meaning of the one Danish term. The problem is that *Tro* can mean 'belief' both in the simple sense of believing a fact to be true and in the religious sense of 'faith'.

To make clear which form of *Tro* he is discussing, Kierkegaard therefore appends certain qualifying phrases to the term. Thus he often describes *Tro* in the sense of belief as '*Tro* . . . in its direct and ordinary meaning as the relationship to the historical'[52] or *Tro sensu laxiori*.[53] *Tro* in the second sense is described as faith 'in the wholly eminent sense'[54] or as faith *sensu strictissimo*.[55] Kierkegaard plays on these two meanings and uses them to take the reader from a consideration of *Tro* as an epistemological concept to an awareness

⁴⁹ Ibid.   ⁵⁰ PF 81.   ⁵¹ Ibid.   ⁵² PF 87.   ⁵³ CUP 285.
⁵⁴ PF 87.   ⁵⁵ CUP 286, 287.

of it as a religious concept. In this chapter we are concerned with *Tro* in the first sense, that is, in its purely epistemological capacity.

The reason *Tro* is able to overcome the barriers standing between the knower and his acquisition of knowledge is that it corresponds exactly to the uncertainty of knowledge. As Collins puts it, 'Historical becoming and belief are exactly proportioned to each other: the former is the physical way, and the latter the cognitive way, of reducing possibility to actuality.'[56] *Tro* corresponds to coming into existence because it is based upon the principle of uncertainty. It does not eliminate this uncertainty by striving after more certain and more comprehensive data in the manner of the empiricist but takes this uncertainty as its foundation for the establishment of knowledge. This uncertainty is then overcome *by an act of will*. That is, the individual *wills* to believe that a particular event has indeed happened or that a perceived object is that which it appears to be.

In contrast, it is now readily apparent that belief is not a knowledge but an act of freedom, an expression of will. It believes the coming into existence and has annulled in itself the incertitude that corresponds to the nothingness of that which is not. It believes the 'thus and so' of that which has come into existence and has annulled in itself the possible 'how' of that which has come into existence, and without denying the possibility of another 'thus and so,' the 'thus and so' of that which has come into existence is nevertheless most certain for belief.[57]

The 'believer' thus makes use of the same tool to acquire knowledge as the sceptic used to deny it. Kierkegaard writes:

Greek scepticism was a withdrawing scepticism (ἐποχή); they doubted not by virtue of knowledge but by virtue of will (deny assent—μετριοπαθεῖν). This implies that doubt can be terminated only in freedom, by an act of will, something every Greek sceptic would understand, inasmuch as he understood himself, but he would not terminate his scepticism precisely because he *willed* to doubt.[58]

The act of knowing, then, is not simply an intellectual process but is a process which involves the whole person. It is not dependent wholly on the cognitive faculties but involves decision, commitment, and will on the part of the knower. This non-cognitive nature of belief comes to the fore in the following passage, in which Kierkegaard draws a comparison between belief and doubt: 'Belief and doubt are not two

---

[56] J. Collins, *The Mind of Kierkegaard* (Princeton, NJ, 1983), 170.   [57] *PF* 83.
[58] *PF* 82 (original emphasis).

kinds of knowledge that can be defined in continuity with each other, for neither of them is a cognitive act, and they are opposite passions.'[59] Knowledge, then, is determined by the subject, not by the object. This does not mean, of course, that the object is abandoned. The object is retained but because of its intrinsic uncertainty its status as knowledge is dependent upon the subject's decision to treat it as such.

To sum up the second solution to the epistemological impasse brought about by scepticism, we can agree with Hannay when he writes that 'Kierkegaard places historical belief in the same bracket as moral and religious belief; it is analogous to these in requiring a decision or choice.'[60] This is, of course, very different from the position adopted by traditional epistemologists. These have tended to make a distinction between knowledge and belief, arguing that the former refers to propositions that the individual regards as certain and beyond dispute whereas the latter refers to propositions which the individual regards as probable though not beyond doubt. For Kierkegaard, however, the term 'knowledge' does not denote 'I assent to this proposition and give my personal authority to it' but 'I have made an act of commitment to this proposition; despite its inherent uncertainty I accept it as true.' One might almost say that for Kierkegaard 'knowledge that' = 'belief in'. He is not, as Pojman would have us believe,[61] making 'a radical distinction between belief and knowledge'. Nor is knowledge 'a qualitatively different phenomenon' from belief. For Kierkegaard knowledge *is* belief.

In Kierkegaard's development of the concept of 'belief' the apophatic strand present in his thought once again becomes apparent. 'Belief', as we saw above, involves commitment and decision to accept a proposition as a piece of knowledge. This does not come about by the cultivation of an objective and impersonal cognitive attitude but by a passionate act of will to accept something as true despite all that might argue against it. Apophatic motifs can be detected here in three respects.

(*a*) Conventional means of acquiring knowledge are discarded by Kierkegaard and replaced by a method based upon the radical uncertainty of knowledge. 'Belief', although a positive concept in that it does permit the possibility of knowledge, is negative in that it is not reducible to intellectual, rational terms but is based upon an

[59] PF 84.   [60] Hannay, *Kierkegaard*, 105.
[61] Pojman, *Logic of Subjectivity*, 98.

aspect of the human self that transcends the merely intellectual. An apophatic motif can be detected here in that the objective, intellectual disposition adopted towards knowledge in traditional epistemologies is replaced by *passion* and *will*.

(*b*) Belief nevertheless retains the uncertainty which it is designed to overcome. This manifests itself as the danger of error. Kierkegaard writes, 'When belief resolves to believe, it runs the risk that it was an error, but nevertheless it wills to believe. One never believes in any other way; if one wants to avoid risk, then one wants to know with certainty that one can swim before going into the water.'[62] An apophatic motif is present here in the danger of error implicit in every act of knowledge and the necessity of the individual's constant renewal of the initial act by which knowledge was established.

(*c*) Finally, because it is acquired by means of belief, knowledge is something intrinsically personal to the single individual. It would be going too far to argue that the individual invents his own knowledge, but we would be justified in asserting that the organization imposed upon sense data by his passionate act of will creates a form of knowledge unique to each knower. An apophatic motif can be detected here in the isolation of each individual in the act of knowing and in the uniqueness of his knowledge.

[62] *PF* 83 n.

4

Truth

KIERKEGAARD's thesis that 'subjectivity is the truth' is perhaps the most controversial of all aspects of his thought. It is impossible to do justice to this issue in the space of a single chapter. We will nevertheless attempt to enumerate the various interpretations of this thesis and advance a theory which, we hope, will go some way to resolving the controversy surrounding this issue.

This chapter falls into five parts. First, a brief survey will be undertaken of the vast literature on Kierkegaard's theory of truth. This will set the scene for our own discussion. Secondly, we will discuss the scope and purpose of Kierkegaard's concept of truth. Thirdly, the basic principle of Kierkegaard's position, namely the correspondence theory of truth, will be considered. This will show that Kierkegaard develops his theory of truth on the basis not of the identity but of the existential division of thought and being. Fourthly, Kierkegaard's concept of subjectivity will be analysed and the attempt made to show that this aims not at eliminating objectivity but merely at shifting the emphasis from the objective to the subjective pole. The fifth section will be concerned with Kierkegaard's understanding of objectivity and will attempt to show that Kierkegaard certainly has an object in mind when speaking of the truth in terms of subjectivity but that this object is of a very special kind. During our discussion, attention will, of course, be paid to any apophatic motifs implicit in Kierkegaard's theory of truth.

I. SURVEY OF LITERATURE ON KIERKEGAARD'S THEORY OF TRUTH

Kierkegaard's thesis that 'subjectivity is the truth' is notoriously difficult to interpret. It is one of the most controversial and most discussed aspects of his thought. I wish now to undertake a brief survey of some of the literature on this controversial topic.

Kierkegaard scholars can be divided into two basic camps. The first considers Kierkegaard's theory to be subjectivist or solipsistic. The second camp, however, argues that Kierkegaard does not deny objectivity but is merely concerned with the human being's relation to the truth.

1. The Subjectivist Camp

To the subjectivist camp belong Theodor Haecker, E. J. Carnell, E. L. Allen, Paul Edwards, Arthur E. Murphy, and, to a lesser extent, Herbert M. Garelick, Regis Jolivet, and James Collins.

Haecker takes a sympathetic view of Kierkegaard's position and praises his thesis that subjectivity is the truth as an insight into the need to 'incarnate the truth'.[1] Unfortunately, however, this insight is 'disguised by errors'.[2] Kierkegaard makes the grave error, Haecker argues, of taking the 'how' as his point of departure, the result of which is ultimately the disappearance of the 'what' and the reduction of truth to the 'how'.[3] This is an error on Kierkegaard's part because the 'what' is indispensable for faith. The human being needs 'the firm, dogmatic what of faith'[4] because at the beginning 'the how is weak and distant'.[5]

According to E. J. Carnell, Kierkegaard's thesis that subjectivity is the truth means that '*any* religious position could be defended, providing a person held the position with sufficient subjective passion'.[6] Carnell also criticizes Kierkegaard's emphasis on the need for passion in one's relation to the truth, writing that 'passion has no more authority to create evidences for the Christian religion than it has to create evidences for the science of obstetrics'.[7]

E. L. Allen rightly perceives that Kierkegaard's interest is in ethical and religious truth. Nevertheless, in his opinion Kierkegaard's thesis that subjectivity is the truth is guilty of undermining truth's objectivity. He writes that, 'The religious interest blinded him to the fact that the scientific outlook is of equal importance.'[8] This cannot be tolerated, Allen goes on to argue, for 'The truth which alone can

[1] T. Haecker, 'Der Begriff der Wahrheit bei Sören Kierkegaard', in *Opuscula* (Munich, 1949), 166.
[2] Ibid. 163.   [3] Ibid. 182.   [4] Ibid.   [5] Ibid. 183.
[6] E. J. Carnell, *The Burden of Søren Kierkegaard* (Exeter, 1965), 169 (original emphasis).
[7] Ibid. 170.
[8] E. L. Allen, *Kierkegaard: His Life and Thought* (London, 1935), 150.

save me is the truth which I choose, not for the hope of salvation by
it, but because, saved or lost, I must acknowledge it to be true.'[9]
Allen also claims that Kierkegaard subscribed to the 'disparagement
of intellect in favour of emotion'.[10] Thus although Allen
acknowledges the existential and religious thrust of Kierkegaard's
deliberations on truth, he nevertheless argues that Kierkegaard's
position is in danger of slipping into subjectivism.

When we turn to Paul Edwards and Arthur Murphy we find the
charge of subjectivism advanced much more forcefully. Edwards
asks us to imagine that 'Kierkegaard was mistaken about the nature
of God and that what God prizes is intellectual rectitude and not the
feverish inwardness that Kierkegaard valued so highly.'[11] Edwards
then envisages God rewarding David Hume with eternal bliss for
being a representative of the former while condemning Kierkegaard
to extinction for advocating the latter. After such a judgement
Kierkegaard would not, Edwards argues, feel vindicated by virtue of
his subjectivity but 'would regard himself defeated and refuted . . .
because although "in the truth" in the subjective sense, it would now
become apparent that he was not also in the truth in the objective
sense'.[12] For Edwards Kierkegaard's position is only valid if the
objective uncertainties which he holds on to with subjective passion
prove to be *objectively* true. Edwards thus makes objectivity the
guarantor of the validity of subjectivity.

Arthur Murphy launches a scathing attack upon Kierkegaard's
conception of truth. He perceives no distinction between subjectivity
and 'sheer egocentricity'[13] and believes that 'Kierkegaard has given
us a kind of truth for cases in which we are told not to bother about
the truth.'[14] Despite this, Murphy believes that Kierkegaard's
position presupposes an objective dimension. Indeed, he scorns
Kierkegaard's theory as 'parasitic for its "existential" significance on
the assumed objective truth of a doctrine about man and God'.[15]
Summing up his interpretation of Kierkegaard's position, Murphy
writes: 'Subjectivity is a disclosure of the reality, not of God, but of
Kierkegaard.'[16]

    [9] Ibid. 150–1.   [10] Ibid. 151.
    [11] P. Edwards, 'Kierkegaard and the "Truth" of Christianity', in P. Edwards and
A. Paps (eds.), *A Modern Introduction to Philosophy* (3rd edn., New York, 1973),
514.   [12] Ibid. 515.
    [13] Arthur E. Murphy, 'On Kierkegaard's Claim that "Truth is Subjectivity"', in
J. H. Gill (ed.), *Essays on Kierkegaard* (Minneapolis, 1969), 96.
    [14] Ibid. 98.   [15] Ibid. 99.   [16] Ibid.

In addition to these 'fully fledged subjectivists' mention ought to be made of three scholars who seem to adopt a milder form of subjectivism, namely, Garelick, Jolivet, and Collins. All these believe that Kierkegaard's thesis contains some element of objectivity but hold that this is swamped by what they regard as Kierkegaard's overemphasis of subjectivity.

Garelick points out that Kierkegaard's principle that subjectivity is the truth 'is a *moral commitment* by the individual, not an alternative to the rational way of knowing reality'.[17] Despite this, however, Garelick must be placed in the subjectivist camp. This is because, as he sees it, subjectivity is for Kierkegaard a goal in itself and not merely the means by which he becomes a Christian: 'Subjectivity is not justified in terms of anything else but justifies everything else.'[18]

Jolivet argues that Kierkegaard is not excluding objectivity but is asserting that the accent in questions of truth should be placed on personal assimilation rather than upon doctrinal content.[19] Nevertheless, Jolivet holds 'that Kierkegaard incontestably has a tendency to depreciate the "objective" for the sake of the purely subjective, and to misunderstand the function of the Church'.[20] Jolivet attributes this to a tension between Kierkegaard's Lutheran background and the implicit Catholicism of his thought.

Collins, like Jolivet, seems to occupy a middle ground between those who accuse Kierkegaard of solipsism and those who argue that there is indeed an objective dimension to Kierkegaard's thought. Although not holding Kierkegaard to be subjectivist, Collins believes that in his subordination of the 'what' to the 'how', Kierkegaard 'fails to understand sufficiently the coercion which the thing rightfully exercises over the mind, in the formation of the speculatively true judgement'.[21]

There are several objections that can be raised against the subjectivist interpretation of Kierkegaard's conception of the truth. First, as Alistair Hannay points out, 'It is not clear...that Kierkegaard employs a sense of "true" confined to the manner or "how" of the believer's believing, and which takes no account of what, for the Christian, must be objectively the case if his belief is to have the significance in reality he supposes it has.'[22] As we shall see in

---

[17] Garelick, *Anti-Christianity*, 21 (original emphasis).   [18] Ibid. 62.
[19] Jolivet, *Introduction*, 169.
[20] Ibid. 172.   [21] Collins, *Mind of Kierkegaard*, 144.
[22] Hannay, *Kierkegaard*, 133.

the course of this chapter, there is much to suggest that Kierkegaard
has a much broader conception of truth than the subjectivist camp
gives him credit for.

Secondly, it is doubtful that Kierkegaard's intention is to establish
a theory for the justification of truth claims. As Hannay points out,
the word 'proof' occurs only very rarely in Kierkegaard's works.[23]
On the basis of this apparent lack of interest in questions of proof, it
is questionable whether Kierkegaard develops the concept of
subjectivity as a means of verifying truth claims.

Thirdly, Edwards makes being a Christian dependent upon
believing '*as a matter of fact* there is a God, that God manifested
himself in the person of Christ, and that human beings are
immortal'.[24] The counter-question we could put to Edwards and to
the other subjectivists is: in what sense can we speak of these as facts?
The problem is precisely that these 'facts' spring the confines of what
is normally understood by the word 'fact'.

Fourthly, in his deliberations on God's behaviour at the Last
Judgement Edwards is guilty of two errors Kierkegaard was at pains
to combat, namely, speculation and the human being's tendency to
attempt to view the truth from a God-like perspective. One of the
points Kierkegaard wishes to make in advancing his thesis that
'subjectivity is the truth' is that human beings are not capable of
occupying the position Edwards takes up in his exposition. Precisely
because we are finite beings and thus incapable of experiencing the
totality of objective truth, we have to be content with subjective
truth. That this truth may prove to be objectively untrue is the risk
we have to take as finite, existing individuals.

2. *The Non-Subjectivist Camp*

The non-subjectivist camp holds that Kierkegaard's thesis does not
dispense with objectivity but is concerned merely with shifting the
emphasis from the objective to the subjective pole. Within this group
there are again many different positions, depending primarily upon
how 'objectivity' is understood. Among the representatives of this
position are Emanuel Hirsch, Günter Rohrmoser, E. D. Klemke,
Liselotte Richter, Romano Guardini, Mark C. Taylor, Walter
Schulz, Hermann Diem, J. Heywood Thomas, Robert Perkins, and
Louis Pojman.

[23] Ibid. 138–9.   [24] Edwards, 'Kierkegaard', 514 (original emphasis).

Hirsch[25] bases his interpretation upon Kierkegaard's definition of Christianity as an 'existential communication'. According to Hirsch, this definition contains two distinct elements. First, 'as something which approaches us from outside, the existential communication of Christianity has naturally presupposed or brought with it a provisional knowledge of what Christianity is.' This knowledge belongs to the sphere of the 'objective-historical'. In this sense, then, there is an objective side to Kierkegaard's thesis that 'subjectivity is the truth'. Secondly, the 'objective-historical' side of Christianity leads not to historical or systematic knowledge but to *Christsein* or *Christwerden*. Indeed, this objective aspect is only disclosed through being actualized in an ethical-religious existence. Only when the Christian actualizes this truth in his own existence can he be said to have a relation to the truth. It is in this sense that subjectivity is the truth.

Rohrmoser[26] also argues that Kierkegaard's thesis presupposes an objective element. He points out that the problem with which Kierkegaard is concerned is that of reintroducing Christianity into Christendom. The truth as such is known. The problem is that the age relates itself to this truth in an untrue way. The issue is thus not one of establishing or discovering the objective truth, but of establishing a relation to a truth that is already known.

Like Hirsch and Rohrmoser, Klemke[27] argues that Christianity is the objective element in Kierkegaard's theory of truth. It is not that Kierkegaard denies the objective pole of the truth relationship but that for him the crucial question is: 'How may I be related to this proclamation, or to the possibility for personal transformation which it presents?' Kierkegaard's answer, as Klemke formulates it, is 'This is a subjective matter.' By this Kierkegaard means that the response to objectivity, i.e. the historical proclamation of the Christian faith, is determined by each individual for himself 'upon the basis of his entire selfhood, rather than merely his intellect'.

Richter[28] argues that Kierkegaard cannot be out to defend a theory of subjectivism since subjectivism, like objectivism, belongs in the sphere of objective reflection. Rather, 'Kierkegaard

[25] Emanuel Hirsch, *Kierkegaard-Studien*, i–iii (Gütersloh, 1930–3), 778–9.
[26] Günter Rohrmoser, 'Die Metaphysik und das Problem der Subjektivität', in *Emanzipation und Freiheit* (Munich, 1970), 159–96.
[27] Klemke, *Studies*, 5.
[28] Liselotte Richter, *Der Begriff der Subjektivität: Ein Beitrag zur christlichen Existenzdarstellung* (Würzburg, 1934), 2.

understands subjectivity as an existential expression for the thinking
subject's concern about himself.' In other words, becoming
'subjective' does not entail the individual's divorcing himself from
objectivity but the attempt to establish a correct relationship to
objectivity.

For Guardini[29] the truth with which Kierkegaard is concerned is
spiritual truth. 'Truth' does not refer to something the individual
correctly grasps but to the necessity of self-commitment in his
relation to the truth and to the actualization of the self that this
brings. Because of this reference to the human self the truth comes to
be defined not according to its object but to its subject.

Like Guardini, Mark Taylor argues that Kierkegaard's theory
of truth must be restricted to the religious sphere. Indeed, Taylor reformulates Kierkegaard's thesis as 'religious truth is
subjectivity'.[30] His interpretation is based on the inclusion of the
term 'appropriation' in Kierkegaard's definition of truth on p. 182 of
the *Concluding Unscientific Postscript*. On the basis of this term he
defines subjectivity as 'the process by which an individual
appropriates what he thinks, or constitutes his actuality by realizing
his possibilities'.[31] Taylor sees Kierkegaard's position as being best
summed up by the phrases 'he is true to' or 'he is faithful to', both of
which presuppose an object.

Schulz[32] believes it to be a grave error to treat Kierkegaard as a
subjectivist. In his opinion, Kierkegaard does not wish to deny the
objectivity of truth but to assert the necessity of *relating oneself* to
the truth. Because objective truth is unattainable, however, this act
of self-relation is transformed into striving. As a result of this
the immediate goal ceases to be objectivity and becomes the
establishment of oneself as a striver.

That Diem belongs to the non-subjectivist camp is made clear by
his criticism of Høffding's argument that Kierkegaard 'sought truth
in the subjective (psychological) sphere,' and 'made it the object of
personal feeling'.[33] Such a conclusion can only be drawn, Diem
argues, if one disregards the whole of Kierkegaard's dialectic. As

---

[29] Romano Guardini, 'Der Ausgangspunkt der Denkbewegung Sören
Kierkegaards', in Schrey, *Søren Kierkegaard*, 76.

[30] Taylor, *Kierkegaard's Pseudonymous Authorship*, 38, 44.

[31] Ibid. 44; cf. *Journey to Selfhood*, 100–1.

[32] Schulz, 'Sören Kierkegaard', in Schrey, *Søren Kierkegaard*, 313–14.

[33] Diem, *Kierkegaard's Dialectic*, 38 n. Diem refers to H. Høffding's *S.
Kierkegaard als Philosoph* (1922), 74 ff.

evidence against the subjectivist position Diem points to p. 182 of the *Postscript*. This passage is concerned, Diem claims, 'to establish what the character of subjectivity must be if it is to be anchored in truth'.[34] It is only on this basis that we can go on to enquire into what truth is objectively, which, according to Diem, means investigating what objectively corresponds to that which the subjective thinker experiences as truth.

Heywood Thomas[35] rejects the argument that Kierkegaard is subjectivist on two grounds. First, he claims that the fact that 'faith is an expression of the individual's concern and that God only exists for subjectivity does not mean that faith creates its object and that subjectivity is subjectivism'. As evidence for this position he cites Book One of the *Postscript*, where Kierkegaard deals with the possibility of treating truth objectively. An analysis of this book will show that Kierkegaard does not reject the objective approach as such but wishes to make clear its limitations. Secondly, the real issue is not the question of objectivity but the question of the relation of the individual to the objectively given truth. Objectivity is not rejected but is merely subordinated to subjectivity. In addition to this, Heywood Thomas points out that part of the meaning of Kierkegaard's thesis is that every assertion must be subjectively appropriated if the truth is indeed to be the truth. This again presupposes an object. On the basis of these considerations Heywood Thomas concludes that the charge of subjectivism made against Kierkegaard cannot be upheld.

Robert Perkins's rejection of subjectivism is particularly vigorous.[36] 'Sometimes', he writes, 'it is said that Kierkegaard's notion of subjective truth allows for even Nazism and sado-masochism.' The error of these views becomes clear, however, when we recall that Kierkegaard is concerned with the edification of the human being, something which does not entail simply believing what one wants to believe but involves believing in a manner which develops the individual religiously and morally. Clearly, this is not the case with Nazism and sado-masochism. As Perkins puts it, 'the actual texturing of upbuilding and subjectivity is sufficient to end such nonsense'.

Finally, mention ought to be made of Louis Pojman's position.

---

[34] Diem, *Kierkegaard's Dialectic*, 49.
[35] J. Heywood Thomas, *Subjectivity and Paradox* (Oxford, 1957), 72.
[36] Perkins, 'Kierkegaard', 16.

Pojman argues that Kierkegaard's thesis presupposes objectivity, although there are passages which seem to indicate that this objectivity is attainable only through subjectivity.

Pojman's argument is extremely complex. In his opinion, there are three incompatible notions of subjectivity present in Kierkegaard's thought, namely 'the reduplicative model of subjectivity or Socratic subjectivity',[37] 'the Platonic or metaphysical model of subjectivity',[38] and 'the necessary-condition or auxiliary model of subjectivity'.[39]

The reduplicative model is understood by Pojman as 'the correspondence theory of subjective truth', i.e. 'truth is a correspondence of a state of affairs (my life) with an idea which it aims to reproduce'.[40] This does not as such rule out objectivity, Pojman argues, but makes clear that 'it will never be reached and that our task is to live within our lights'.[41]

The Platonic model of subjectivity is a form of recollection. By increasing his subjectivity the individual comes to discover 'objective' truths. As evidence Pojman cites *Pap.* V B 40, X A 299; *E/O* ii. 171 (Swenson translation); and *CUP* 206, all of which seem to indicate that some sort of objectivity can be established on the basis of subjectivity. He concludes, 'It would seem, then, that if a person is maximally subjective over some proposition, he can be sure that the proposition is true. That is, maximal subjectivity is a sufficient condition for having metaphysical knowledge, even when it is of the highest kind, centred on the absolute paradox.'[42]

The third form of subjectivity, the necessary-condition model, falls between the reduplicative and the Platonic models. This states that 'if the truth is attainable, it must be attained through subjectivity and not objectivity'.[43] Subjectivity does not guarantee truth but is a necessary condition for it.

These three forms of subjectivity are, according to Pojman, incompatible. They all contain some element of objectivity but this varies according to the form of subjectivity under discussion. Pojman attributes this incompatibility to Kierkegaard's lack of interest in logical connections.

Against the basic argument of the non-subjectivist camp no substantial objections can, in my opinion, be raised. In the

---

[37] Pojman, *Logic of Subjectivity*, 63–5.   [38] Ibid. 64, 68.
[39] Ibid. 64, 71.   [40] Ibid. 67.   [41] Ibid.
[42] Ibid. 71.   [43] Ibid.

following, I intend to take up this argument and to examine in some detail the nature of the objective element in Kierkegaard's conception of truth. In the course of this examination we shall also, of course, be constantly alert to any apophatic elements present in Kierkegaard's thought. Our first task is that of determining the aim and scope of Kierkegaard's theory of truth.

II. THE SCOPE AND PURPOSE OF KIERKEGAARD'S CONCEPTION OF TRUTH

1. *The Existential Dimension of Truth*

The first point we must make is that Kierkegaard is not interested in constructing a philosophical theory. His aim is rather to elucidate the nature of the human being's relationship to the truth. Although this sometimes resembles the work of a philosopher intent on establishing a truth theory, Kierkegaard's interests are not so much philosophical as existential and religious. That is, he is anxious to find a truth which can give his life *meaning*. This is made clear in an early journal entry:

The crucial thing is to find a truth which is truth *for me*, to find *the idea for which I am willing to live and die*. Of what use would it be to me to discover a so-called objective truth, to work through the philosophical systems so that I could, if asked, make critical judgements about them, could point out the fallacies in each system; of what use would it be to me to be able to develop a theory of the state, getting details from various sources and combining them into a whole, and constructing a world I did not live in but merely held up for others to see; of what use would it be to me to be able to explain the meaning of Christianity . . . if it had no deeper meaning *for me and for my life*? . . . Of what use would it be to me for truth to stand before me, cold and naked, not caring whether or not I acknowledged it, making me uneasy rather than trustingly receptive. I certainly do not deny that I still accept an *imperative of knowledge* and that through it men may be influenced, but *then it must come alive in me*, and *this* is what I now recognize as the most important of all.[44]

---

[44] *JP* v. 5100 (original emphasis). Cf. *CUP* 34 n., where Kierkegaard quotes an anecdote from Plutarch's *Moralia* about Eudamidas who, on being told that the aged Xenocrates was a wise man engaged in the search for virtue, asked, 'But when does he then propose to use it?'

Further evidence for the existential thrust of Kierkegaard's conception of truth is provided when we turn to Kierkegaard's works themselves. A close examination will show them to be peppered with references to the existential dimension of the truth. Thus in the *Concluding Unscientific Postscript*, for example, Kierkegaard writes that the truth with which he is concerned is 'essential truth', which he defines as 'the truth which is essentially related to existence'.[45]

This emphasis upon the *existential* nature of truth also reveals the implicit apophaticism of Kierkegaard's thought. As we have seen, for Kierkegaard the question of truth is first and foremost a question about one's personal existence and how one is to structure this existence in such a way that it can acquire *meaning*. This stress on *existential* meaning places truth beyond the competence of theories that treat truth objectively, the consequence of which is that from the objective perspective truth is 'hidden'.

2. *The* Terminus ad quem *of Truth: Eternal Happiness*

The existential nature of the truth is made particularly evident by Kierkegaard's introduction of the concept of 'eternal happiness'.[46] This concept is important for our discussion for two reasons. First, eternal happiness constitutes the *terminus ad quem* of truth. That is, the goal towards which the individual is striving in his quest for the truth is that of acquiring an eternal happiness. Secondly, Kierkegaard's development of the concept of eternal happiness makes particularly apparent the apophatic strand in his thought.

Like most of Kierkegaard's key concepts eternal happiness is very difficult to define.[47] Indeed, Kierkegaard argues that a definition is

---

[45] *CUP* 178 n.

[46] *En evig Salighed.* This expression is difficult to translate because of the variety of meanings the word *Salighed* possesses. Most commentators opt for 'happiness'. The problem with this translation is that 'happiness' can easily acquire aesthetic connotations which distract from the religious meaning of the term. A better translation would perhaps be 'blessedness', which is the term Hannay and Taylor opt for. However, since the most commonly employed translation is 'happiness', we will retain this term.

[47] Opinions vary among Kierkegaard commentators as to how to define this term. Blass argues that 'happiness' means being a self and the predication of 'eternity' expresses the fact that this happiness consists in the perfect and eternal actualization of the essence of the human being. However, because the human being can attain selfhood only by establishing a relationship with God, the concept of an eternal happiness is expanded and comes occasionally to be employed by Kierkegaard as a

in fact impossible. Eternal happiness is the 'poorest of all conceptions'[48] and any attempt to define it would automatically reduce it to an aesthetic category.[49] In fact, to talk about it at all is an indication that one does *not* talk about it.[50] Nor can an eternal happiness be proved to exist. If such an attempt were made, eternal happiness would *eo ipso* 'be non-existent, since the existence of the absolute ethical good can be proved only by the individual himself expressing it existentially in existence'.[51] Furthermore, an eternal happiness is only observable on the basis of its mode of acquisition,[52] but this is an observation that I can carry out only with regard to myself.[53] I am thus not in the position to judge whether other individuals sustain a relationship to an eternal happiness.

In this emphasis on the inaccessibility of eternal happiness to analysis and description the apophatic strand in Kierkegaard's thought again becomes apparent. This can be seen in the fact that one of the principal features of eternal happiness is that it is indefinable. Only the individual who comes to acquire an eternal happiness by structuring his life in accordance with it can have some insight into its nature. This insight, however, cannot be expressed. As we have seen, to attempt to do so would mean either transferring eternal happiness into the sphere of objective thought, where it does not and cannot belong, or reducing it to an aesthetic concept. Both procedures would entail the negation of eternal happiness. The individual who stands in relation to an eternal happiness is thus unable to articulate what it is he stands in relation to. Consequently,

---

synonym for God (J. L. Blass, *Die Krise der Freiheit im Denken Sören Kierkegaards: Untersuchungen zur Konstitution der Subjektivität* (Ratingen bei Düsseldorf, 1969), 140). For Sløk (*Die Anthropologie Kierkegaards*, 122), eternal happiness means becoming an eternally valid self. Weisshaupt also interprets 'eternity' to mean 'validity' and understands the terms 'absolute *telos*', 'absolute good', as well as 'eternal happiness', to describe the 'continual validity' of existence. These terms express the meaning of human existence. That which the self should become as dictated by this meaning is its eternal happiness (K. Weisshaupt, *Die Zeitlichkeit der Wahrheit: Eine Untersuchung zum Wahrheitsbegriff Søren Kierkegaards* (Freiburg, 1973), 114). By far the fullest treatment of this concept, however, is Abrahim H. Khan's, *Salighed as Happiness?* We cannot do justice to Khan's thorough and detailed analysis of *Salighed* here. It is sufficient to note that he writes: 'For Kierkegaard, *Salighed* is primarily an ethico-religious ideality that is constitutive of human personality. As such it is not an object for assessment but a criterion for one's life' (p. 84). Khan also points out that Kierkegaard interprets *Salighed* 'to show that true selfhood is acquired on the basis of one's helplessness before God' (p. 85).

[48] *CUP* 352.   [49] *CUP* 349, 351–2.   [50] *CUP* 350–1.   [51] *CUP* 379.
[52] *CUP* 383, cf. 347–9, 352.   [53] *CUP* 346, 352–3.

the upshot of Kierkegaard's position is not only that the truth as such is 'hidden' from the existing individual, as we saw earlier, but so too is the *terminus ad quem* of truth.

Despite the impossibility of arriving at a definition of eternal happiness, however, Kierkegaard does make some comments which enable us to gain a limited comprehension of the nature of this concept. It is helpful if we divide these comments into two groups, namely those that refer to the *form* of eternal happiness and those that refer to its *content*.

The most explicit references Kierkegaard makes to eternal happiness are descriptions of its form. Thus we are informed that eternal happiness is the highest[54] or absolute[55] good. Although this good, like eternal happiness itself, cannot be described,[56] its very name gives us some indication of how Kierkegaard understands eternal happiness, namely, as the highest good possible for the human being.

A further indication of the form of eternal happiness is provided by the connection Kierkegaard makes between eternal happiness and the 'absolute *telos*'. Indeed, these two concepts are often employed interchangeably.[57] Again, although the absolute *telos* cannot be described but 'exists for the individual only when he yields it an absolute devotion',[58] its very name indicates one of the characteristics of eternal happiness, namely, that it is the highest goal for the human being.

As an initial definition, then, eternal happiness is the highest good and the goal of human existence.

Although this may serve as an initial definition, eternal happiness is in fact more complex than this. As mentioned above, this concept not only possesses a form but also has a content. It is, however, exceedingly difficult to reach a full and clear comprehension of this content. This lack of clarity is most probably deliberate policy on Kierkegaard's part. If an eternal happiness is the highest good, then its content is to a certain degree dependent upon what the individual conceives such a good to be, as well as upon the degree in which he comes to structure his life according to it. If we link this with Kierkegaard's theory of stages, the content of eternal happiness

---

[54] *CUP* 19, 116, 348–50, 381, 545.   [55] *CUP* 347, 382–3, 407.
[56] *CUP* 382–3, 407.
[57] *CUP* 352, 355–6, 360, 362, 404, 468, 497.   [58] *CUP* 355.

could be understood as being determined by the human being's progression through the spheres of existence. If this is the case, then another apophatic motif would seem to be present. Namely, if eternal happiness is dependent upon progress through the spheres of existence, we can speak of an eternal happiness being hidden from the individual according to the distance that still remains between him and the highest sphere of existence.

Despite the fluidity of the concept, however, Kierkegaard does indeed seem to have a specific content in mind in his deliberations on eternal happiness. Although individuals in lower spheres of existence may not realize it, the ultimate goal of their quest for an eternal happiness is God. That this is the case is indicated by a number of considerations.

The clearest indication of this is that in certain passages Kierkegaard seems to employ 'eternal happiness' as a synonym for 'God'.[59] In addition to this, there are a number of statements which indicate that the term is closely connected with the God-relationship. For example, it is sometimes employed to mean 'eternal life' or 'immortality'[60] and, as Taylor points out,[61] in the sphere of religiousness B it appears to be synonymous with salvation. Further evidence of the essentially religious nature of eternal happiness is provided by the problem Kierkegaard sets himself in *Philosophical Fragments* and *Concluding Unscientific Postscript*: 'Can a historical point of departure be given for an eternal consciousness; how can such a point of departure be of more than historical interest; can an eternal happiness be built on historical knowledge?'[62] The historical point of departure in question is, of course, the Incarnation. This juxtaposition of eternal happiness with the Incarnation would again seem to indicate that Kierkegaard conceives of there being a close relationship between eternal happiness and God.[63] However, in defining the content of eternal happiness in this way Kierkegaard is not making it any less opaque. As we shall see in Chapter 6, Kierkegaard adopts an apophatic understanding of God, a fact which means that a description of eternal happiness in theistic terms is itself apophatic.

---

[59] *CUP* 432, 446; cf. 472, 483, where Kierkegaard seems to shift from one term to the other with no apparent distinction in meaning.

[60] *CUP* 496.   [61] Taylor, *Kierkegaard's Pseudonymous Authorship*, 240.

[62] *PF* 1; *CUP* 18; cf. *CUP* 86–7, 241–2, 323–4, 330, 340, 345.

[63] Cf. the relation Kierkegaard posits between eternal happiness and Christianity in *CUP* 20; cf. 19, 545.

Having investigated the goal towards which Kierkegaard's concept of truth is directed, it is now necessary to discuss the foundation upon which he constructs this concept.

III. THE STRUCTURE OF TRUTH: TRUTH AS THE IDENTITY OF THOUGHT AND BEING

Kierkegaard takes as his starting-point the correspondence theory of truth, namely, the thesis that truth consists in the identity of thought and being. He has, however, severe reservations about the form in which this theory has come down to him. Before it can serve as the basis for the development of a valid concept of the truth, it must therefore be subjected to stringent criticism and revision.

1. *The Meaning of Being*

Kierkegaard's first attack concentrates on the meaning of 'being'. He argues that before we can make use of the traditional formulation of the correspondence theory we must establish what is meant by the term 'being'.

According to Kierkegaard being can be defined in two ways. First, it can be defined as empirical being, i.e. being is identified with concrete existence.[64] Existence or empirical being, however, is never finished. This is because everything in the sphere of existence is in a continual and never-ending process of change. Indeed, empirical being is not being at all in the strict sense but is *becoming*. This has serious consequences for the truth. Because empirical being is incomplete and in a process of becoming it is impossible to establish a genuine identity between thought and being. Because one of its elements is incomplete, the correspondence of thought and being that constitutes the truth is also incomplete. The truth thus becomes a 'desideratum' or 'an approximation'.[65] In addition to this, the incompleteness of empirical being has a retroactive effect on the whole process of attempting to establish the truth. The lack of a conclusion makes it impossible not only to bring to an end such a process of

---

[64] *CUP* 169.   [65] Ibid.

development towards the truth, but also to embark upon such a process in the first place.[66]

The difficulties of the empirical position can be avoided, however, if being is understood idealistically, i.e. 'as the abstract reflection of, or the abstract prototype for, what being is as concrete empirical being'.[67] There is now nothing to prevent us from understanding being as finished because the identity of thought and being is, from the standpoint of abstract thought, always finished. But this approach contains a fundamental weakness. It reduces the thought-being formula to a tautology. The being that is united with thought is merely the abstract form (i.e. the concept) of being. Consequently, 'Thought and being mean one and the same thing, and the correspondence spoken of is merely an abstract self-identity.'[68]

If we are to develop a concept of truth that is viable for human existence, then, there are two things we must avoid. On the one hand, we must avoid allowing the concreteness of being to cause truth to become an impossibility. On the other hand, however, we must avoid reducing being to an abstraction.

2. *The Problem of the Thinker's Relation to the Truth*

Kierkegaard's second criticism of the correspondence theory stems from his belief that it fails adequately to express the thinker's relation to the truth. This is because traditional forms of the theory have tended to work according to the principles of objective reflection. The problem with this is that, as we saw in our discussion of dialectics in Chapter 2, objective reflection emphasizes the predominance of thought over being, thus causing the thinker to direct his thought away from his own personal being.[69] With respect to the truth this means that the task becomes that of establishing *objective* truth, a task which involves pointing one's thoughts away from one's relationship with the object held to be the truth towards a consideration of the object itself. Once the validity of the object is established, it is argued, then a relationship to it follows as a matter of course.

---

[66] Should the thinker nevertheless make a beginning 'such a beginning is not the consequence of an immanent movement of thought, but is effected through a resolution of the will, essentially in the strength of faith' (*CUP* 169).
[67] *CUP* 170.   [68] Ibid., cf. 112.   [69] *CUP* 178.

When the question of truth is raised in an objective manner, reflection is directed objectively to the truth, as an object to which the knower is related. Reflection is not focused upon the relationship, however, but upon the question of whether it is the truth to which the knower is related. If only the object to which he is related is the truth, the subject is accounted to be in the truth.[70]

This approach has three important consequences for an understanding of the truth.

First, objective reflection causes 'the subject and his subjectivity [to] become indifferent'.[71] The inquirer is interested only in the objective truth of the object concerned. He is not interested in considering his own relationship to this object and the significance this might have for the acquisition of an eternal happiness.

The inquiring, speculating, and knowing subject thus raises a question of truth. But he does not raise the question of a subjective truth, the truth of appropriation and assimilation. The inquiring subject is indeed interested; but he is not infinitely and personally and passionately interested on behalf of his own eternal happiness for his relationship to this truth.[72]

Yet it is precisely the individual's subjectivity[73] and passionate interest in the truth[74] that determine his relation to an eternal happiness. With objective reflection's elimination of these concepts, however, any such relation simply disappears.

Secondly, even if the objective inquirer invests his inquiry with subjectivity and passion, he can never establish the truth in such a way that it can become the basis for an eternal happiness. The reason for this is that absolute certitude is required if eternal happiness is to be achieved by objective means. Kierkegaard writes, 'In relation to an eternal happiness, and an infinite passionate interest in its behalf (in which latter alone the former can exist), an iota is of importance, of infinite importance.'[75] The consequence of this is that the objectively inquiring individual embarks upon a never-ending process of approximation. He becomes enmeshed in a constant collation, selection, and analysis of 'objective' facts in the attempt to establish with certitude that it is *this* object upon which an eternal happiness should be based. Such an approximation, however, is 'essentially incommensurable with an infinite personal interest in an

[70] Ibid.   [71] *CUP* 173.   [72] *CUP* 23.   [73] *CUP* 105.
[74] *CUP* 28, 33; cf. 54.   [75] *CUP* 28.

eternal happiness'.[76] Attempts to base an eternal happiness upon, for example, the absolute historicity of the Bible[77] or upon one's church membership[78] are doomed to failure. The necessary certainty can simply not be attained. Such attempts succeed only in plunging the individual into despair.[79]

Thirdly, through being treated as an object, truth ultimately becomes a matter of indifference to the individual engaged in its inquiry. Objective reflection results in such 'truths' as mathematics and historical knowledge. Such 'truths' are indifferent because they are of no decisive significance to the existence of the individual himself.[80]

If we are to avoid the errors of traditional versions of the correspondence theory, then, we must reject objective reflection and make use of subjective reflection. This is necessary because, as we saw in our analysis of Kierkegaard's dialectics, subjective reflection is concerned with precisely that which for objective reflection is a matter of indifference, namely the subject and his relationship to the truth: 'When the question of the truth is raised subjectively, reflection is directed subjectively to the nature of the individual's relationship.'[81] For Kierkegaard this means that thought is not to be pointed away from the subject but 'must probe more and more deeply into the subject and his subjectivity'.[82] The individual himself is the place where the truth is to be found.

This stress on the individual as the place where truth is to be found means that the crucial thing is not that the individual establish that the object believed to be the truth is indeed the truth, but that he establish the correct *relationship* to this object: 'If only the mode of this relationship is in the truth, the individual is in the truth even if he should happen to be thus related to what is not true.'[83] And, as Kierkegaard writes with reference to the question of God's existence: 'Objectively, reflection is directed to the problem of whether this object is the true God; subjectively, reflection is directed to the question whether the individual is related to something *in such a manner* that his relationship is in truth a God-relationship.'[84] It is, then, not the establishment of the validity of an object but the establishment of a proper relationship that constitutes the truth.

The question now arises as to how subjective reflection is able to

---

[76] *CUP* 26.   [77] *CUP* 27–8.   [78] *CUP* 42–3.   [79] *CUP* 28, 43.
[80] *CUP* 173.   [81] *CUP* 178.   [82] *CUP* 171, cf. 175.   [83] *CUP* 178.
[84] Ibid. (original emphasis).

unite thought and being and thereby establish the truth. If we link the above discussion with our analysis of ethical knowledge in the previous chapter, an answer is readily provided. Truth is established when the human being unites thought and being in his own personal existence by constructing his existence (being) according to his conception (thought) of the truth. That is, by acting upon what one conceives to be the truth, one actualizes this conception in one's own being. This conception of the truth thus ceases to be an abstract possibility and is anchored in the concrete existence of the individual human being, thereby re-establishing the identity of thought and being that constitutes the truth.

By making the existence of the single individual the sphere in which thought and being are reunited, truth becomes subjective. It is now necessary to examine in detail the nature of this subjectivity and its significance for our investigation of the apophatic nature of Kierkegaard's thought.

IV. SUBJECTIVITY

Subjectivity is a complex term encompassing a diversity of meaning often overlooked by commentators, particularly by those critical of Kierkegaard. Pojman indicates the complexity of the term when he writes:

On the surface at least, it would seem that the term 'subjectivity' in Kierkegaard's work signifies not a simple concept but a set of concepts, related to each other but not identical. At various times, the term stands for inwardness in general, passionate striving for some object, the emotions, the action of the will, acquiring a belief, the act of faith, the voice of conscience, the process of reduplicating an ideal, and the process of introspection, as well as intuition.[85]

In my opinion this gamut of meanings can be reduced to two distinct but closely related concepts, namely, subjectivity as *relationship* and subjectivity as the *selfhood* of the existing individual.

1. *Subjectivity as Relationship*

Kierkegaard formulates the relational dimension of subjectivity in a variety of different ways.

[85] Pojman, *Logic of Subjectivity*, 55.

(a) The 'How' and 'What' of the Truth

This formulation is aimed at drawing attention to the fact that it is the relationship (the 'how') and not the object (the 'what') of the relationship that determines the truth. Kierkegaard writes:

The objective accent falls upon WHAT is said, the subjective accent on HOW it is said. . . . Objectively the interest is focused merely on the thought-content, subjectively on the inwardness. At its maximum this inward 'how' is the passion of the infinite, and the passion of the infinite is the truth. But the passion of the infinite is precisely subjectivity, and thus subjectivity becomes the truth. . . . It is the passion of the infinite that is the decisive factor and not its content, for its content is precisely itself. In this manner subjectivity and the subjective 'how' constitute the truth.[86]

What Kierkegaard means by this is that truth is only truth to the degree in which the individual relates himself to the object or proposition held to be the truth. To regard the 'what' as the criterion of truth is to embark, as we have already seen, on an endless approximation process,[87] with the result that the existing individual never comes to have the opportunity to exist in the truth he is so anxious to grasp objectively. The problem of existing in the truth is only solved if we dispense with the attempt to grasp the truth objectively and concentrate on our relationship to the truth. As Kierkegaard more briefly puts it, 'The mode of apprehension of the truth is precisely the truth.'[88]

Indeed, since it is the relationship that is decisive, it is possible to be in the truth even when the individual is related to an object which is not the truth.

If one who lives in the midst of Christendom goes up to the house of God, the house of the true God, with the true conception of God in his knowledge, and prays, but prays in a false spirit; and one who lives in an idolatrous community prays with the entire passion of the infinite, although his eyes rest upon the image of an idol: where is there most truth? The one prays in truth to God though he worships an idol; the other prays falsely to the true God, and hence worships in fact an idol.[89]

---

[86] *CUP* 181 (original emphasis), cf. 442, 540; *JP* iv. 4537, 4550, 4558, 4868; v. 5791, 5792.
[87] *CUP* 539, cf. 541. [88] *CUP* 287, cf. 115. [89] *CUP* 179–80, 542.

(b) The Way

Kierkegaard also describes truth as 'the way'.[90] As was the case with his emphasis upon the 'how' of truth, this description stresses the importance of the relationship rather than the need to establish objectively certain results.

(c) Appropriation

A further aspect of subjectivity is 'appropriation'. This term draws out more explicitly the nature of the relational dimension of the truth. The individual is not called upon simply to know the truth, but is required to *appropriate* it. He is called upon to make this truth his own by actualizing it in *his* own existence. This is succinctly expressed in the *Concept of Anxiety*.

What I am speaking about is very plain and simple, namely, that truth is for the particular individual only as he himself produces it in action. If the truth is for the individual in any other way, or if he prevents the truth from being for him in that way, we have a phenomenon of the demonic. Truth has always had many loud proclaimers, but the question is whether a person will in the deepest sense acknowledge the truth, will allow it to permeate his whole being, will accept all its consequences, and not have an emergency hiding place for himself and a Judas kiss for the consequence.[91]

(d) Reduplication

This idea of appropriating the truth is also expressed by the concept of reduplication.[92] According to Kierkegaard, 'to reduplicate is to "exist" in what one understands',[93] something which is succinctly summed up in the following passage: 'No, truth in its very being is the reduplication in me, in thee, in him, so that my, that thy, that his life, approximately, in the striving to attain it, is the very being of truth, is a *life*, as the truth was in Christ, for he was the truth.'[94]

(e) Inwardness

Inwardness is closely related to subjectivity. Indeed there are many

   [90] *TC* 202–6.   [91] *CA* 138.
   [92] See Malantschuk for a detailed analysis of this concept: G. Malantschuk, 'Begrebet Fordobelse hos Søren Kierkegaard', in *Kierkegaardiana*, ii (1957), 43–53.
   [93] *TC* 133.   [94] *TC* 201 (original emphasis).

passages in which Kierkegaard seems to employ inwardness interchangeably with subjectivity.[95] For this reason some commentators have come to regard the two concepts as synonymous.[96] Despite the closeness of the relationship between the two concepts, however, they are in my opinion to be distinguished. Subjectivity is the all-embracing term for the individual's relationship to the truth. Inwardness, on the other hand, describes the nature of the subjective 'how' that is required on the part of the existing individual in his relationship to the truth. As Hannay points out, 'The concept of inwardness is an important, indeed the central, element in Kierkegaard's answer to the question of what is required of subjectivity for it to grasp "the" problem of the *Postscript*: the subject's relationship to Christianity.'[97]

When we attempt to ascertain the precise content of this concept and the contribution it makes to the individual's relation to the truth, however, we run up against the problem that so often confronts us when reading Kierkegaard. Like so many of Kierkegaard's concepts the nature of inwardness is such that it is impossible to arrive at a full and clear definition. Kierkegaard himself notes this and remarks that 'it is no doubt difficult to give a definition of inwardness'.[98] Nevertheless, he does give us some hints from which we can gain an impression of the meaning of inwardness and its importance for the individual's relation to the truth.

The most important feature of inwardness is that it seems to be a form of introspection. Kierkegaard describes inwardness as the individual's 'reflection into himself' or 'relation to himself'.[99] What this entails is made clear by the following journal entry: 'In order to swim, one strips naked—in order to seek the truth, one must strip in a far more inward sense, must take off a much more internal attire of thoughts, opinions, selfishness, etc. before one is sufficiently

---

[95] In some passages inwardness seems to be equated with subjectivity (*CUP* 33, 42, 51, 266; *JP* iv. 4537). Similarly, in the title of his main chapter on subjectivity (*CUP* 169) inwardness seems to be equated with subjective truth. Elsewhere Kierkegaard shifts from subjectivity to inwardness (*JP* iv. 4550) or from inwardness to subjectivity (*CUP* 226) with no apparent change in meaning. In *CUP* 154 he states that inwardness means becoming subjective, and in *CA* 141 inwardness in conjunction with certitude is said to equal subjectivity.

[96] M. Theunissen and W. Greve (eds.), *Materialien zur Philosophie Søren Kierkegaards* (Frankfurt am Main, 1979), 36; Collins, *Mind of Kierkegaard*, 141; Price, *Narrow Pass*, 126.

[97] Hannay, *Kierkegaard*, 128.   [98] *CA* 146.

[99] *CUP* 391; *CA* 142; *PV* 42-3, 69; cf. *CUP* 37.

naked.'[100] Inwardness, then, is the individual's probing into himself in such a way that those elements which impede his expression and embodiment of the truth are removed. Consequently, like subjectivity, inwardness becomes the truth[101] because by stripping away those elements which stand in the way of the truth the individual comes to acquire a form which truly corresponds to the truth and as such can itself be said to be the truth.

In Kierkegaard's introduction of the concept of inwardness the inherent apophatic nature of his thought once again becomes apparent. Indeed, the concept of inwardness is particularly important for our investigation because here the apophaticism of Kierkegaard's thought ceases to be merely implicit and becomes *explicit*. Apophatic motifs are observable, first, in general statements about the nature of inwardness and, secondly, in the fact that Kierkegaard refers explicitly to inwardness as hidden.

(i) General statements on inwardness which indicate the apophatic strand in Kierkegaard's thought consist primarily of references to the incommensurability of the inward with the outward.[102] This means that inwardness is hidden because it is impossible to translate it into an outwardly observable form.

(ii) There are a number of passages in which Kierkegaard explicitly describes hiddenness as one of the qualities of inwardness. Again, like the general statements on inwardness, these passages emphasize the discrepancy that may arise between the inward and the outward.

Hidden inwardness can manifest itself in a number of different ways. Thus hidden inwardness is a feature of 'humour', the transitional stage between the ethical and the religious spheres. Humour is an example of hidden inwardness by virtue of the fact that although it 'has to do with the paradox . . . it cautiously keeps itself within immanence, and it constantly seems as if it were aware of something different—hence the jest'.[103] That is, humour is an example of hidden inwardness because it expresses its relation to the paradox immanently, yet immanence is a form which is not capable

---

[100] *JP* iv. 4889, cf. 4453 and Kierkegaard's concept of becoming nothing before God in the next chapter.

[101] *CUP* 226; *PF* 219; *TC* 87–8; cf. *CUP* 71.

[102] *CUP* 83–4, 263–4, 364, 366, 370–2; *SLW* 428, 441–2; *JP* ii. 2111; cf. *E/O* i. 3–4, 169, 177–8, 438; *CUP* 123, 126, 481; *SLW* 476.

[103] *CUP* 473 n.; cf. 476, 489, 493.

of expressing the paradox. The external expression thus belies the internal condition.

Another example of hidden inwardness is guilt. If the experience of guilt is so overwhelming that it cannot find a suitable punishment, the individual is deprived of the external outlet which would alleviate his plight. Consequently, guilt becomes trapped in hidden inwardness. As Kierkegaard puts it, 'The eternal recollection of guilt cannot be expressed outwardly, it is incommensurable with such expression, since every outward expression finitizes guilt.'[104]

The most important use of the term 'hidden inwardness', however, is reserved for religiousness, particularly Christian religiousness. Religiousness will be dealt with in the next chapter. Here it is enough to point out that hidden inwardness manifests itself in the discrepancy between the religious existence of the individual and its outward form. The Christian does not express his Christianity through public demonstrations of piety but conceals it behind an opaque exterior.[105]

(f) Striving

The relationship that the individual is called upon to develop is not finished when the individual has acquired the correct subjective disposition towards the truth. Because the existing individual is in time, his decision to base his relation to the truth on a subjective 'how' rather than on an objective 'what' is never completed. If the existing individual is to sustain his subjective relationship to the truth he must continually reiterate and reaffirm his initial decision. The consequence of this is that the 'how' of truth is transformed into a striving.

But the 'how' which is thus subjectively accentuated precisely because the subject is an existing individual, is also subject to a dialectic with respect to time. In the passionate moment of decision, where the road swings away from objective knowledge, it seems as if the infinite decision were thereby realized. But in the same moment the existing individual finds himself in the

---

[104] *CUP* 492; cf. 479, 487, 489.

[105] *CUP* 424, 450 n., 473 n., 476, 489. It should be noted that towards the end of his life Kierkegaard rejected the principle of hidden inwardness, regarding it as a betrayal of Christianity. The danger is that the individual may employ this principle as a means of conforming to the world (*JP* ii. 2119, 2125), thereby avoiding the renunciation that Christianity demands (*TC* 90–1; *JP* ii. 2119, 2125).

temporal order, and the subjective 'how' is transformed into a striving, a striving which receives indeed its impulse and a repeated renewal from the decisive passion of the infinite, but is nevertheless a striving.[106]

The complete correspondence of thought and being that constitutes the truth is never a reality for the human being. It always remains 'only an expectation of the creature'.[107]

Summing up this section, we can say that in the first instance subjectivity appears to be an inward relationship on the part of the existing individual to the truth. On this basis 'subjectivity is the truth' would seem to mean that it is not the object but the manner of the individual's personal relationship to this object that constitutes the truth.

The implicit apophaticism of this becomes apparent when we consider the upshot of this relational form of subjectivity. First, apophatic motifs can be detected in the fact that the truth is hidden from the individual if his subjectivity has not reached the required intensity. That is, conceiving of truth as a relationship means that the individual is only in the truth according to the intensity of this relationship. Conversely, we can say that the individual is removed from the truth according to the discrepancy between the intensity of his relationship and the intensity of the ideal or 'true' relationship. There thus arises what we might call a 'dialectic of inwardness' between the truth the individual believes he has and the truth of a more correct, i.e. more inward and subjective, relationship. This means that the existing individual is at any one time both partially in the truth and partially excluded from the truth. The latter, of course, is always the greater and in this sense we can speak of truth being 'hidden'. The truth the individual has at any given stage is only a faint echo of the 'true' truth, despite the fact that he himself may regard it as the highest truth.

The problem that now confronts us is to ascertain how Kierkegaard can move from the insight that subjectivity is decisive for the individual's understanding of the truth to the assertion that subjectivity itself is the truth. We can only make sense of this progression if we posit a second meaning of subjectivity.

---

[106] *CUP* 182; cf. *JP* iv. 4537; v. 5791, 5792.   [107] *CUP* 176.

2. Subjectivity as Selfhood

The second meaning of subjectivity is 'becoming a subject', i.e. becoming a proper self or person.[108] Apart from the etymological relation between 'subject' and 'subjectivity', there are several considerations which seem to indicate that Kierkegaard conceived of subjectivity in terms of selfhood.[109]

First, there are a number of passages in Kierkegaard's works where he clearly equates subjectivity with being or becoming a subject. He writes, for example, that 'Christianity teaches that the way is to become subjective, i.e. *to become a subject in truth*.'[110] Similarly, a little later he speaks of becoming a subject as 'the highest task confronting a human being',[111] an epithet he usually applies to subjectivity itself.[112] Further evidence for this use is contained in the title Kierkegaard gives to a section in his consideration of the nature of subjectivity, namely, 'The simultaneity of the individual factors of subjectivity in the existing subject'.[113] Here subjectivity clearly refers to the structure of the human person.

Secondly, there are several passages in which Kierkegaard suddenly switches from 'subjectivity' to 'subject' with no apparent change in meaning.[114] In addition to this, there are several places where 'subjectivity' and 'subject' stand in close proximity to each other.[115]

Thirdly, the interpretation of subjectivity as selfhood makes intelligible Kierkegaard's assertion that 'subjectivity is *untruth*'.[116] If we

---

[108] That 'subject' means 'person' or 'self' is indicated by a number of passages in which it would be possible to substitute the latter for the former without changing the meaning of the text (see *CUP* 149, 151, 154, 171, 173, 177–8, 186, 273, 281, 474–5, 517, 540). In addition to this, Kierkegaard sometimes changes in the course of a passage from 'subject' to 'self' (see, for example, *CUP* 305). And on one occasion in *The Sickness unto Death*, 'subjectivity' is equated with the 'single individual' (*SD* 122). Furthermore, Kierkegaard often complains that when speculative philosophy deals with the subject, it treats it not as a genuine, existing human self but as humanity in the abstract.

[109] In advocating this position I find myself in agreement with Emanuel Hirsch (*Kierkegaard-Studien*, 785) and H. M. Junghans (n. 61 in his translation of *CUP*: *Abschließende unwissenschaftliche Nachschrift*, i (Gütersloh, 1982)). Anz also makes more or less the same point in his statement that 'the principle of subjectivity is only another formula for the definition of spirit as a synthesis of the finite and the infinite' (*Kierkegaard und der deutsche Idealismus*, 64).

[110] *CUP* 117 (emphasis added).   [111] *CUP* 119, cf. 116.

[112] *CUP* 141–2, 145–6, 149, 151.   [113] *CUP* 307.

[114] *CUP* 116, 149; *JP* iv. 4537.   [115] *CUP* 112, 171, 173.

[116] *CUP* 185 (emphasis added). Subjectivity as untruth will be dealt with in the next chapter.

interpreted this only in accordance with the first sense of subjectivity described above, this statement would seem to be a simple negation of the assertion that truth must be conceived of in terms of relationship. Kierkegaard would then seem to be guilty of an astonishing self-contradiction. By understanding subjectivity to refer to the subject, however, this contradiction is resolved. It then becomes clear that Kierkegaard is making the point that the *human being* is in untruth, i.e. that *the human being is a sinner*. This interpretation fits in well with the context, which goes on to give a brief analysis of original sin. [117] It also explains how Kierkegaard can move smoothly from the assertion that subjectivity is untruth to statements such as 'but the *subject* cannot be untruth eternally'. [118] When he wishes to consider why subjectivity is untruth he switches to an analysis of the subject.

Finally, our interpretation of subjectivity as selfhood would tie in nicely with Kierkegaard's concept of the self as a synthesis or relation. In Chapter 2 we saw that the existential division of thought and being posited the human being as a compound of the contradictory elements of infinitude and finitude, eternity and time, etc. To overcome the contradiction between these elements and to constitute himself as a genuine self, the human being had to establish a proper relation or synthesis between them. In his formulation of truth in terms of subjectivity Kierkegaard is making the same point from a different perspective. Truth for the existing individual is to become what one should be or, to put it in the terms employed in Chapter 2, to unite the contradictory elements of the self into a coherent whole.

It would seem, then, that there are two forms of subjectivity present in Kierkegaard's thought, namely, subjectivity as relationship to the truth, and subjectivity as the individual's 'subject-ness'. The question that now arises is: what is the relation between these two forms of subjectivity?

In my opinion both forms of subjectivity reflect Kierkegaard's basic principle that truth only exists (as far as the human being is concerned) when it is actualized in the existence of the single individual. The difference between the two forms is primarily one of emphasis. The first form of subjectivity expresses the insight that truth 'is' to the degree in which I decisively and passionately grasp it as the truth. The *relationship* is decisive. The second form of

117 *CUP* 186–7.   118 *CUP* 186 (emphasis added).

subjectivity makes the point that this relationship to the truth involves becoming a self. 'Truth' in this sense occurs when the individual, by means of his relationship to the truth, has come to actualize himself as a 'true' self. Both forms of subjectivity come together in such statements as 'the truth is the subject's trans-formation in himself'.[119]

This is the sense in which it is possible to be in the truth even if one is related to an object which is not the truth. The decisive factor is the impact the relation to the object held to be the truth has on the structure of the self. If the object serves as an occasion for a higher synthesis of the constituent elements of the self, if it aids the individual in bringing thought and being together within his own existence, then the individual can be said to be in the truth even if the object to which he relates himself is, from the objective perspective, false.

The development of truth in terms of subjectivity has considerable significance for our investigation of Kierkegaard as a negative theologian. Apophatic motifs are present in the fact that the truth is hidden when the structuring of the self has not yet reached the level truth requires. This is due either to truth failing to have the necessary impact on the self or to an inadequate comprehension of the truth on the part of the individual, with the result that his self comes to reflect this inadequacy. In either case the individual has failed to structure his self to conform to the truth. The extent of this failure determines to what degree truth is hidden. The consequence of this is that a similar dialectic arises to that of the dialectic of inwardness, namely, a dialectic between what the individual is and what he should be. On the one hand, the individual is in the truth according to the degree in which he has become a self. On the other hand, he is distanced from the truth according to the degree in which he has not yet become a 'true' self. In this sense, it is again possible to speak of truth being 'hidden'.

Furthermore, the transferral of truth to the realm of subjectivity means that my relation to the truth is unintelligible to my fellow human beings. This is because subjectivity is a sphere which is only accessible to the individual himself and to God. To an observer the question of whether a particular individual actually sustains a

[119] *CUP* 38.

relationship to the truth is unanswerable. Indeed, the very attempt to ascertain the nature or state of another individual's subjectivity is illegitimate.

V. OBJECTIVITY

In the course of our analysis of Kierkegaard's thesis that subjectivity is the truth, we have claimed that he does not abandon the objective pole of the truth-relationship but has a specific kind of object in mind. It is now necessary to justify this claim by investigating what Kierkegaard understands by 'object'.

Like subjectivity, the term 'object' is employed ambiguously by Kierkegaard. As we have seen, Kierkegaard seems to understand truth in the first instance as that in relation to which the individual develops his subjectivity. This would seem to imply that truth is an object. However, in certain passages in his works Kierkegaard seems to adopt a more radical position and to dispense with the objective pole of truth altogether, arguing, as we have seen, that the relationship itself is the truth. Can these two positions be reconciled or is Kierkegaard inconsistent?

That Kierkegaard is not out to deny the objectivity of truth is indicated by a number of considerations. An entry in the journals makes particularly clear that he does not conceive of the truth as object-less: 'In the relation between an established order and the new within Christianity, the rule is quite simply this: the new is not a new *what* but a new *how* of the old *what*.'[120] Similarly, in the *Postscript* Kierkegaard concedes that 'from an objective standpoint Christianity is a *res in facto posita*,'[121] and admits the possibility of dealing with the truth of Christianity in an objective manner. Other indications that Kierkegaard's theory of truth does indeed have an objective pole are his assertions that 'human knowledge...has objective reality,'[122] and that Christianity is not something produced by the human intellect.[123] Further evidence is provided by his treatment of the 'world-historical'. He does not reject the world-historical as such but wishes merely to subordinate it to subjective

---

[120] *JP* iv. 4558.   [121] *CUP* 23.   [122] *JP* ii. 2269.
[123] *JP* iii. 3276, cf. ii. 2266.

truth. As he puts it, 'First then the ethical, the task of becoming subjective, and afterwards the world-historical.'[124]

On the other hand, there are, as we have seen, some passages where Kierkegaard seems to argue that objectivity is posited by means of subjectivity. Indeed, on at least one occasion, Kierkegaard seems to argue that subjectivity *replaces* objectivity: 'Just as in the preceding objective reflection, when the objectivity had come into being, the subjectivity had vanished, so here the subjectivity of the subject becomes the final stage, and objectivity a vanishing factor'.[125] Despite such passages, which seem to contradict the statements Kierkegaard makes concerning the validity of objectivity, I do not believe there is necessarily a contradiction here. The main thrust of Kierkegaard's position is not that objectivity is invalid but that truth is only truth for the human being when it is appropriated subjectively and becomes part of the individual's personal existence. Objectivity is not eliminated but is subordinated to the human being's subjectivity. Another journal entry sheds light on Kierkegaard's position here. He writes, 'Objectivity is believed to be superior to subjectivity, but it is just the opposite; that is to say, an objectivity which is *within* a corresponding subjectivity is the finale.'[126] It is thus not a question of denying objectivity but of finding a correct match between objectivity and subjectivity.

We have seen, then, that Kierkegaard seems to presuppose some sort of objectivity in his theory of truth. The question we must now answer is that of the nature of this objectivity.

In our opinion Kierkegaard has a very specific type of object in mind in his formulation of the principle that subjectivity is the truth. Described from the objective standpoint this object is an 'objective uncertainty'. The most important passages in which Kierkegaard deals with this are: 'An objective uncertainty held fast in an appropriation-process of the most passionate inwardness is the truth, the highest truth attainable for an existing individual';[127] and: 'The truth is precisely the venture which chooses an objective uncertainty with the passion of the infinite.'[128] What is of significance here is the connection Kierkegaard makes between truth

[124] *CUP* 142. Kierkegaard holds, of course, that the ethical tasks posed by existence will never allow the individual the time to embark upon a consideration of the world-historical. Nevertheless, this passage makes clear that Kierkegaard does not reject objectivity outright.

[125] *CUP* 175–6.   [126] *JP* vi. 6360 (emphasis added).   [127] *CUP* 182.

[128] Ibid.

and the concepts of 'appropriation' and 'choice'. Both these concepts require an object. 'Appropriation' requires something to appropriate. It cannot exist in isolation but exists in relation to the thing it wishes to appropriate. Similarly, choice is not an abstract act but involves choosing *something*. Both concepts therefore seem to presuppose the existence of an object. From the two passages quoted above it seems clear that the object the individual is called upon to appropriate or choose is 'an objective uncertainty'.[129] The truth-object must therefore be of a very specific kind. It is something which is not accessible to an objective approach. This does not mean that the object ceases to be an object or that Kierkegaard abandons the objective pole of the truth-relationship. It means rather that the truth-objects with which he is concerned are of such a kind that the individual's relation to them cannot be based on an objective relationship. If we look at the form of 'objectivity' brought about by subjectivity we will ascertain that it pertains only to objects of existential significance to the human being. That is, objectivity only comes about when, on the basis of his passionate commitment to a proposition, the individual comes to regard it as so certain that it becomes an objective reality for him. There are several 'objects' which would seem to fulfil the criterion of being objects which are not accessible to an objective approach to the truth.

(a) Existential Issues

By 'existential issues' we mean such questions as: 'What [does] it mean to die?'[130] 'What does it mean to be immortal?'[131] 'What does it mean that I am to thank God for the good He bestows upon me?'[132] 'What does it mean to get married?'[133] It is possible to embark upon an impartial and objective analysis of any one of these questions, drawing up a list of propositions or rules for their explication. If we remain here, however, we miss the point of all these questions. These questions, which all have to do with what it is to be a human being, are only properly understood when I apply them to myself. Marriage, for example, remains an abstract proposition until I myself marry. None of these issues can be dealt

---

[129] In the decisive Christian sphere of existence, Kierkegaard corrects this by stating that the objective uncertainty, which is the Socratic position, has become the certainty of the absurd (*CUP* 188).

[130] *CUP* 147.   [131] *CUP* 152.   [132] *CUP* 158.   [133] *CUP* 160.

with definitively by means of an objective approach. They can only be resolved when the single individual poses them *subjectively*.

(b) Christianity

Christianity is not an objective doctrine but an 'existential communication'. By this Kierkegaard means that Christianity and being a Christian do not consist of assenting to a list of doctrinal propositions but of appropriating and living according to these propositions.[134] Christianity has an 'objective' side in that it does indeed put forward certain 'propositions'. These propositions only become 'true', however, on their appropriation and actualization by the individual. The truth of Christianity, then, consists not in an objective, scientific attempt to 'prove' Christianity but in becoming and living as a Christian.

(c) God

God is another 'object' which, although discussable in objective terms, only truly becomes a reality for the human being when approached subjectively. The problem is that all objective evidence for God's existence is ambiguous.[135] On the one hand, the individual is confronted by phenomena in nature which would seem to argue for the existence of a divine creator. On the other hand, however, there exists much in nature that 'disturbs my mind and excites anxiety'.[136] The consequence of this is that the individual can never reach absolute certainty as to whether there is a God or not. If he nevertheless wishes to assert the validity of this 'object', it is not by objective means but by a subjective leap of faith.[137]

(d) The Incarnation

The Incarnation is from the objective point of view uncertain. Unlike normal historical facts, which can be compared with each other and thereby acquire a certain degree of plausibility, the Incarnation falls outside our conception of a historical fact. From the objective,

---

[134] *JP* iv. 4548, 4549, 4553, 4564, cf. i. 578.
[135] Kierkegaard's treatment of the arguments for the existence of God is considered in Ch. 6.
[136] *CUP* 182.   [137] See next chapter.

rational perspective this event is inconceivable, indeed, it is *paradoxical*. If we are nevertheless to hold on to it as a historical fact it must be on the basis of intense personal decision and commitment despite its fundamental historical uncertainty.[138]

(e) The Absolute Paradox

That the 'how' of subjectivity does indeed have an object but that this object is not accessible to objectivity becomes clear in the following passage: 'The thing of being a Christian is not determined by the *what* of Christianity but by the *how* of the Christian. This *how* can only correspond with one thing, the absolute paradox.'[139] Truth for Kierkegaard does indeed have an object, but this is an object which from the objective perspective is absolutely paradoxical.

On the basis of these examples it would seem that Kierkegaard does indeed have some sort of object in mind when he speaks of subjectivity as being the truth. However, as these examples make clear, this object is of a very peculiar nature. First, it is an object that is objectively uncertain and not accessible to normal means of verification. Secondly, the 'objects' with which Kierkegaard is concerned are all objects upon which the human being can base an eternal happiness.[140] Kierkegaard's thesis that subjectivity is the truth applies, then, only to issues of significance for human existence. It is *not* aimed at establishing a principle of verification for truth-claims in general.

Summing up Kierkegaard's position on objectivity, then, we can say that truth does indeed possess an objective element. The accusation of subjectivism is thus unjustified. The difficulty with Kierkegaard's position is that this objective element is not accessible to an objective approach. Its 'objectivity' consists, first, in the individual's treating it as such and, secondly, in his providing it with an 'objective' existence by actualizing it in his own existence.[141] Objectivity is thus subordinated to subjectivity by Kierkegaard. Such a truth is difficult to grasp because the principle of verification employed with regard to objective forms of truth is not applicable.

---

[138] See Ch. 7.   [139] *CUP* 540, cf. 542 n.; *JP* iv. 4550.

[140] This, of course, makes the 'objects' concerned even more uncertain, as the question is now not only one of whether I believe in this object but also of whether I believe that I can base an eternal happiness upon it.

[141] This is how I understand Kierkegaard's statement that at its highest, subjectivity becomes objectivity.

For Kierkegaard truth is not verified by objective analysis but by living it.

The significance of our analysis of objectivity for our investigation of Kierkegaard as negative theologian is that it brings to the fore three more apophatic motifs. These motifs emerge in the following areas.

1. Objectivity in the normal sense of the word is not possible. The 'objectivity' of a fact is dependent upon its appropriation by the individual. Absolute objectivity thus lies outside the sphere of the existing individual. Because of this, truth, in the absolute sense, is 'hidden'.

2. Objectivity exists only for the individual human being, i.e. objectivity is dependent upon the subjectivity of the existing individual. A fact is 'objective' in so far as *I* believe it to be so. This means, of course, that from the perspective of a 'non-believer', this 'fact' may be merely subjective in the negative sense of having no basis in reality. Truth is 'hidden', then, in that the objectivity one individual attributes to it does not necessarily constitute objectivity for another individual. My relationship to the truth is thus concealed from my fellow human beings and vice versa.

3. The 'object' of truth is not accessible to logical, rational analysis. It is 'objectively uncertain' and can only be approached by risking a relationship in the face of this uncertainty. The 'object' itself, however, remains essentially 'hidden'.

5

The Stages of Existence

IN his theory of stages or spheres of existence Kierkegaard ties together many of the elements that we have considered separately in previous chapters. In Chapter 2 we saw how Kierkegaard was concerned to develop a form of thought that would do justice to the existential position of the human being, namely, that the human being is subject to the existential division of thought and being. In Chapter 3 we saw that the intrinsic uncertainty contained in existence means that the only way to overcome scepticism and acquire knowledge is by means of 'belief'. In Chapter 4 we saw that subjectivity is the means by which the human being establishes a relationship to the truth. In the stages of existence, these three elements come together. An individual's stage or sphere of existence is determined by his conception of what truth is, his belief in this truth despite the obstacles that may stand in his way, and his subjective appropriation and actualization of this truth in his concrete, personal existence. We shall now examine the various stages of existence and consider to what extent apophatic motifs appear in them.

I. THE AESTHETIC STAGE

The lowest sphere of existence is the aesthetic sphere. In this sphere the individual is unaware of the contradiction of being an infinite and eternal self placed in finite and temporal existence. He conceives of himself solely in terms of the physical, the finite, and the temporal, ignoring the infinite, eternal, and spiritual aspects of the self.

This emphasis on finitude and temporality means that the self comes to be conceived of primarily in terms of particularity. That is, it is understood as a conglomeration of talents and urges particular to the individual.[1] A fulfilled existence is then regarded as the successful cultivation of these talents and the satisfaction of these urges.

[1] E/O ii. 225.

Consequently, the fundamental principle of the aesthetic sphere is enjoyment.[2]

The result of living according to the principle of enjoyment is that the individual exists in 'the aesthetic dialectic between fortune and misfortune'.[3] As long as a successful relationship is sustained between the individual and the external world upon which he is dependent for his enjoyment, he is happy. However, should something interrupt this relationship, then he becomes unhappy. This interruption is not seen, however, as a manifestation of the contradiction of being an infinite and eternal self placed in the finitude and temporality of existence. Nor is it seen as indicative of the fundamental inadequacy of the aesthetic mode of existence. Rather, the aesthete considers it to be a temporary problem caused by the unfortunate intervention of an external force. As Kierkegaard puts it: 'Immediacy, the aesthetic, finds no contradiction in the fact of existing: to exist is one thing, and the contradiction is something else which comes from without.'[4]

Because the existential contradiction is understood as a problem of the individual's relationship with the external world the suffering it causes is considered to be accidental.[5] That is, suffering is not understood as a reflection of the contradiction of being an infinite and eternal self confined in finite and temporal existence, but is regarded as the result of the disruption of the pleasurable relationship between self and environment. The individual simply hopes that the impediment to his happiness will disappear and allow him to return to his original state.[6]

The aesthete, then, is 'undialectical in himself'.[7] He externalizes the existential contradiction, transforming it into a dialectic between the self and its environment.

The significance of this for our investigation of the apophatic nature of Kierkegaard's thought is twofold. First, an apophatic motif is present in the fact that truth is infinitely distanced from the aesthetic individual. None of the presuppositions necessary for a relationship to the truth is fulfilled. The discrepancy between the truth of the aesthetic sphere and truth in its absolute form is total. In

---

[2] E/O ii. 179–84, 190–1, 229; CUP 256, 258, cf. 261.
[3] CUP 397, cf. 388.   [4] CUP 507.   [5] CUP 398, 400, 404–5.
[6] CUP 388–9, 397.   [7] CUP 412, 478, 507.

addition to this, the relation of the aesthete to this inadequate conception of truth is external. This has the result that the inward relationship constitutive of the truth is lacking. Because the aesthete is so far removed from fulfilling the presuppositions of a relationship to the truth, we can speak of the truth, and *eo ipso* the establishment of a God-relationship and the acquisition of an eternal happiness, as being absolutely hidden from him.

Secondly, the aesthete is hidden from himself and from other selves. He is hidden from himself because he has not recognized what he truly is but identifies his self with peripheral attributes and talents. He is hidden from other selves because he does not structure his existence according to universally acknowledged norms but lives according to his own private quirks. He is hidden in his particularity and is thus unintelligible to his fellows.[8]

Because of its fundamental inadequacy it is impossible for the human being to remain in the aesthetic sphere. The structure of the human self is such that it is incapable of sustaining long-term an aesthetic mode of existence. The spirit is suppressed by such an existence and sooner or later attempts to break out in an effort to actualize itself on a higher plane.[9] The dissolution of the aesthetic mode of existence that this entails casts the individual into despair, but it is precisely this despair which offers him an escape from his plight. Despair is 'personality's doubt',[10] and as such is the starting-point for a reassessment of the self's mode of existence. Should the individual 'choose despair',[11] that is, accept the inadequacy of the aesthetic stage, then the dominance of the aesthetic is broken and the way opened to higher actualization and fulfilment. It is to a consideration of the sphere of existence that the self enters on choosing despair that we now turn.

II. THE ETHICAL STAGE

The ethical individual is the individual who has chosen despair. Through this choice he discards his aesthetic or finite self and takes on the 'absolute self or my self according to its absolute validity'.[12]

---

[8] Cf. *CUP* 227. [9] See Kierkegaard's portrayal of Nero in *E/O* ii. 185–8.
[10] *E/O* ii. 211. [11] *E/O* ii. 211, 218–19; cf. *CUP* 235.
[12] *E/O* ii. 219.

What Kierkegaard means by this is that in the act of choice, the individual draws together into a coherent whole his dissipated aesthetic personality. As he puts it, 'In the choosing the personality declares itself in its inner infinity and in turn the personality is thereby consolidated.'[13]

This act of self-choice overcomes the existential contradiction by virtue of the fact that the consolidation it posits involves the individual's structuring of his particularity according to the 'universal-human'.[14] The universal-human is identified with the norms of bourgeois society,[15] which is seen as being undergirded by God.[16] In participating in and contributing to social institutions the human being is thus also establishing a God-relationship. In this grafting of his particularity and finitude on to the God-given ethical norms of bourgeois society, the existential contradiction between thought and being, finitude and infinitude is overcome.

Apophatic motifs are only hinted at in the ethical sphere. Indeed, one of the ways in which the self consolidates itself results not in hiddenness but in self-revelation.[17] Despite this, however, there are one or two explicit references to our theme. These arise primarily from Judge William's anxiety to avoid the externalization of the ethical as a catalogue of duties. By stressing above all the inward nature of the ethical, Judge William isolates individuals from each other. We all stand under ethical categories and are all called upon to 'realize the universal', but how we understand these categories and how we realize the universal is something each one of us must decide for himself. As Judge William, again with reference to marriage, puts it: 'Ethics tells him only that he should marry, it does not say whom. Ethics explains to him the universal in the differences, and he transfigures the differences in the universal.'[18] Because an ethical act such as marriage involves the fusion and subordination of the particular, i.e. the individual's unique, personal attributes, talents, and characteristics, with the universal, such an act, despite its public nature, belongs uniquely to the individual and is only partly

---

[13] *E/O* ii. 167, cf. 270.   [14] See esp. *E/O* ii. 328–32.

[15] Thus Kierkegaard, or rather his pseudonym Judge William, sees the self as 'not only a personal self but a social, a civic self' (*E/O* ii. 262).

[16] As Kierkegaard puts it with regard to the ethical consolidation of the love-relationship in marriage, 'In the resolution [the lover] will, through the universal, place himself in relationship with God' (*SLW* 164, cf. 122).

[17] *CUP* 227, 231, 450; *E/O* ii. 322–3; cf. *CUP* 227, 446 n.; *E/O* ii. 116–19.
[18] *E/O* ii. 305.

intelligible to external observers. Correspondingly, although the ethical individual understands himself as a member of a social group, there is a limitation to his capacity to aid another or be aided in the realization of the universal. One human being can aid his fellow only by making him aware of 'the reality of choosing'.[19] Beyond this, however, he is on his own.[20] In this limitation of our intelligibility to others and their intelligibility to us, apophatic motifs can be detected even in the ethical sphere.

The most important form of apophaticism in the ethical sphere, however, is implicit rather than explicit. This implicit apophaticism manifests itself in the ethical sphere's fundamental inadequacy. Despite the higher degree of truth the ethical possesses in relation to the aesthetic sphere, the ethically existing individual is, like his aesthetic predecessor, not in the full sense of the word in the truth. This is because the ethicist's solution of the existential contradiction takes place as 'self-assertion'.[21] Although the ethicist has internalized the dialectic posited by the existential contradiction, the 'ultimate basis is not dialectic in itself, inasmuch as the self which is at the basis is used to overcome and assert itself'.[22] The self is seen as standing above the dialectic, as it were, from which position it then organizes the constituent elements of the dialectic and overcomes the existential contradiction by means of its own powers. This places a limitation upon the inwardness acquired through the ethicist's choice of despair and *eo ipso* his relationship to the truth.

In addition to this, the ethical sphere also fails to fulfil its own demand that the individual choose himself. Although the ethicist can wrench himself loose of the aesthetic sphere by choosing despair, this cannot result in his 'winning himself',[23] as Judge William asserts. The individual needs all his strength for the initial act of despair and thus 'cannot by [himself] come back'.[24] In fact, all the ethicist achieves is to work himself deeper into despair.[25]

Apophatic motifs can be detected, then, in that although the ethical sphere is an advance on its aesthetic predecessor, it still remains infinitely distanced from the truth and the God-relationship this entails.

---

[19] *E/O* ii. 176.   [20] Cf. *E/O* ii. 176, 302.   [21] *CUP* 507.
[22] Ibid.   [23] *CUP* 230.
[24] Ibid.   [25] *SD* 14.

III. RELIGIOUSNESS A

The next sphere of existence is general religiousness or 'religiousness A'.[26] Here the individual has come to discover that the ethical sphere is inadequate. The happy relationship established between the infinite and finite through adherence to the norms laid down by society cannot be sustained. The consequence of this is that the contradiction of being an infinite, eternal self placed in finite and temporal existence again comes to the fore. If this contradiction is to be resolved a new way of bringing together the infinite and the finite must be found.

Kierkegaard tackles this in two ways. First, he makes recourse to the Socratic-Platonic doctrine of recollection. According to this doctrine the human being is in innate possession of the essential truth. This truth he has by virtue of his participation in the realm of essence prior to his earthly existence. On coming into existence, however, his awareness of this essential truth is dulled. If he is to be brought to a comprehension of this truth he must be made to 'recollect' it.[27] This recollection can be assisted by a teacher who, by means of certain probing questions, can 'bring to birth' the truth innate within the human being. Once the human being has come to rediscover this essential truth, the task becomes that of transforming existence into a form capable of expressing this truth.[28] This means subordinating the finite and temporal elements of the self acquired on coming into existence to the essential truth.

Secondly, Kierkegaard considers the individual's attempt to overcome the existential contradiction in terms of the relationship to God. With the breakdown of the ethical sphere, the individual discovers that his God-relationship, which previously had been mediated through the norms of bourgeois society, collapses. A new basis for the God-relationship is thus required. According to Kierkegaard, this new basis is acquired when we establish a uniquely personal relationship with God that is free of ethical intermediaries. For the establishment of such a relationship it is necessary that the individual clear away those elements which impede it. This means above all subordinating all finite ends to the absolute *telos* that is God.

Both of Kierkegaard's approaches result in the same conclusion,

---

[26] *CUP* 493–8, cf. 505–9, 512–13, 515–16, 518–19, 535–6.
[27] *PF* 96–7; cf. *R* 149.   [28] *CUP* 184, cf. 508–9.

namely, that the human being is called upon to reduce existence or the finite and temporal elements of the self to the greatest degree possible in order to allow the eternal truth to express itself and a genuine God-relationship to be established. If the individual is successful in this, the existential contradiction is resolved.[29]

This process is carried out in two movements.

(a) The Movement of Infinity

As its name implies, this movement consists of infinitude's breaking out from the finite confines within which it had been imprisoned in the ethical sphere. Thereby it separates the individual from the ethical sphere of existence and lays the foundation for the religious mode of existence. This process of breaking away from the finite is itself made up of two movements. First, there is the movement whereby the individual comes to collect his powers and focus them on one particular object or live according to one particular principle. This is important because it gives his life a structure.[30]

Secondly, there is the 'infinite movement of resignation'.[31] Having constructed his existence according to a single principle, the individual must then give up all hope of realizing this principle. He must 'resign' himself to the impossibility of its becoming a reality.[32] This does not mean, however, that the 'knight of resignation', as Kierkegaard calls the 'resigned' individual, is to give up the principle upon which he has constructed his existence. On the contrary, if he were to do this, he could not make the movement of infinity necessary for the establishment of a religious mode of existence. The individual is rather to hold on to this principle and to believe in its realization despite all the difficulties that confront him.[33] In doing so, Kierkegaard asserts, 'the individual has emptied himself in the infinite'.[34]

Through making this act of resignation, the individual achieves two things. First, he receives his 'eternal consciousness'.[35] That is, he becomes conscious of the eternal. Secondly, the individual has acquired the form upon which a God-relationship can be based. As Kierkegaard puts it in the *Postscript*, 'resignation looks to see that the individual has an absolute direction toward the absolute *telos*'.[36]

---

[29] *CUP* 507.   [30] *FT* 42–3.
[31] *FT* 115; cf. 37–8, 46–8, 115, 119; *CUP* 353.   [32] *FT* 43–5.
[33] See *FT* 44–6.   [34] *FT* 69.   [35] *FT* 48, cf. 46.
[36] *CUP* 396.

(b) The Movement of Faith

The negation of the individual's reliance upon himself is only the first movement in the individual's relation to the absolute *telos* and his development as a self. If he is to become a genuine self and establish a relationship with the absolute *telos*, a second movement has to occur whereby the human being is rescued from his resignation and restored as a whole person. The movement by which this healing is achieved is faith. In this movement the individual is saved from the despair of the first movement and is reconstituted as a whole self by virtue of his relation to God.

We now wish to examine the various components of religiousness A in detail and draw out the apophatic elements we believe to be present.

1. *Suffering*

Suffering arises from the individual's attempt to transform his existence into a form capable of sustaining a God-relationship. The importance of suffering is that it sweeps away those elements which impede the establishment of a God-relationship. As Kierkegaard puts it, 'Immediacy expires in suffering; in suffering, religiosity begins to breathe.'[37]

The reason for this is that, according to Kierkegaard, a true relationship can only be established between equal parties. If one of the parties is unequal, then he must adapt himself to the position of the other. Because God is utterly transcendent of the human being, however, this 'equality' must be expressed not 'through superhuman exertion to approach nearer to God',[38] but through 'humility'.[39] This entails sweeping away those elements which impede the God-relationship or, as Kierkegaard puts it, 'dying to immediacy', a process which means 'becoming nothing'[40] or 'annihilating oneself'. It is in this process of becoming 'equal' with God that suffering lies.

This suffering has its ground in the fact that the individual is in his immediacy absolutely committed to relative ends; its significance lies in the transposition of the relationship, the dying away from immediacy, or in the

---

[37] *CUP* 390.   [38] *CUP* 439.   [39] *CUP* 439–40.
[40] *CUP* 412, 432–7, 452.

expression existentially of the principle that the individual can do absolutely nothing of himself, but is as nothing before God.[41]

Apophatic motifs can be detected here in two respects. First, suffering becomes the *mark* of the God-relationship. As Kierkegaard puts it:

For suffering is precisely the expression for the God-relationship, that is, the religious suffering, which signalizes the God-relationship and the fact that the individual has not arrived at happiness by emancipating himself from a religious relationship to an absolute *telos*.[42]

This is apophatic because a negative category, namely, suffering, is both the criterion and indicator of a positive category, namely, the God-relationship. As Kierkegaard puts it, 'Here again the negative is the mark by which the God-relationship is recognized, and self-annihilation is the essential form for the God-relationship.'[43] Suffering is what we might term the 'incognito' of the God-relationship.

Secondly, an apophatic motif can be detected in Kierkegaard's emphasis that suffering is only determinative of a God-relationship when it manifests itself inwardly. As Frater Taciturnus puts it, 'The religious does not consist in an immediate relation between strength and suffering, but in the internal, when this relates itself to itself.'[44] Should suffering manifest itself outwardly, it indicates that the individual suffers merely aesthetically and *eo ipso* does not stand in a God-relationship.[45] Apophaticism is present here in that the movement of faith expressed through suffering is not intelligible to the outside observer. It is a movement made in the inwardness of the self and as such is not accessible to external observation.[46]

---

[41] *CUP* 412.   [42] *CUP* 405, cf. 407.   [43] *CUP* 412.

[44] *SLW* 467–8.

[45] *CUP* 405. It should be mentioned here that Kierkegaard seems to have revised this position in the last years of his life. In his later works he places great emphasis on the physical suffering of the Christian in his conflict with the world. 'Dying away' from the world seems to take on the literal meaning of martyring oneself as a witness to the Christian faith in a hostile world. This alteration in Kierkegaard's position mirrors the transition we saw in Ch. 4 from 'hidden inwardness' to the demand that the Christian express his faith openly in the world. This is not the place to go into the reasons for Kierkegaard's change of position but a plausible suggestion is that Kierkegaard's treatment at the hands of the satirical magazine *The Corsair* may have played an important role.

[46] Cf. *SLW* 458.

2. *Guilt*

Guilt arises from the fact that while the individual is engaged in dying away from immediacy, time is lost which should have been spent in relation to the absolute *telos*. That is, the human being is guilty because he cannot begin immediately with the God-relationship but must first acquire a form capable of sustaining such a relationship.

Thus things go backwards: the task is presented to the individual in existence, and just as he is ready to cut at once a fine figure . . . and wants to begin, it is discovered that a new beginning is necessary, the beginning upon the immense detour of dying from immediacy, and just when the beginning is about to be made at this point, it is discovered that there, since time has meanwhile been passing, an ill beginning is made, and that the beginning must be made by becoming guilty and from that moment increasing the total capital guilt by a new guilt at a usurious rate of interest.[47]

In attempting to move towards the absolute *telos*, then, the individual succeeds only in increasing his distance from it. This has two consequences. First, guilt becomes a 'total determinant',[48] that is, it is not merely an aspect or episode in the human being's life but defines his existence as a whole.[49] Secondly, 'guilt is the expression for the strongest self-assertion of existence'[50] and is 'the first deep plunge into existence'.[51] What Kierkegaard means by this is that through guilt the individual has reached a heightened concreteness with regard to his own existence. Guilt makes him aware of himself as a specific individual with a specific past and present. Guilt is an expression of his awareness of this and his acceptance of responsibility for it. To reformulate Judge William's exhortation to choose oneself, we could say that the guilty individual has indeed chosen himself but as guilty. Thereby the individual has chosen not an ideal self but his real self.

It might be assumed that guilt makes a God-relationship impossible. Such an assumption is indeed to a certain extent correct, for guilt makes impossible the establishment of a God-relationship on an ethical basis. This assumption, however, is incorrect if it is

---

[47] *CUP* 469.   [48] *CUP* 471.

[49] Ibid. The position which understands guilt to be due to isolated instances of unethical behaviour is described by Kierkegaard as childish, comparative, or aesthetic guilt (*CUP* 473–4, 478).

[50] *CUP* 470.   [51] *CUP* 473, cf. 469–70.

understood to mean that guilt rules out *all* possibility of a relationship with God. This is incorrect because guilt plays a crucial role in bringing the human being into a relationship with God on a higher plane. Kierkegaard writes:

One might think that this consciousness [of guilt] is an expression of the fact that one is not related to it [i.e. an eternal happiness], the decisive expression of the fact that one is lost and the relationship is relinquished. The answer is not difficult. Precisely because it is an exister who is to relate himself, while guilt is at the same time the most concrete expression of existence, the consciousness of guilt is the expression for the relationship.[52]

How does guilt accomplish this? How is it that a negative category such as guilt can bring about such a positive result as the establishment of a relationship with God? This seems to occur in two ways.

First, guilt results in a higher resolution of the existential contradiction. This is because it establishes a correct relationship between finitude and infinitude, eternity and temporality. In confessing his guilt, the human being accepts the inadequacy of the finite as a vehicle for overcoming the existential contradiction. We cannot establish a relationship to the absolute *telos* on *our* terms, but must allow the infinite to dictate the terms of the relationship. To put it another way, guilt represents the most advanced form of self-annihilation or 'dying away' from the world to date.[53] By conceiving of himself as guilty, the human being sweeps away those elements of his self which stand in the way of a full expression of the infinite.

Secondly, guilt results in a higher degree of subjectivity and *eo ipso* truth. As we saw in the previous chapter, intensity of subjectivity is one of the factors that determines to what degree the individual is in the truth. With his discovery that he is guilty subjectivity reaches a qualitatively higher level. Guilt forces the individual to immerse himself in his own existence. That is, guilt compels him to reassess himself, to examine his subjectivity and reconstruct it on the basis of the insights gained through his discovery of himself as guilty. Since subjectivity is the decisive factor in the individual's relation to the truth, guilt, by forcing the individual to re-examine his subjectivity, acts as the occasion for the construction of a more adequate relation to the truth.

In these two ways, then, guilt marks not a retreat but an advance. As Kierkegaard puts it, guilt, although a 'backwards movement' is at

---

[52] *CUP* 470, cf. 473–4.   [53] Cf. *CUP* 468–9, 474, 479.

the same time 'a forward movement, in so far as going forward means going deeper into something'.[54]

In Kierkegaard's treatment of guilt the inherent apophaticism of his thought becomes, I believe, particularly prominent. This apophaticism appears above all in the nature of the God-relationship that guilt posits. This relationship is not direct and immediate but is based on *disrelationship*. As Kierkegaard puts it, 'the exister cannot get a grip on the relationship because the disrelationship is constantly placing itself between as the expression for the relationship.'[55] Strange as it sounds, it is precisely this disrelationship that constitutes the relationship, since 'it is the expression for the relationship by reason of the fact that it expresses the incompatibility or disrelationship'.[56] Kierkegaard throws light on these paradoxical statements by describing the God-relationship as a 'repellent relationship'.[57] What he means by this is that, in moving away from God, the individual actually comes to establish a more genuine relationship with God. This repellent relationship is more genuine than a direct relationship because it expresses the incompatibility of God and humanity, the infinite and the finite. In this idea of the God-relationship as a *dis*relationship, the apophatic strand in Kierkegaard's thought is clearly visible.

3. Paradox

The apophaticism implicit in this term becomes immediately apparent when we attempt to define it. Because the paradox is paradoxical it is not accessible to logical analysis. As a result of this, any discussion of the paradox must necessarily be limited. We can examine its *form*, but its content remains shrouded in mystery. In addition to this, a further difficulty arises from the fact that Kierkegaard employs the paradox in a number of different ways with little or no attempt to explain the relationship between them. They are merely placed side by side as different approaches to religiousness A.[58] Here we wish to limit our discussion to the paradoxes in which Kierkegaard's apophaticism becomes apparent.

[54] *CUP* 469.   [55] *CUP* 473.   [56] Ibid., cf. 476–7.   [57] *CUP* 474.
[58] Some scholars have attempted to establish a relationship between the various paradoxes. Schröer (*Denkform der Paradoxalität*, 71), for example, argues that the Abrahamic and Socratic paradoxes are based on the same ontological principle, namely, 'subjectivity, existence, passion, the single individual is the truth'.

(a) Repetition

This is the term Kierkegaard employs to describe the restitution of what the individual had regarded as irrevocably lost.[59] As we saw earlier, the movement of infinity entails the concentration of the individual's energies on a single principle or object, followed by an 'infinite movement of resignation' whereby he then gives up all hope of realizing this principle or obtaining this object. Thereby the individual's connection with the finite is dissolved, leaving him moving in the direction of the infinite with no anchor in the finite. Because, however, the human being is a synthesis of both the infinite and the finite, a life lived exclusively in the infinite is not a viable proposition. If the self is to be reconstituted, then, a return to the finite must be brought about.

The problem is that human powers are exhausted in making the first movement of the religious sphere, the movement of infinity. This means that the individual does not have the strength to make the second movement, i.e. the movement of faith by which a return to the finite is effected.[60] If this is the case, how then is a repetition possible? Kierkegaard's answer is that it is not.[61] A return to the finite is an impossibility because it completely transcends the capacity of the human being to make it.

But for God the impossible is possible.[62] Despite the fact that from the human perspective repetition is utterly impossible, God may choose to restore to the individual that which the latter believed he had lost forever. This means, however, that from the human perspective repetition is a paradox, for it contradicts both the actuality of the human being and what is humanly possible. As the young man of *Repetition* says of Job: 'So there is a repetition, after all. When does it occur? Well, that is hard to say in any human language. When did it occur for Job? When every *thinkable* human certainty and probability were impossible.'[63]

At this point we once again see the intrinsic apophaticism of Kierkegaard's thought coming to the fore. Human powers, including

---

[59] The fullest discussions of 'repetition' of which I am aware are: F. Sontag, 'The Role of Repetition', *Bibliotheca Kierkegaardiana*, 3 (Copenhagen, 1980), 283–94, and L. Reimer, 'Die Wiederholung als Problem der Erlösung bei Kierkegaard', in Theunissen and Greve (eds.), *Materialien zur Philosophie Søren Kierkegaards*, 302–46.

[60] *FT* 49–50.   [61] *FT* 16, 34, 42, 47–8, 51.   [62] *FT* 38–40, 46; *SD* 71.

[63] *R* 212 (original emphasis); cf. 185, 305, 313, 321, 324; *CUP* 235; *CA* 18.

reason, are exhausted in the movement of infinity. Consequently, the 'repetition' by which the individual recovers what was thought to be lost irrevocably is something that can neither be achieved nor comprehended by means of human powers. That it nevertheless comes about is a marvel that is simply incomprehensible to the human being. In the limit that the paradox places upon human capacity another apophatic motif is revealed.

(b) The Socratic Paradox

In the *Postscript* the paradox is given a broader and more general conceptual basis. This general paradox is described by Kierkegaard as the Socratic paradox.[64]

The Socratic paradox arises from the incompatibility of eternal truth and existence.[65] Unlike the ethical individual, the individual in religiousness A is aware of this incompatibility and realizes that the finite can never serve as a vehicle for the eternal. The paradox is that, despite this incompatibility, existence remains the sphere in which a relationship to the truth must be established. This relationship is sustained by means of suffering and guilt, which, as we saw earlier, are based on the fundamental incompatibility of eternity and existence. Apophaticism is present here in that the fundamental incompatibility of the eternal truth with existence has the result that the truth is recognized by its incompatibility with or 'repellence' to existence[66] and by its absurdity to human reason.[67] The correct existential attitude on the part of the individual towards the eternal truth thus becomes one not of understanding but of Socratic ignorance.[68]

4. *Faith*

Perhaps the clearest example of the apophaticism implicit in religiousness A is its portrayal of faith. Apophatic motifs can be detected in the following areas.

---

[64] *CUP* 186. [65] *CUP* 162, 177–8, 180, 186. [66] *CUP* 183.
[67] *CUP* 387 n.
[68] See *CUP* 180, 183.

(a) The Structure of the God-Relationship

Perhaps the most powerful expression of the apophatic strand in religiousness A is the negative structure it imposes upon the God-relationship. We saw in our analysis of dialectics in Chapter 2 that a negative form is an essential prerequisite for anyone who wishes to think existentially, i.e. in a way which is relevant to existence. In the same way, negativity is decisive for the individual who wishes to exist religiously.

Just as the highest principles of thought can for an existing individual be proved only negatively ... so also it is the case that the existential relationship to the absolute good is for an existing individual determined only through the negative—the relation to an eternal happiness only through suffering, just as also the certainty of the faith which sustains a relationship to an eternal happiness is determined through its uncertainty.[69]

A God-relationship is only possible, then, when the individual relates himself negatively to it.

This does not mean, however, that religiousness has no positive form or is not a positive category. The point Kierkegaard wishes to make is that the individual only attains to this positivity on the basis of negativity.

The negative does not come upon the scene once for all, later to be replaced by the positive; but the positive is constantly wrapped up in the negative, and the negative is its criterion, so that the regulative principle *ne quid nimis* does not here find any application.[70]

Without the negative, then, the positive cannot come about. Should the individual attempt to bypass the negative or hold that, having established a relationship to the absolute *telos* by means of negativity, he can now dispense with the negative and progress to a purely positive relationship, he falls back into aesthetic[71] or childish forms of religiousness.[72] Even when the individual has established a relation to the absolute *telos*, then, the principle of negativity remains in force. It is the criterion or sign of the religious[73] and 'the

---

[69] *CUP* 407, cf. 438; *SLW* 443–4.
[70] *CUP* 467.   [71] See *CUP* 399 n., 405–6.
[72] See 'Childish Christianity' (*CUP* 520–37).
[73] *CUP* 387, 414, 421, 474–5, 497–8, 506.

mark by which the God-relationship is recognized'.[74] In this emphasis on negativity as the criterion of the God-relationship the apophatic structure of Kierkegaard's thought is apparent.

(b) The Paradoxicality of Faith

The apophatic dimension of religiousness A is also indicated by Kierkegaard's emphasis on the paradoxical nature of faith. If, as we saw earlier, repetition is a paradox, then the response of the individual to this paradox must be equally paradoxical.

Faith is paradoxical for two reasons. First, it is the mirror image of the paradoxical movement by which God makes possible the impossible.[75] The 'knight of faith' believes that, despite its impossibility, God will restore to him what he has lost.

He does exactly the same as the other knight did [i.e. the knight of resignation]: he infinitely renounces the love that is the substance of his life, he is reconciled in pain. But then the marvel happens; he makes one more movement even more wonderful than all the others, for he says: Nevertheless I have faith that I will get her—that is, by virtue of the absurd, by virtue of the fact that for God all things are possible.[76]

The absurdity of God's making the impossible possible is answered by faith in the possibility of the impossible.

Secondly, faith is a paradox because it cannot be rationally justified or explained. It is a movement made 'by virtue of the absurd',[77] i.e. the knight of faith believes in repetition despite the fact that this flies in the face of all logic and common sense. Thus Abraham believes that God will return Isaac to him despite the fact that God himself has ordered him to sacrifice his son.[78]

The apophatic dimension of Kierkegaard's thought emerges here in his emphasis upon the non-rationality of faith. It is, as we have seen, a marvel, and 'begins precisely where thought stops'.[79] As Kierkegaard puts it with reference to Abraham, 'By faith Abraham emigrated from the land of his fathers and became an alien in the promised land. He left one thing behind, took one thing along: he left behind his worldly understanding, and he took along his faith.'[80]

---

[74] CUP 412.   [75] FT 38, cf. 36, 40–1.   [76] FT 46, cf. 17.
[77] FT passim, but see esp. FT 35–6, 40–1, 46–50, 56–7, 69.
[78] FT 115.   [79] FT 53.   [80] FT 17, cf. 36.

(c) The Uncertainty of Faith

The apophatic strand running through religiousness A is also very prominent in Kierkegaard's emphasis on the *necessity* of uncertainty in faith. Without uncertainty there can be no faith. Faith needs room to 'venture',[81] that is, room to make the passionate leap whereby the individual comes to believe. This room is provided by uncertainty, which 'tortures forth the passionate certainty of faith'.[82]

Certainty, however, removes this room. It 'lurks at the door of faith and threatens to devour it'.[83] To base a God-relationship on certainty is akin to basing a love-relationship on a certificate of marriage[84] or on the certainty that one is loved.[85] The person who acts in such a way has 'lost the Idea constitutive of the inwardness of love'.[86] Similarly, certainty eliminates the passion that is decisive for faith: 'For if passion is eliminated, faith no longer exists, and certainty and passion do not go together.'[87] Kierkegaard sums up his position in the following statement: 'The uncertainty is the criterion, and the certainty without the uncertainty is the criterion for the absence of a God-relationship.'[88] In making uncertainty rather than certainty the criterion of faith, the apophatic strand in Kierkegaard's thought once again becomes apparent.

5. The Unintelligibility of the Knight of Faith

Another important characteristic of religiousness A in which apophatic motifs are to be found is Kierkegaard's emphasis upon the unintelligibility of the religious individual and his inability to communicate his God-relationship to his fellow human beings. There are four reasons for this unintelligibility.

(*a*) As we saw in our analysis of dialectics in Chapter 2, thought is based upon the principle of abstraction. That is, thought functions by abstracting a generic concept or 'universal' from particularities. This universal then comes to act as a token for all instances and forms of the particularity from which it was originally abstracted. If, however, a particularity is not susceptible to abstraction, if it is a unique instance on the basis of which no universal can be constructed, then thought breaks down. This is precisely the case with the faith that compels Abraham to sacrifice Isaac. It is a unique instance which simply cannot be translated into a universal. As Johannes de Silentio puts it:

This paradox [of faith] cannot be mediated, for it depends specifically on this: that the single individual is only the single individual.[89]

Faith itself cannot be mediated into the universal, for thereby it is cancelled. Faith is this paradox, and the single individual simply cannot make himself understandable to anyone.[90]

Consequently, thought grinds to a halt[91] and the observer can only look on in amazement.[92]

(b) The knight of faith cannot communicate. He cannot make himself intelligible to others. The reason for this is that, like thought, language is based on universals.[93] That is, information is conveyed by relaying concepts known both to communicator and recipient. If, however, a particularity is incapable of being expressed as a universal, then there is no point of contact between the would-be communicator and the intended recipient of his communication. This is precisely the problem with Abraham. His intention to sacrifice Isaac is so alien to the categories of human thought that there exists no term by which he can explain himself to his fellows. As Kierkegaard puts it, 'The paradox of faith has lost the intermediary, that is, the universal.'[94] Consequently, Abraham cannot speak.[95]

(c) The religious individual is not outwardly recognizable. His basis in the absurd is not perceptible. Indeed, it is possible for the knight of faith to appear to be an example of bourgeois philistinism.[96] Because of this incommensurability between the knight's appearance and his basis in the absurdity of faith it is possible that everyone or no one might be such a knight.[97] There is simply no way of being certain. This, Kierkegaard states, is the religious individual's 'incognito'.[98]

(d) The religious individual never arrives at a result. There are two reasons for this. First, 'The religious lies in the internal. Here the result cannot be shown in the external.'[99] In religiousness 'the scene

---

[89] *FT* 70.   [90] *FT* 71.   [91] *FT* 53, cf. 33, 56.

[92] *FT* 36–7, 47; cf. the description of the knight's movement of faith as a 'marvel' (*FT* 36, 41, 46, 48, 51, 67, 120; *R* 185).

[93] *FT* 60: 'As soon as I speak, I express the universal'; *FT* 113: 'The relief provided by speaking is that it translates me into the universal.'

[94] *FT* 71.   [95] *FT* 60, 113; cf. *SLW* 351; *R* 201.   [96] *FT* 38.

[97] *FT* 38; *CUP* 424, 446, 452, cf. 457.

[98] *CUP* 446 n., 452.   [99] *SLW* 441.

is in the internal, in thoughts and dispositions that cannot be seen, not even with a night telescope'.[100] Consequently, 'the religious outcome, indifferent toward the external, is assured only in the internal, that is, in faith'.[101]

Secondly, the religious individual never actually arrives at a result. The reason for this is that it is impossible to achieve a finished and complete God-relationship. Any human being 'who believes he has finished...has lost'.[102] The individual never *is* religious, he never *has* an absolute relation to the absolute *telos*, but is in the process of *becoming* religious and is *on the way* to having an absolute relation to the absolute *telos*.

On the basis of our analysis, it seems clear that religiousness A is permeated with apophatic elements. Religiousness A, however, although a considerable advance on previous stages, is still not the highest sphere of existence. The reason is that although the religious individual has reached a far higher expression of the truth than was the case in earlier spheres of existence, this expression of the truth still remains infinitely distanced from truth in its absolute form. The superiority the religious sphere possesses over the aesthetic and ethical spheres is thus merely relative and pales into insignificance when brought into relation with absolute truth. As a consequence, truth still remains essentially hidden even in the higher sphere of religiousness A.

Despite the continued hiddenness of the truth, however, the conception of truth prevalent in religiousness A *does* mark an advance on lower spheres. This is precisely because the religious individual is *aware* of his distance from the truth and structures his life accordingly. Nothingness before God, suffering, and guilt all express the individual's awareness and acceptance of the fact that, first, the truth lies beyond his grasp and, secondly, that he is unworthy to receive it. This awareness that he is removed from the truth is the highest truth to which the individual can attain. We thus have the paradoxical situation of truth being less hidden in the religious sphere by virtue of the individual's awareness and existential expression of this hiddenness. This paradoxical state of affairs once again points to the inherent apophaticism of Kierkegaard's thought.

---

[100] *SLW* 442.   [101] Ibid.   [102] *SLW* 443.

IV. RELIGIOUSNESS B

Religiousness A is not, however, the highest sphere of human existence. Although it does not collapse in the manner of the ethical sphere—indeed, it is possible to remain in this sphere for the whole of one's life—it nevertheless contains a fundamental inadequacy. This inadequacy is its *immanence*.

This immanence takes two closely related forms. First, there is a fundamental affinity between existence and the eternal or, in Kierkegaard's words, 'eternity . . . sustains everything by the immanence which lies at the base of it.'[103] The eternal is seen as undergirding existence, as being the fundament upon which existence rests. There is thus a fundamental continuity between eternity and existence.

Secondly, religiousness A is based upon the principle of 'an evolution within the total definition of human nature'.[104] It assumes that each individual possesses the condition necessary for a relationship to the eternal and the relationship both to God and the truth that this entails. There is thus a fundamental continuity between the individual and the eternal.

Now according to Kierkegaard there are several problems with religiousness A's emphasis upon immanence. One of its most serious weaknesses is that it robs existence, time, and history of their significance. Because the existential task is understood as the rediscovery of the eternal, existence is important only in so far as it is the realm in which this is to take place. In itself, however, existence, along with time and history, is of no importance. As Kierkegaard puts it, 'In religiousness A there is constantly a possibility of revoking existence into the eternity behind.'[105]

A further problem with religiousness A is that it 'has nothing dialectical in the second instance'.[106] That is, the dialectic at work in religiousness A exists only between the individual and his relation to an eternal happiness. As Kierkegaard puts it:

Religiousness A is the dialectic of inward transformation; it is the relation to an eternal happiness which is not conditioned by anything but is the dialectic inward appropriation of the relationship, and so is conditioned only by the inwardness of the appropriation and its dialectic.[107]

---

[103] *CUP* 506.   [104] *CUP* 496.   [105] *CUP* 516.   [106] *CUP* 515.
[107] *CUP* 494, cf. 496–7, 508–9.

Eternal happiness itself, however, and eternity's relation to existence are non-dialectical. As a consequence, the inwardness of religiousness A is limited and *eo ipso* the individual's relation to the truth. If a heightened degree of inwardness is to come about, it can only be on the basis of a mode of existence in which both the individual's relation to the eternal and the eternal itself are dialectical.

Finally, what if religiousness A's assumption that there exists an immanent relationship between existence and eternity is wrong? What if the individual does not possess the condition necessary for a relationship to the eternal? What if, far from eternity undergirding existence, they are in fact separated by an unbridgeable chasm? Then an approach based upon the principle of immanence would be fundamentally mistaken. That this is the case is Kierkegaard's firm conviction. He attempts to solve the problems of religiousness A by his development of 'paradoxical religiousness' or 'religiousness B'.

Religiousness A is not cancelled by religiousness B but is taken up and sharpened. Indeed, it is not possible to progress to religiousness B unless one has already reached the sphere of religiousness A.[108] It forms, as Kierkegaard puts it, the *'terminus a quo* for B'.[109] What B retains is A's emphasis on self-annihilation as the means by which the self is moulded into a form capable of sustaining a relationship to the eternal. Where B goes beyond A, however, is in its qualification of the eternal itself. It is no longer merely the individual's relation to the eternal that is the issue, but the eternal itself. Kierkegaard writes:

> Religiousness B, as henceforth it is to be called, or the paradoxical religiousness, as it has hitherto been called, or the religiousness which has the dialectical in the second instance, does on the contrary posit conditions, of such a sort that they are not merely deeper dialectical apprehensions of inwardness, but are a definite something which defines more closely the eternal happiness (whereas in A the only closer definitions are the closer definitions of inward apprehension), not defining more closely the individual apprehension of it, but defining more closely the eternal happiness itself, though not as a task for thought, but paradoxically as a repellent to produce new pathos.[110]

The element that brings about this decisive change between religiousness A and B is 'the absolute paradox'. In the following sections we wish to consider the nature of this 'absolute paradox' before

---

[108] *CUP* 494.   [109] *CUP* 496 (original emphasis).   [110] *CUP* 494.

going on to discuss the other two distinctive categories of religiousness B, namely sin and faith. In the course of this discussion we
will, of course, be attentive to any apophatic motifs that might
appear.

1. *The Absolute Paradox*

The paradox determinative of religiousness B in fact comprises two
paradoxes, namely, what we choose to call the 'objective' and 'subjective' paradoxes. Together these raise the paradox of religiousness
A to such a pitch that the paradox becomes absolute.

(a) *The Objective Paradox*

By 'objective paradox' we mean the composition of the paradox itself
rather than the paradox's relation to the individual (this is the subjective paradox). This paradox can be considered from a philosophical and a theological perspective. Both perspectives are
summed up in a journal entry in which Kierkegaard states that an
examination of the 'paradox [of] the God-man...is to be
developed solely out of the idea, and yet with constant reference to
Christ's appearance'.[111]

The philosophical treatment of the paradox is, as the above-
quoted passage makes clear, concerned with the 'idea' of the God-
man. That is, it is concerned with the philosophical principle
contained in the doctrine of the Incarnation.

We saw earlier that the paradox of religiousness A arises from the
incompatibility of the eternal and temporal, the infinite and the
finite. Despite this incompatibility, however, a fundamental affinity
exists between eternity and existence. This affinity allows the individual to overcome the incompatibility by means of 'recollecting'
the eternal and structuring his existence accordingly. Thereby the
existential contradiction is resolved. In religiousness B, however, the
immanent relationship with the eternal that makes possible religiousness A's resolution of the existential contradiction is dissolved.
This is done by eternity itself entering into time. With this, recollection becomes impossible. Eternity is no longer outside existence,
undergirding and sustaining it, but is directly present within existence itself. It is this that constitutes the absolute paradox.

---

[111] *JP* iii. 3074.

Kierkegaard remarks: 'The eternal truth has come into being in time: this is the paradox.'[112]

With eternity's entry into time, a synthesis occurs between qualities that are mutually exclusive. This is succinctly expressed in the *Fragments*: 'The paradox specifically unites the contradictories, is the eternalizing of the historical and the historicizing of the eternal.'[113] This juxtaposition of eternity and temporality within existence is paradoxical because these two terms are fundamental opposites and simply cannot be brought together into a coherent whole. Either something is eternal or it is temporal. To say it is both is a paradox.

The theological treatment of the paradox describes the paradox not in terms of the relation between the philosophical concepts of eternity and time, infinitude and finitude, but in terms of the relationship between God and existence. This occurs in such expressions as 'the god has been',[114] 'the god has been in human form',[115] 'the god has come into existence',[116] 'the god has existed',[117] as well as in such 'Christological' titles as the 'God-in-time' and the 'God-man'.[118] Unlike their philosophical counterparts the theological expressions of the paradox have no parallel in religiousness A. In religiousness A God is always transcendent of existence. In religiousness B, however, God has become present in existence itself as an individual human being. He has transformed himself into a form which stands in absolute opposition to his nature. As Kierkegaard puts it, God's presence in time 'is not something simply historical, but the historical which only against its nature can be such'.[119] It is this 'punctualization' and individualization of the omnipotent, omniscient, and omnipresent God that constitutes the absolute paradox. Kierkegaard writes: 'That God has existed in human form, has been born, grown up, and so forth, is surely the paradox *sensu strictissimo*, the absolute paradox.'[120]

In summary, the objective paradox consists of God/eternity's

---

[112] *CUP* 187, cf. 191, 242, 316.   [113] *PF* 61; cf. *JP* iii. 3085, 3089.

[114] *PF* 87.   [115] *PF* 103.   [116] *PF* 87.   [117] *PF* 87; *JP* iii. 3085.

[118] There are some instances where philosophical and theological formulations stand side by side; e.g. *CUP* 512: 'The historical assertion is that the Deity, the Eternal, came into being at a definite moment in time as an individual man.'

[119] *CUP* 512.

[120] *CUP* 194–5, cf. 188, 515, 528; *PF* 62, 107. Since it is based on the absurdity of God's presence in time, Christianity itself is a paradox (*CUP* 95, 192–4, 197–8, 200, 206, 515; cf. also *CUP* 480; *SD* 83, 100) and an absurdity (*CUP* 191–2, 338, 496).

presence in time. This is an *absolute* paradox because it is a contradiction for God to become human and eternity to enter time, and be united with precisely those elements with which they cannot be united.

(b) The Subjective Paradox

This paradox results from the human being's inability to grasp the objective paradox. This inability is due to the fact that the principles according to which thought functions are not applicable to the paradox. We saw in our analysis of religiousness A that thought was unable to make Abraham intelligible because Abraham, as the single individual in an absolute relationship with God, was not accessible to the principle of universality upon which thought is based. With regard to the absolute paradox the problem thought faces is even greater.

As we saw in our examination of epistemology in Chapter 3, Kierkegaard holds that for thinking to take place thought has to translate actuality into possibility. In this way, an object is given a form accessible to thought. The principle of possibility, however, cannot deal with the paradox. The reason for this is that thought only functions where possibility is dominant. In the case of the paradox, however, actuality is dominant.[121] This dominance of actuality over possibility, which, I believe, is an alternative way of speaking of the precedence of the particular over the universal, precludes the assimilation of the paradox into possibility and thereby its capacity to be thought.

If the thinker with a resolving *posse* comes upon an *esse* that he cannot resolve, he must say: this is something I cannot think. He thus suspends his thinking with respect to it; and if he nevertheless persists in trying to establish a relationship to this reality as a reality, he does not do so by way of thought, but paradoxically.[122]

The paradox, then, is incomprehensible. Thought is simply incapable of gaining purchase upon it.

In this limitation of reason by the paradox the apophatic strand in Kierkegaard's thought once again becomes apparent. Indeed, Kierkegaard argues that any attempt to explain the paradox, any

---

[121] *CUP* 514; cf. 95, 285, 512.
[122] *CUP* 285 (original emphasis), cf. 95, 512, 514–15.

procedure which entails the application of reason to the paradox in order to make it acceptable for human thought, is fundamentally mistaken. Such activity is akin to the nonsense of attempting to express an inexpressible joy.[123] It robs the paradox of its force and reduces it to a mere 'rhetorical expression'.[124] A true understanding of the paradox does not mean, then, attempting to make the paradox intelligible. Such an understanding of the paradox is a misunderstanding.[125] A true explanation will rather attempt to explain what the paradox is, and this means explaining that the paradox is unintelligible.[126] As Kierkegaard succinctly puts it, 'in connection with the absolute paradox, the only understanding possible is that it cannot be understood'.[127] Indeed, the pressure of the paradox on reason is so great that reason becomes 'a clod and a dunce'.[128] Consequently, certainty with regard to the absolute paradox is unattainable. The best the human being can hope for is a militant certainty in which he continually affirms his belief in the paradox in the face of its absurdity.[129] In this emphasis on the incomprehensibility of the paradox and its inaccessibility to reason, the apophatic nature of Kierkegaard's thought has again become apparent.

2. Sin

We saw earlier that religiousness A is based on an immanent relationship between existence and eternity. It was pointed out that the individual's relation to the eternal is determined by his recollection of his fundamental affinity with the eternal. With the entry of the eternal into time, however, all this changes. Eternity's presence in time posits a breach between existence and eternity. As Kierkegaard puts it, 'the exister and the eternal in time get eternity as an obstacle between them.'[130] As a result, the immanent relation between eternity and existence is dissolved and recollection is no longer a viable option.

The significance of this for existence is radical. It cancels out the circular movement of recollection and replaces it with a *linear* movement. The movement of the individual is thus not towards the eternal but *away* from it. As Kierkegaard puts it, through eternity's

---

[123] *CUP* 198.   [124] *CUP* 197.   [125] Cf. *CUP* 514.
[126] *CUP* 196–8, 500, 512; *JP* iii. 3092.
[127] *CUP* 195, cf. 514 for the opposite formulation.   [128] *PF* 53.
[129] *CUP* 203.   [130] *CUP* 474.

presence in existence 'the stamp of existence'[131] is brought to bear on the individual a second time. To the first 'stamp' by which the individual came into existence is added a second stamp which imprisons him in existence by making recollection impossible. Thereby all continuity with the eternal truth is severed. With this discovery the individual comes retrospectively to see the transition of coming into existence not as an unfortunate but repairable removal from the eternal (this is religiousness A) but as a fundamental separation.

This separation from the eternal has two consequences. First, the human being has lost the condition necessary for a relationship to the eternal / truth / God. Eternity's presence in time makes clear that the human being lacks the eternal determinant constitutive of a relationship to the eternal truth. Secondly, the principle that subjectivity is the truth must be replaced by the principle that subjectivity is *untruth*.[132] Because the human being lacks the eternal determinant, subjective development leads him not towards the truth but to a greater consciousness of his untruth. This separation from the eternal and awareness of untruth is described by Kierkegaard as *sin*.[133]

With the introduction of the concept of sin the implicit apophaticism of Kierkegaard's thought becomes particularly prominent. First and foremost, apophaticism is present in the *paradoxicality* of sin. There are several reasons for this paradoxicality.

(*a*) Because it is a consequence of the absolute paradox of eternity's presence in time, sin shares in the paradoxicality of this primary paradox.[134]

(*b*) Reason functions according to the principle of immanence. Sin, however, is based on a breach of immanence, a 'leap',[135] and thus lies outside reason's sphere of competence.

(*c*) The human being cannot know what sin is because it is impossible for him to know what perfection is and therefore the distance from perfection that constitutes sin.[136]

(*d*) If the human being is to acquire a knowledge of sin he is dependent upon outside instruction: 'The consciousness of sin is the paradoxical, and in turn, quite consistently with this, the

---

[131] *CUP* 186, cf. 201.   [132] *CUP* 185–6.
[133] *CUP* 186, 192, 241, 316, 516–17.   [134] Cf. *CUP* 474.
[135] *CA* 32, 47, 93, 111–12.   [136] *SD* 96.

paradoxical thing is that the exister does not discover this by himself, but comes to know it from without.'[137]

Many of the apophatic elements contained in Kierkegaard's concept of paradox have been dealt with elsewhere and do not need to be re-examined here. Here it suffices to point to the intrinsic unknowability of sin and the individual's epistemological dependence in acquiring an awareness of his sin. In this emphasis on human incapacity the apophatic dimension of Kierkegaard's thought once again becomes visible.

Secondly, the concept of sin indicates the apophatic dimension of Kierkegaard's thought by virtue of the fact that it marks a *positive* step in the development of the self. According to Kierkegaard, the self is constituted by that which it takes as its criterion.[138] The self acquires its highest form when it takes Christ as its criterion. This does not mean, however, that one conceives of oneself as Christ's equal. On the contrary, by taking Christ as criterion we become conscious of our *inequality* with him or, to put it in more traditional terms, we become aware of our sin. It is precisely this consciousness of sin that marks the highest development of the self. As Kierkegaard puts it, 'the more self there is, the more intense is sin'.[139] An apophatic motif is present here in that it is precisely through the negative category of sin that the human being comes to achieve selfhood. It is not a positive assessment of the human being's capacity but a negative one that constitutes the way to becoming a genuine self.

Thirdly, apophatic elements can be detected in the fact that sin is the means by which the individual comes to establish a God-relationship. As Kierkegaard puts it, 'Sin is a decisive expression for the religious mode of existence.'[140] Like guilt in religiousness A, sin places the human being in the correct position before God, namely, one of absolute disrelationship. It is precisely this disrelationship that constitutes the human being's relationship with God. By being utterly removed from God, the human being is in the correct position before God and by virtue of being in the correct position before God stands in relationship with him. There thus exists a dialectic whereby the individual comes close to God through his distance (i.e. sin) and distant from God through his closeness. Kierkegaard writes: 'The most offensive forwardness toward God is at the greatest distance; in order to be forward toward God, a person must go far away; if he

---

[137] *CUP* 475 n.   [138] *SD* 79.   [139] *SD* 114.   [140] *CUP* 239.

comes closer, he cannot be forward, and if he is forward, this *eo ipso* means that he is far away.'[141] In this dialectic between the negativity of sin and the positivity of the God-relationship, the inherent apophaticism of Kierkegaard's thought again becomes apparent.

3. Faith

The response to the absolute paradox and the crisis into which this plunges the individual is faith. This response must address two problems.[142]

(a) *The epistemological problem.* As we saw in our analysis of Kierkegaard's epistemology in Chapter 3, certitude with respect to historical events is impossible. The individual is simply not in the position to collect the material necessary to establish the certainty of such events and even if this were possible the problem of the interpretation of this material would still remain. As we saw earlier, Kierkegaard attempts to overcome this problem by the development of the concept of 'belief'. By an act of will the individual *decides* to believe that a historical event is true despite all that might argue against it.

With regard to the historical event of God's entry into time the epistemological problem the individual faces is compounded in two ways. First, in dealing with the Incarnation, the individual is faced not only with the general problem of accepting a historical event as true but with accepting an event that 'is not a direct historical fact but a fact based upon a self-contradiction'.[143] Secondly, the paradoxical event of God's presence in time is that upon which it is proposed to base an eternal happiness. This proposal contains 'two dialectical contradictions'.[144] The first of these is 'the basing of one's eternal happiness upon the relation to something historical'.[145] This is a contradiction because historical events, simply because they are historical and therefore contingent and conditioned, cannot be carriers of eternal truth.[146] Thus to regard a particular historical event as decisive for an eternal happiness is a contradiction.[147] As Kierkegaard graphically puts it: 'Every Christian is such only by being nailed to the paradox of having based his eternal happiness upon the

---

[141] *SD* 114, cf. 122.

[142] It is its confrontation with these two problems that distinguishes faith in religiousness B from that of religiousness A.

[143] *PF* 87. [144] *CUP* 513. [145] Ibid. [146] See *CUP* 86 ff.

[147] Cf. *CUP* 90.

relation to something historical.'[148] The second dialectical contradiction is that the historical datum upon which the individual intends to base his eternal happiness 'is compounded in a way contradictory to all thinking'.[149] That is, the contradiction of basing one's eternal happiness on a historical event is increased still further by the fact that the historical event in question is itself contradictory. The individual is thus proposing to base something that is absolutely decisive, namely, his eternal happiness, on something that is absolutely uncertain.

If we are to accept the paradoxical event of God's presence in time, first, as historical and, secondly, as something upon which we can base an eternal happiness, an organ must be found which permits this acceptance despite all that may argue against it.

(b) *The anthropological problem.* The absolute paradox not only plunges the individual into an epistemological crisis but also into a crisis of the self. As we saw earlier, the presence of the eternal in time causes a breach between the human being and the eternal truth, thereby positing him as a sinner. If the individual is to be rescued from this plight, an organ must be found which overcomes sin and reconstitutes the individual as a whole self.

The means by which both the epistemological and anthropological problems are solved is the *leap of faith.* This leap is 'the qualitative transition from non-belief'.[150] It is the means by which the individual comes to accept the historical reality of the Christ-event despite its paradoxicality, and the means by which the human being comes to base an eternal happiness upon this most paradoxical and uncertain of events.[151] Furthermore, it is also the means by which sin is overcome. Kierkegaard rejects the common assumption that virtue is the opposite of sin and argues that faith is sin's true opposite.[152] It is only through faith that sin is annulled or, in Kierkegaard's words, 'the only thing that is truly able to disarm the sophistry of sin is faith'.[153]

According to Kierkegaard, then, faith is the organ which overcomes the epistemological and anthropological difficulties associated with the absolute paradox.

We now wish to examine Kierkegaard's concept of faith in more

---

[148] *CUP* 512.   [149] *CUP* 513.   [150] *CUP* 15, cf. 340.
[151] *CUP* 86, 90; *JP* iii. 2354.
[152] *SD* 82–3, 124, 131.   [153] *CA* 117.

detail. This examination is motivated by two factors. First, we wish to examine how faith overcomes the epistemological and anthropological crises into which the absolute paradox plunges the human being. Secondly, we shall attempt to show that the concept of faith reveals the apophatic strand in Kierkegaard's thought particularly clearly.

(a) Faith Sensu Strictissimo

Faith *sensu strictissimo*[154] or, as Kierkegaard alternatively describes it, 'faith *sensu eminentiori*'[155] would seem at first sight to be a heightened form of belief or 'faith *sensu laxiori*'. To a certain extent this is true. Like belief, faith *sensu strictissimo* is concerned with the problem of accepting a historical event as true. Despite this similarity, however, Kierkegaard holds that there is a qualitative distinction between faith and belief. Faith in the eminent sense, he asserts, is in a sphere of its own.[156]

There are three reasons for this. First, faith is concerned with a past event that is qualitatively different from all other events. This qualitatively different event calls forth a qualitatively different response. This response falls into two parts.

(i) Faith is structurally different from belief. Unlike belief, which only has to cope with the uncertainty brought about by the transition of coming into existence, faith must 'bear the stamp of having a relationship to God's having come into being'.[157]

(ii) Faith's aim differs from that of belief. We saw earlier how belief aimed at establishing the historical certainty of an event in the face of doubt and uncertainty. The aim, then, was to establish some sort of certainty despite all the difficulties. In the case of the absolute paradox, however, this does not apply. The absolute paradox is 'something which can become historical only in direct opposition to all human reason'.[158] Consequently, it is illegitimate to strive after historical certainty. The paradox must be accepted as absurd and believed as such.[159] Unlike belief, then, faith does not aim at establishing the certainty of its object.

Following on from this, faith is not a form of knowledge. Faith

---

[154] *CUP* 188, 286–7.   [155] *CUP* 185, cf. *PF* 87.
[156] *CUP* 291; *JP* ii. 1125.
[157] *CUP* 188, cf. 189–90; *PF* 87.   [158] *CUP* 189.   [159] *CUP* 190.

transcends knowledge and cannot be expressed in epistemological terms. This too can be divided into two sections.

(i) The object of faith is not something we can *know*. This is because 'all knowledge is either knowledge of the eternal, which excludes the temporal and the historical as inconsequential, or it is purely historical knowledge, and no knowledge can have as its object this absurdity that the eternal is the historical'.[160] As the paradoxical combination of eternity and history, then, the paradox withdraws itself from the sphere of knowledge.

(ii) Faith is not cognitive, epistemological, or intellectual but is an *existential* response to the absolute paradox.[161] As Kierkegaard so often emphasizes, Christianity is not a doctrine but an existential communication. In responding to this communication the human being must respond not merely intellectually but with his *whole* self.

Thirdly, unlike belief, faith is *not* an act of will. Now there are passages in Kierkegaard's works which would seem to indicate exactly the opposite. First, there are a number of passages where Kierkegaard explicitly refers to faith as an act of will.[162] Secondly, there are several passages which, although not specifically mentioning the will, imply the use of will in relation to faith. Examples of such passages are the identification of subjective truth with faith,[163] the setting aside of reason in order to grasp the paradox,[164] and the leap of faith. All of these imply a conscious act of will. On the other hand, there are a number of passages which could be cited as evidence that Kierkegaard argues that faith is *not* an act of will. The clearest of these occurs in the *Fragments*, where Kierkegaard expressly states that faith is *not* an act of will.[165] In the course of this chapter we will attempt to resolve these two contradictory positions.[166] First, how-

---

[160] *PF* 62; cf. *JP* ii. 1111.   [161] See *CUP* 290.
[162] *JP* ii. 1094, 1130; *Pap*. IV B 87: 2.
[163] *CUP* 182.   [164] *PF* 59.   [165] *PF* 62.
[166] Price attempts to reconcile these two positions by arguing 'that what Kierkegaard is really denying is that faith is an act of "willed understanding"' (*Narrow Pass*, 129). Price believes that Kierkegaard's argument is directed against the popular assumption that faith is a provisional form of knowledge which we have to make do with until replaced with something more adequate. Stengren, on the other hand, sees the contradiction arising through the anti-Hegelianism of Kierkegaard's works. The different positions must be understood as attacks on different aspects of Hegel's system ('Faith', *Kierkegaardiana*, xii. 83). Taylor (*Kierkegaard's Pseudonymous Authorship*, 314) adopts a very different approach from the two aforementioned scholars. He ascribes the ambiguity of Kierkegaard's statements on faith to a tension between grace and response. Kierkegaard is against the understanding of grace that eliminates will but at the same time, in view of his consciousness of human sinfulness

ever, we should turn to the main theme of our discussion and consider to what extent apophatic motifs have emerged in our analysis of faith so far.

In my opinion, apophatic motifs appear in the following areas. First, Kierkegaard's severing of the link between faith and knowledge and the emphasis on faith as an existential response mean that faith is non-rational. Consequently, reason and logic are simply not able to gain purchase upon it. Indeed, to acquire faith these must be set aside in what Kierkegaard calls the 'crucifixion'[167] or 'martyrdom of understanding'.[168] Faith, then, is not acquired by means of logical deduction[169] but by means of a leap that transcends the understanding.[170] The only understanding of faith possible is that it cannot be understood. In this limitation of reason the inherent apophaticism of Kierkegaard's thought again becomes apparent.

Secondly, like faith in religiousness A, faith in religiousness B is itself paradoxical. This is because the object upon which it is based, namely, eternity/God's presence in time, is absolutely paradoxical. Kierkegaard writes: 'But then is faith just as paradoxical as the paradox? Quite so. How else could it have its object in the paradox and be happy in its relation to it? Faith itself is a wonder, and everything that is true of the paradox is also true of faith.'[171] In this emphasis on the non-rationality and paradoxicality of faith, the apophatic nature of Kierkegaard's thought is again revealed.

(b) Faith and Inwardness

The epistemological and anthropological crises into which the paradox thrusts the individual can only be met with radically increased inwardness. In the case of the epistemological crisis the individual's inwardness is increased by the absurdity of the paradox. The human being no longer has an objective fact upon which he can exercise his reasoning powers, but has an absolute uncertainty which reason cannot deal with. As a consequence, the paradox thrusts the individual away. If he is nevertheless to sustain a relation to the

and the significance this has for the will, it is necessary that he retain it. Consequently, he concludes that faith is a function both of God's grace and of the human being's will. The ambiguity in his statements on faith is a reflection of this. As we shall see later, this is the most satisfactory solution to this problem.

[167] CUP 496, 500–1, 531.   [168] CUP 208–9, 503, cf. 505.
[169] Cf. PF 94–5 n.
[170] Cf. CUP 340.   [171] PF 65.

paradox, it can only be on the basis of a radically increased inwardness which accepts the absurdity and uncertainty of the paradox. Kierkegaard writes:

> It is certain only that it is absurd, and precisely on that account it incites to an infinitely greater tension in the corresponding inwardness. The Socratic inwardness in existing is an analogue to faith; only that the inwardness of faith, corresponding as it does, not to the repulsion of the Socratic ignorance, but to the repulsion exerted by the absurd, is infinitely more profound.[172]

In the case of the anthropological crisis, inwardness is increased by the individual's awareness of sin. We saw earlier that the paradox results in the replacement of the principle 'subjectivity is the truth' with the principle 'subjectivity is the untruth'. As a consequence, the task of the existing individual becomes more difficult. He cannot begin immediately on the quest for a relationship with the eternal truth because an obstacle has been placed in his way. This 'has the effect of making the inwardness far more intensive'.[173] Indeed, Kierkegaard writes: 'It is impossible to express with more intensive inwardness the principle that subjectivity is truth, than when subjectivity is in the first instance untruth, and yet subjectivity is the truth.'[174] Both crises, then, result in increased inwardness.

It is this inwardness that Kierkegaard sees as forming the basis of the individual's escape from his crises. The difficulty in his relationship to the eternal truth is now so great that he can only sustain a relationship to it on the basis of the highest possible degree of inwardness, namely, passion. It is this passion that constitutes faith.[175]

(c) Faith and the Condition

So far two facts have emerged in our discussion of the nature of faith. First, we have established that faith is not an intellectual but an existential response. Secondly, we have ascertained that the nature of this response is passionate inwardness. Kierkegaard's third approach is to analyse the relationship between faith and the 'condition'.

We saw earlier that eternity's entry into time shows that the

[172] *CUP* 184; cf. 188, 192, 201, 510, 540.   [173] *CUP* 185.
[174] *CUP* 191, cf. 240.
[175] *PF* 54, 59; *CUP* 118; cf. *PF* 92; *CUP* 30–1, 179, 182, 185 n., 209, 540.

human being does not possess the condition requisite for a relationship to the eternal truth. This, we saw, posits the human being as
a sinner. If, despite his sin, he is to come into a relationship with the
eternal truth, he must be provided with this condition *from outside*.
This condition is provided by the God-in-time.[176]

God's entry into time, then, not only posits the individual as a
sinner but also provides him with the condition necessary to escape
from this plight. The question we must now deal with is that of the
nature of this condition.

Unfortunately, as soon as we embark upon an analysis of this
concept, we run into the old problem of Kierkegaard's reluctance to
provide straightforward definitions. We are thus compelled to ascertain the meaning of this term on the basis of its usage. This usage,
however, is ambiguous. In some passages Kierkegaard seems to
understand the condition as the consciousness of sin.[177] The problem here is that it is difficult to see how the consciousness of sin could
rescue the human being from the plight—which itself is, of course,
sin—into which he has been thrust by God's entry into time. Elsewhere Kierkegaard speaks of the condition as 'faith'.[178] Here the
problem is that, if faith is the condition, faith would cease to be a free
response and become something bestowed upon the individual from
outside. If this is the case, then the freedom of the individual to
choose—which is a crucial category in Kierkegaard's thought—
would seem to be overridden.

The first step towards resolving these problems is to ask ourselves
what would rescue the human being from the plight into which the
absolute paradox has plunged him. As we have seen, this plight is
sin. It would thus lie near at hand to understand the condition of a
relationship to the eternal as the removal, i.e. *forgiveness*, of sin.

There are two arguments in favour of this. First, there are passages
in which Kierkegaard links forgiveness with faith or related concepts. An example of such a passage is to be found in the journals,
where Kierkegaard writes that, 'To believe the forgiveness of one's
sins is the decisive crisis whereby the human being becomes
spirit.'[179] Secondly, if we understand forgiveness of sins as the condition, then the contradiction between Kierkegaard's statements that

[176] PF 14–15, 17, 56, 62, 64–5, 69–70, 100, 103; CUP 508–10.
[177] PF 93; CUP 517.
[178] PF 59, cf. Pap. V B 6:2 (draft version of PF 59, quoted in PF 197), where
Kierkegaard states this explicitly.
[179] JP i. 67.

faith both is and is not an act of will, is resolved and the problem of faith itself being the condition is solved. These problems are solved by the fact that forgiveness is a two-sided concept. There must be both a person who forgives and a person who is forgiven. Faith is *not* an act of will, since forgiveness of sins is not something that can be produced by willing it. Forgiveness must come from the injured party. It cannot be acquired by means of the immanent development of the self. In this sense, then, faith is *not* an act of will. On the other hand, forgiveness is without effect if the recipient does not will to accept it. We could understand faith as an act of will, then, in that it requires a conscious decision to accept the forgiveness offered.

The same explanation applies to Kierkegaard's statement that faith is the condition. We can speak of faith as a condition that is provided by an outside agent in the sense that faith is dependent upon the external provision of the forgiveness of sins. In the forgiveness of sins, the foundation is laid for faith. Once the condition of the forgiveness of sins has been provided, however, the individual is again placed before the choice of accepting or rejecting it.[180] Hence Kierkegaard's statement that, 'If I do not possess the condition . . . then all my willing is of no avail, even though, once the condition is given, that which was valid for the Socratic is again valid.'[181]

This linking of the condition of faith with the forgiveness of sins once again brings Kierkegaard's apophaticism to the fore. This is because it makes clear again the paradoxicality of faith. Faith is paradoxical because, like faith in religiousness A, it entails belief in the possibility of the impossible. Here, however, this impossibility acquires a new dimension which transforms an impossible possibility into the absolute paradox. This new dimension is the forgiveness of sins. For Kierkegaard this is 'a paradox *sensu strictiori*, because the existing individual is stamped as a sinner, by which existence is accentuated a second time, and because it purports to be an eternal decision in time with retroactive power to annul the past, and because it is linked with the existence of God in time'.[182] In this emphasis upon the paradoxicality of forgiveness, Kierkegaard is

---

[180] Although faith offers the way out of sin, if the individual rejects the offer of forgiveness of sins provided by the Incarnation, that is, if he is *offended* by the absolute paradox, sin returns in even stronger form. This offence is a heightened form of sin, because the individual defiantly chooses to remain in his sin and repudiates forgiveness. See *SD* 113–24.

[181] *PF* 63.   [182] *CUP* 201, cf. 204, 479 n.; *JP* iii. 3085.

again emphasizing the intrinsic unintelligibility of faith. Here again, then, we can observe the apophaticism of Kierkegaard's thought.

(d) The Uncertainty of Faith

We saw earlier that faith in religiousness A is conditioned by uncertainty. In religiousness B, this is heightened by the paradoxicality of the object to which faith is directed. Because of the paradoxicality of the object of faith as well as that of faith itself, the faith-full individual must continually live with the risk that he may be wrong. Rather than shying away from faith and its uncertainty, however, the individual should hold on to it despite its uncertainty. Indeed, uncertainty is the mechanism by which an individual's faith is both sustained and deepened. Kierkegaard writes:

Without risk there is no faith. Faith is precisely the contradiction between the infinite passion of the individual's inwardness and the objective uncertainty. If I am capable of grasping God objectively, I do not believe, but precisely because I cannot do this I must believe. If I wish to preserve myself in faith I must constantly be intent upon holding fast the objective uncertainty, so as to remain out upon the deep, over seventy thousand fathoms of water, still preserving my faith.[183]

Apophatic motifs are present in two respects:

An apophatic motif can be detected in the assertion that uncertainty is essential to faith. Here we again confront the dialectic between a negative form and a positive result that we have so often come across in Kierkegaard's thought. Here this dialectic expresses itself in the principle that to reach the positive category of faith we must pass through the negative category of uncertainty. As Kierkegaard puts it, 'the certainty of faith . . . has in every moment the infinite dialectic of uncertainty present with it.'[184] Faith, if it is to remain as faith, must always be in peril of its life. In this emphasis upon uncertainty as essential to faith, the apophaticism of Kierkegaard's thought again becomes apparent.

A further apophatic motif is visible in the denial that the human being can ever rest easy in the certain knowledge that he has a relationship to God. Indeed, certainty in one's relationship to God is 'the one certain sign that the individual does not stand in a relationship to God'.[185] There is only one certainty in the

---

[183] CUP 182, cf. 188.   [184] CUP 53; cf. PF 108.   [185] CUP 406.

God-relationship and that is that it is uncertain and must be continually won anew by the individual in the face of its uncertainty. As Kierkegaard puts it, the assurance of faith is 'not an assurance once for all, but a daily acquisition of the sure spirit of faith through the infinite personal passionate interest'.[186] In Kierkegaard's stress on uncertainty as the mark of a God-relationship, the apophatic nature of his thought once again comes to the fore.

Summing up, religiousness B is the highest sphere of existence because it most adequately expresses the relationship between God and the human being. It also achieves the most adequate solution to the existential division to which the human being is subject. Having said this, however, we have seen that the advance of religiousness B over the other spheres is not the result of increased closeness to God but of its awareness of the human being's distance from God, namely that the human being is a sinner. This insight, however, places the human being in a correct relationship with God. It also enables him to resolve the existential contradiction because by his understanding himself as a sinner the elements that constitute his self are brought into as correct a relationship as is possible within the confines of human existence. To express this with reference to the truth, we could say that through his awareness of his absolute separation from the truth, the individual has reached the highest expression of and relation to the truth that is possible for the human being. In this emphasis on one's nearness to God only coming about through the increased awareness of one's distance from God the apophatic strand inherent in Kierkegaard's thought has come powerfully to the fore.

With our discussion of the stages of existence we have come to the end of our treatment of the apophatic nature of Kierkegaard's thought from the anthropological perspective. We have established, I believe, that there is an apophatic undercurrent running through Kierkegaard's thought. We have seen that Kierkegaard has developed an epistemology based on uncertainty. We have seen that he develops a theory of truth based not on the principle of objective verifiability but on the non-verifiable principles of inwardness, subjectivity, and passion. Finally, we have seen that he develops a theory of stages of existence in which the human being progresses through

---

[186] *CUP* 53.

higher spheres of existence according to his awareness of the hidden-ness of truth and the remoteness of God.

The apophatic motifs that have become apparent in Kierkegaard's anthropology are important for our discussion of Kierkegaard as negative theologian in two ways. First, they show that for Kier-kegaard key factors determinative both of the human being's under-standing of the world in which he lives and of his development as a self are inaccessible or 'hidden'. The human being is simply unable by means of his own powers to acquire (certain) knowledge and estab-lish a relationship to the (objective) truth. Furthermore, because he is in sin, even his development as a self is flawed. All these factors impose a fundamental limitation on the human being which makes impossible a direct and objective relationship to God. Indeed, as we saw in our discussion of religiousness A and B, progress is only made when the human being accepts these limitations and constructs a God-relationship on their basis. Consequently, God is hidden not only because he does not manifest himself in a direct and obvious way, as we shall now go on to see, but also because the human being is fundamentally limited.

Secondly, our discussion of the apophatic motifs present in Kier-kegaard's anthropology is important because it is ultimately towards the question of our knowledge of and relationship to God that this anthropology is directed. Thus his epistemology is concerned ulti-mately with how we can know both God and the paradoxical event of the Incarnation. Similarly, truth is first and foremost religious truth and the stages of existence chart the human being's progress towards a higher understanding of this truth and the God-relationship this entails.

We will now leave the anthropological dimension of Kier-kegaard's apophaticism and turn to a consideration of its theological basis.

6

God

IN this and the following chapter we wish to turn our attention to the theological dimension of Kierkegaard's apophaticism. That is, we shall be concerned to show that apophatic motifs arise not only from Kierkegaard's emphasis on the limitations and incapacity of the human being but also from his understanding of God and his Christology. We turn first to an analysis of Kierkegaard's understanding of God.

Our treatment of Kierkegaard's doctrine of God falls into three parts. The first part will deal with how Kierkegaard defines the term 'God'. The second part will consider Kierkegaard's treatment of the arguments for the existence of God. Finally, the third part will be concerned with examining how human beings acquire knowledge of God. In the course of this discussion we will, of course, attempt to bring to the fore the apophaticism we believe to be implicit in Kierkegaard's thought.[1]

I. THE CONCEPT OF GOD

The first point we must make in dealing with Kierkegaard's concept of God is that he believes that the very attempt to establish such a concept is fundamentally mistaken. There are two reasons for this. First, God is the unknown.

But what is this unknown against which the understanding in its paradoxical passion collides and which even disturbs man and his self-knowledge? It is the unknown. But it is not a human being, in so far as he knows man, or

---

[1] There is, of course, a development in the individual's concept of God according to which sphere of existence he has reached. Here, however, we wish to concentrate upon the general concept of God and not upon the various forms it acquires in the different stages.

anything else that he knows. Therefore, let us call this unknown *the god*.[2]

This unknown that is God, however, is not unknown because the individual lacks knowledge. God is unknown because human reason is simply not capable of grasping him. To gain purchase on God, reason would have to be above God. God would then be subject to its laws and open to examination and explication. God, however, is the creator of the world and it is he who has ordained its laws and principles, including those of reason. Consequently, God is above reason and as such is unknown. As Kierkegaard puts it, he is 'the frontier that is continually arrived at'[3] but never crossed. In this emphasis on the breakdown of reason when confronted by the Divine we can see a very powerful apophatic motif coming to the fore. Because reason is incapable of grasping God, God becomes the Unknown, a concept that bears a striking resemblance to the hidden God of negative theology.

Secondly, Kierkegaard holds that an individual who sustains a God-relationship feels no need of a definition of God. He writes: 'Whoever lives in daily and festive communion with the thought that there is a God could hardly wish to spoil this for himself, or see it spoiled, by piecing together a definition of what God is.'[4] Kierkegaard does not mean that a concept of God is irrelevant. The point he wishes to make is that the relationship we sustain to God transcends our conceptualization of him. To attempt to define God is to put him at a distance, to stand outside our relationship with him and to treat him not as a partner in a relationship but as an external object.

That this is Kierkegaard's meaning becomes clear when we examine the context of the above-quoted passage. This passage occurs in the course of a discussion on the nature of 'earnestness'. Kierkegaard remarks that, as far as he is aware, there does not exist a single definition of earnestness. This fact pleases him 'because in relation to existential concepts it always indicates a greater discretion to abstain from definitions'.[5] The reason for this is that exis-

---

[2] *PF* 39 (original emphasis). Kierkegaard employs the term 'the god' in two ways. First, it refers, as is the case here, to God in general. Secondly, it refers, as will become clear in our consideration of Kierkegaard's Christology, to God's presence in time in the Incarnation.

[3] *PF* 44.   [4] *CA* 147, cf. 212.   [5] Ibid.

tential concepts are known not on the basis of definition but through personal experience. A definition of love, for example, cannot do justice to what love truly is. True comprehension of love is only acquired when one is in it. The same applies to God. I only truly know God when I sustain a relationship to him. And if I sustain a relationship to him, why should I jeopardize this in the objectifying process of defining him?[6]

In this reversal of the bond between the concept of God and the God-relationship another apophatic motif becomes apparent. We have seen that Kierkegaard rejects the position which would first establish the meaning of a concept before going on to consider the possibility of a relationship to that which the concept describes. That is, the *relationship* takes precedence over the concept. Indeed, Kierkegaard goes further than this and argues that a person who stands in a relationship to God will feel no need to attempt to establish a conceptual understanding of that to which he relates himself. Kierkegaard is thus denying both the right and the competence of the intellect to grasp what is involved when speaking of God. In this denial, we can again detect the implicit apophaticism of Kierkegaard's thought.

On the basis of Kierkegaard's emphasis on God as the Unknown and the precedence he gives to the God-relationship, the reader might conclude that it is impossible to say anything about God. This seems to be Garelick's opinion, who interprets Kierkegaard's position to mean that 'for us he [God] can be anything, including the Unlimited-limiting-Himself by being evil, good, finite, or all or none of these possibilities'.[7] Such an interpretation is, in my view, mistaken. Although denying that the human being can ever come to a full comprehension of the mystery that is God, Kierkegaard nevertheless believes that conceptuality does indeed have a role to play in our relationship with God. An example of this role can be found in Kierkegaard's discussion of prayer.

Kierkegaard writes that in order to pray, 'Intellectually I need to have an entirely clear conception of God, of myself, of my relation to God, and of the dialectics of the particular relationship which is that of prayer.'[8] If we are to avoid confusing God, ourselves, and prayer with other things, then, it is necessary that we construct an adequate

---

[6] *JP* ii. 1348, cf. 1343; *CUP* 484.   [7] Garelick, *Anti-Christianity*, 47.
[8] *CUP* 145.

concept of God. In enabling us to construct such a concept conceptuality plays an important role.

However, in constructing a concept of God we must not allow it to usurp the priority of the God-relationship or employ it to explain or define God. Conceptuality must therefore be subordinated to the relationship the individual has with God. Consequently, the only legitimate way of developing a concept of God is to explore it *from within*. As Kierkegaard puts it, 'God is a highest conception, not to be explained in terms of other things, but explainable only by exploring more and more profoundly the conception itself.'[9] The only way to achieve a greater understanding of what the concept 'God' entails, then, is to begin on the basis of the concept itself and to work out its connotations. In doing this, it is quite legitimate to employ terms drawn from human experience as long as we understand that they do not grasp God's essence but merely provide us with useful pointers towards the content of the highest conception that is God.

Now Kierkegaard's development of a concept of God might seem to argue against our assertion that apophatic motifs can be detected in his reversal of the bond between the concept of God and the God-relationship. This, however, would be a mistaken assumption for two reasons. First, the relationship *always* has precedence over the concept. Secondly, Kierkegaard denies to the concept of God anything more than theoretical significance. The concept, as we saw above, is 'not to be explained in terms of other things'. The terms we apply to God are merely the unfolding of the inherent possibilities and permutations of the concept. Consequently, they cannot tell us anything that is not already contained in the concept. This means not only that the apophatic motifs we detected earlier are retained but that new apophatic elements are added to them. First, apophaticism is present in Kierkegaard's denial that external terms are capable of explaining the concept of God. Such a capacity could only be acquired if we were able to stand outside the concept of God and examine it as an object 'under laboratory conditions'. Because the concept 'God' is the absolute highest concept, however, this is not possible. It is only when the individual stands 'within' the concept by establishing a relationship with God that the concept acquires a meaning. But then, of course, the individual has, as we have seen, no interest in conceptualization.

Secondly, the terms Kierkegaard employs to draw out the content

[9] *CUP* 197.

of the concept of God are themselves determined by apophatic elements. We now wish to look more closely at these terms and to investigate their inherent apophaticism.

In much of his understanding of God Kierkegaard simply accepts traditional descriptions of God. Thus he describes God as omniscient,[10] omnipotent,[11] and omnipresent.[12] Similarly, God is described as infinite[13] and eternal,[14] as love[15] and truth.[16] Other traditional terms which feature in Kierkegaard's works are descriptions of God as the examiner who puts human beings to the test,[17] as judge,[18] as righteous,[19] as spirit,[20] as Father,[21] and as the Unmoved Mover.[22]

It is worth noting here that although these various descriptions of God give us an idea of the content of the concept 'God', they do not aid us in coming to an objective definition. This is because they themselves are concepts which are just as difficult to grasp as the concept they are intended to define. 'Omnipotence', for example, does not help us to grasp what God is, because the term omnipotence itself transcends our capacity to comprehend it. Thus, these terms, although allowing us to gain some idea of the content of the concept 'God', do *not* provide us with a definition of God. They are merely propositions which allow us to attain a certain idea of the scope and significance of the term 'God'. In this denial of *objective* descriptive powers to the concepts we apply to God and his emphasis that they too participate in God's fundamental hiddenness, the apophatic nature of Kierkegaard's thought once again comes to the fore.

Perhaps the most important evidence for the apophatic nature of Kierkegaard's understanding of God, however, is his emphasis on transcendence. He is, of course, by no means the originator of this term but he gives it a uniquely intense and vigorous formulation. For

---

[10] *CUP* 368.   [11] *CUP* 124; *E/O* ii. 30, 315; *SD* 38–41, 71, 150; *FT* 119.

[12] *CUP* 219–20, 235, 368, 424, 432; *E/O* ii. 167; *CA* 86; *SD* 121; *JP* i. 698; iii. 2743.

[13] *CUP* 145, 195; *CA* 112.

[14] *CUP* 195, 217, 271, 296, 368, 512; *TC* 192; *E/O* i. 237; ii. 58, 167, 177, 189, 206, 217, 232, 236, 246; *SLW* 237, 317; *CA* 196.

[15] *TC* 137; *JP* ii. 1328, 1367, 1368, 1401, 1446; iii. 3450; cf. ii. 1321.

[16] *PV* 119.   [17] *TC* 182, 188; *PV* 114; *CA* 48, 172; *JP* ii. 1401.

[18] *CUP* 247; *SD* 123.   [19] *SLW* 317.

[20] *CUP* 124, 217–18; *E/O* ii. 20, 48–9; *SLW* 100, 169; *PV* 48.

[21] *SD* 128, 141; *TC* 34, 79–81, 106, 134, 167, 176–7; *JP* ii. 1413, cf. ii. 1321, 1322.

[22] *PF* 24–5; *CUP* 277; *TC* 66; *JP* ii. 1332, 1348, 1379; but cf. *CUP* 387 n.

Kierkegaard God is the wholly Other who is separated from humankind by 'the deep gulf of qualitative difference'.[23] There are three reasons for this.

(*a*) God and humankind belong in different spheres. The human being belongs in the sphere of existence. God, however, belongs in the sphere of the infinite and the eternal.[24]

(*b*) God is utterly independent of the human being. He does not need the human being for his designs,[25] although he is, of course, quite prepared to make use of him.[26] God's willingness to make use of the human being does not imply, however, that God needs the human being. As we saw in the previous chapter, all things are possible for God and, if the need arose, he could create an untold number of geniuses to do his bidding.[27]

(*c*) The human being is a sinner. It is this which posits 'the most chasmal qualitative abyss'[28] between God and the human being. With this the difference between God and humankind is increased by a qualitative degree. In Kierkegaard's words, 'If the difference is infinite between God who is in heaven and thee who art on earth, the difference is infinitely greater between the holy One and the sinner.'[29]

In this emphasis on transcendence, the apophatic strand of Kierkegaard's thought once again comes to the fore. The transcendence of God, as we have seen, posits a qualitative abyss between the Divine and the human. This separation means that if no measures are taken to bridge the abyss, God is hidden from humankind.

It is now necessary to establish whether the concept of God that Kierkegaard has developed has any reality. We must now consider the question: does God exist?

II. THE EXISTENCE OF GOD

The question of God's existence must be prefaced with a consideration of the applicability of the term 'existence' to God. This term has a breadth of meaning in Kierkegaard's works which it is impossible

---

[23] *SD* 99, cf. 117, 127; *PF* 44–5; *CUP* 369; *TC* 31, 67, 139; *JP* ii. 1323, 1383.
[24] *CUP* 195.
[25] *CUP* 122, 140, 233.   [26] *CUP* 140.   [27] *CUP* 233 n.
[28] *SD* 122, cf. 121; *PF* 46–7.   [29] *CD* 368.

to consider here. It suffices to point out that Kierkegaard makes a distinction between what he calls 'factual being' and 'ideal being'.

Factual being is what could perhaps be better defined as 'concrete existence', i.e. it is the designation for all that physically exists in the universe.[30] Ideal being, however, refers not to the concrete, physical existence of a thing but to its ideal form. That is, it designates the existence of a thing as an idea and not as an independent, concrete reality.[31]

The problem confronting us when considering the question of God's existence is thus that of establishing whether God has any factual being, that is, whether 'God' is merely an idea or whether he is a genuinely existent being. As Kierkegaard puts it, 'the difficulty is to grasp factual being and to bring God's ideality into factual being.'[32] This problem is further compounded by the fact that if God does possess factual being, it is of a different order to that of existent things. This is probably what prompts Kierkegaard's initially surprising assertion that God does not exist. He writes: 'God does not think, he creates; God does not exist, He is eternal.'[33] Kierkegaard certainly does not wish to deny that there is a God. The point he wishes to make is that the existence of God is of a qualitatively different kind from that of other things. Unlike existent things God's existence is not subject to the ontological division to which existence is subject. Nor is God limited by time and space but is transcendent of them.

Despite this complication, however, the fundamental problem remains the same. Does God possess real being? Is God a living reality or is he a mere concept, existing only in human imagination? We now wish to consider how Kierkegaard deals with these questions.

For Kierkegaard the whole exercise of attempting to prove God's existence is fundamentally mistaken. As he puts it, 'The idea of proving the existence of God is of all things the most ridiculous.'[34] In his opinion, every attempt to prove or disprove the existence of God is both intellectually and existentially invalid.

Its intellectual invalidity stems from the inability of thought to deal with real existence. There are two reasons for this. First, *deductive* reasoning is incapable of dealing with existence. Deduction is always dependent upon a given. It always reasons *from* something *to*

---

[30] *PF* 41–2; cf. 'empirical being' in *CUP* 169.   [31] *PF* 42 n.   [32] Ibid.
[33] *CUP* 296; cf. *JP* ii. 1347.   [34] *JP* ii. 1334.

something. It can therefore only proceed by presupposing that which it intends to prove. Only on the basis of such a presupposition can the argument get going.

It hardly occurs to the understanding to want to demonstrate that this unknown (the god) exists. If, namely, the god does not exist, then of course it is impossible to demonstrate it. But if he does exist, then it is foolishness to want to demonstrate it, since I, in the very moment the demonstration commences, would presuppose it not as doubtful—which a presupposition cannot be, inasmuch as it is a presupposition—but as decided, because otherwise I would not begin, easily perceiving that the whole thing would be impossible if he did not exist.[35]

Deductive reason becomes entangled in a circular movement in which it presupposes what it should prove, and proves merely what it has presupposed. Consequently, it fails in its attempt to prove that God exists.

Secondly, *inductive* reasoning is incapable of proving God's existence. The problem with this form of reasoning is that it always incorporates more into the premiss than is actually present. As we saw in Chapter 3, Kierkegaard holds that, 'As soon as I frame a law from experience, I insert something more into it than there is in the experience.'[36] The thinker places a framework upon his experience which does not arise from the experience itself. Consequently, the conclusion does not unfold as the natural consequence of the premiss but involves a 'leap' on the thinker's part, whereby he *decides* to understand the premiss in terms of the desired conclusion.

And how does the existence of the god emerge from the demonstration? Does it happen straightway? Is it not here as it is with the Cartesian dolls? As soon as I let go of the doll, it stands on its head. As soon as I let go of it—consequently, I have to let go of it. So also with the demonstration—so long as I am holding on to the demonstration (that is, continue to be one who is demonstrating), the existence does not emerge, if for no other reason than that I am in the process of demonstrating it, but when I let go of the demonstration, the existence is there. Yet this letting go, even that is surely something; it is, after all, *meine Zuthat*. Does it not have to be taken into account, this diminutive moment, however brief it is—it does not have to be long, because it is a *leap*.[37]

The inductive method fails as a means of proving God's existence because it is not a reasoning process but a non-intellectual commitment to *believe* something.

[35] *PF* 39.   [36] *JP* i. 1072.   [37] *PF* 42–3 (original emphasis).

Not only are attempts to prove God's existence intellectually invalid, they are also existentially invalid. Arguments for the existence
of God distort the human being's relationship to God. Kierkegaard
illustrates this by likening God to a king. The proper relationship to
a king is one of 'subjection and submission'.[38] This is how a subject
acknowledges the existence of a king. To ignore the king's presence
and then to proceed to prove his existence is to make a fool of him.[39]
This, however, is exactly how the human being proceeds with God.
He should 'prove' God's existence by an act of submission, i.e. he
should *worship*.[40] Instead, he ignores God and then commits the
'shameless affront' of 'proving his existence before his very nose'.[41]
As Kierkegaard puts it in a journal entry, 'This is the way man acts
toward God—he forgets that God exists and ponders whether it is
proper, acceptable, to have a God.'[42]

We now wish to turn to a consideration of Kierkegaard's criticism
of specific arguments for the existence of God.

1. *The Ontological Argument*

The ontological argument is, in Kierkegaard's opinion, an example
of a fallacious deductive argument. As we saw earlier, the weakness
of deduction is that it presupposes the existence of that which it
intends to prove. The ontological argument is a classic example of
this.

Thus when it is argued that God must possess all perfections, or that the
highest being must have all perfections, existence is a perfection; *ergo*, God
or the highest being must exist: this entire movement of thought is deceptive.
For if God is not really conceived as existing in the first part of the argument,
the argument cannot even get started. It would then read about as follows:
'A supreme being who does not exist must possess all perfections, including
that of existence: *ergo*, a supreme being who does not exist does exist.' This
would be a strange conclusion. Either the supreme being was non-existent in
the premises, and came into existence in the conclusion, which is quite
impossible; or he was existent in the premises, in which case he cannot come
into existence in the conclusion. For in the latter case we have in the conclusion merely a deceptive form for the logical development of a concept, a
deceptive circumlocution for a presupposition. Otherwise the argument
must remain purely hypothetical. If a supreme being is assumed to exist, he
must also be assumed in possession of all perfections; *ergo*, a supreme being

---

[38] *CUP* 485.   [39] Ibid.; cf. *CA* 151 n.; *TC* 225; *JP* ii. 1342, 1345.
[40] Ibid.   [41] Ibid.   [42] *JP* ii. 1342.

must exist—if he exists. By drawing a conclusion within an hypothesis we can surely never make the conclusion independent of the hypothesis.... When the argument is finished, the existence of God is as hypothetical as it was before, but within the hypothesis we have made the advance of establishing a logical connection between the notion of a supreme being and being as itself a perfection.[43]

To put it more briefly, the ontological argument fails because it is unable to make a valid transition from the analysis of concepts to their actual existence. It remains imprisoned within ideal being and is incapable of making the only movement which would constitute proof, namely, the transition to factual being.

In addition to this, Kierkegaard holds that the ontological argument is tautological. This comes to the fore in his criticism of Spinoza's version of the ontological argument.

Spinoza's argument is that *essentia involvit existentiam*, that is, existence is not an accidental property but is the natural corollary of essence. Kierkegaard considers Spinoza's formulation of the relation between essence and existence valid and praises its profundity,[44] for 'Spinoza ... by immersing himself in the concept of God, aims to bring being out of it by means of thought, but, please note, not as an accidental quality but as a qualification of essence.'[45] Nevertheless, despite his profundity, a fundamental weakness is present in Spinoza's treatment of the ontological argument. He arrives at his insight that *essentia involvit existentiam* by means of the argument that the more perfect an entity is, the more being it must have. This, however, is tautological for two reasons. First, Spinoza's statement amounts to nothing more than the assertion: 'the more perfect, the more being; the more being, the more perfect'.[46] Secondly, Spinoza 'explains *perfectio* by *realitas, esse*', the consequence of which is that Spinoza's statement degenerates into the tautology: 'the more it is, the more it is'.[47] At best, then, Spinoza's argument can be understood as the unfolding of the inner content of a concept. As an argument for the existence of God, however, it is a failure.

2. The Argument from Design

Kierkegaard attacks the argument from design on two fronts.

First, he attacks it because it is an inductive argument. As we saw

---

[43] *CUP* 298; cf. *JP* iii. 3615.   [44] *PF* 41 n.   [45] Ibid.   [46] Ibid.
[47] Ibid.

earlier, induction is dependent upon incorporating an element into
the reasoning process which is not contained in the premiss. The
argument from design is a classic example of this. The problem is
that God does not reveal himself *directly* in existence. As Kierkegaard puts it, 'He is in the creation, and present everywhere in it,
but directly he is not there.'[48] As a result, nature becomes ambiguous,[49] making impossible a direct progression to the conclusion that
God exists. Consequently, if we are to perceive God in the natural
world, we must read more into nature than nature itself contains.
Kierkegaard writes, 'The observer of nature does not have a result
immediately set before him, but must by himself be at pains to find it,
and thereby the direct relationship is broken.'[50] The element we
must incorporate into our observation of nature is faith. Once we
have faith nature loses its ambiguity and the believing individual
comes to see God everywhere.[51] If, however, nature is ambiguous
and it is necessary to resort to non-rational elements to remove this
ambiguity, nature is disqualified as a reliable source for evidence of
God's existence.

Kierkegaard's second line of attack stems from his criticism of the
deductive approach. The problem is that in attempting to prove
God's existence on the basis of his activity in the natural world, we
are presupposing that nature contains evidence of such activity.
Kierkegaard discusses this problem by examining the nature of the
relationship between Napoleon and his works.[52] We can only prove,
he argues, that certain works were performed by Napoleon if we
presuppose the existence of Napoleon. Presupposing Napoleon's
existence, we can then go on to explain certain works on the basis of
his existence. That is, certain deeds could be interpreted as being of
the kind that Napoleon would perform, if Napoleon does in fact
exist. Kierkegaard sums up the problems of this position in the
following passage.

If one wanted to demonstrate Napoleon's existence from Napoleon's works,
would it not be most curious, since his existence certainly explains the works
but the works do not demonstrate *his* existence unless I have already in
advance interpreted the word 'his' in such a way as to have assumed that he
exists. . . . If I call the works Napoleon's works, then the demonstration is
superfluous, since I have already mentioned his name. If I ignore this, I can

48 *CUP* 218, cf. 220; *PF* 42; *TC* 155.   49 *CUP* 182.   50 *CUP* 218.
51 *CUP* 221.   52 *PF* 40–1.

never demonstrate from the works that they are Napoleon's but demonstrate (purely ideally) that such works are the works of a great general etc.[53]

The same applies to the relation between God and nature. As a 'work', nature presupposes a 'worker' that has brought it into existence. Thus although the worker himself may not be present, the work he has performed constitutes evidence of his existence. In this way, we can prove on the basis of nature that God exists. The problem with this argument, Kierkegaard argues, is that it presupposes that which it should prove. By understanding nature as a work we have already assumed the existence of a worker, thereby pre-empting the conclusion to which our argument should lead. Kierkegaard writes:

From what works do I demonstrate it? From the works regarded ideally—that is, as they do not appear directly and immediately. But then I do not demonstrate it from the works, after all, but only develop the ideality I have presupposed; trusting in *that*, I even dare to defy all objections, even those that have not yet arisen. By beginning, then, I have presupposed the ideality, have presupposed that I will succeed in accomplishing it, but what else is that but presupposing that the god exists and actually beginning with trust in him.[54]

Like the ontological argument, then, the argument from design fails to prove the existence of God.

Our analysis of Kierkegaard's treatment of the arguments for the existence of God has again, we contend, brought to the fore the inherent apophaticism of his thought. In his rejection of these arguments, Kierkegaard indicates quite clearly that God is inaccessible to human investigative methods. These methods fail intellectually because they cannot make the transition from conceptual to real existence. They fail existentially because they eliminate the submission and faith that constitute the proper relationship of the human being to God. In this emphasis upon God's inaccessibility to rational enquiry, the apophaticism of Kierkegaard's thought again becomes apparent.

III. THE KNOWLEDGE OF GOD

Our investigation of Kierkegaard's understanding of God has revealed to us two things. First, the concept of God is subordinate to the God-relationship and, secondly, all attempts at proving God's exist-

---

[53] Ibid. (original emphasis).   [54] *PF* 42 (original emphasis).

ence are illegitimate and doomed to failure. In view of this, the question that now arises is: how can we acquire knowledge of God? This section will be concerned with investigating how Kierkegaard attempts to solve this problem and with drawing out the apophatic motifs present in his solution.

If we are unable to acquire knowledge of God by means of our own efforts, we are necessarily dependent upon God's revelation of himself. According to Kierkegaard, God has revealed himself in a special and a general revelation. The special revelation is, of course, the Incarnation. As Taylor[55] points out, the Incarnation is the only detailed treatment of God's relationship with the world that we find in Kierkegaard's works. Nevertheless, Kierkegaard does consider to some degree the possibility of a general revelation independent of the Incarnation, although, as Taylor points out, this lacks detail. In this section we will concentrate on this general revelation, leaving the consideration of God's special revelation in the Person of Christ to the next chapter.

Kierkegaard begins his discussion by vigorously attacking what he regards as two fundamentally erroneous approaches to the knowledge of God, namely, the aesthetic and the Hegelian approaches.

(a) *The aesthetic approach.* This approach accepts only *direct* revelation as constituting knowledge of God. Kierkegaard rejects this, scoffing at those who would only become attentive to God, 'If God... had taken on the figure of a very rare and tremendously large green bird, with a red beak, sitting in a tree on the mound, and perhaps even whistling in an unheard of manner',[56] or 'If God were to reveal himself in human form and grant a direct relationship, by giving himself, for example, the figure of a man six yards tall'.[57] The reason for Kierkegaard's rejection of this approach is that, in his opinion, it makes a genuine God-relationship impossible. A direct revelation is a 'deception' because human beings then 'have their attention called to what is untrue, and this direction of attention is at the same time the impossibility of the truth'.[58] A direct revelation annihilates the uncertainty which spurs the individual on to make the leap of faith. Secure in the direct knowledge that God has granted him, the individual ceases to strive, with the result that the subjectivity and inwardness which constitute the truth and determine the self's development are negated. As Kierkegaard puts it, 'As soon

[55] Taylor, *Kierkegaard's Pseudonymous Authorship*, 367.   [56] CUP 219.
[57] CUP 220.   [58] Ibid.

as I take the dialectical away, I become superstitious, and attempt to cheat God of each moment's strenuous reacquisition of that which has once been acquired.'[59] The end result is that God becomes an idol,[60] and the individual's God-relationship degenerates into paganism.[61]

But God does not reveal himself in this way. To avoid the distortions prevalent in the aesthetic approach he does not reveal himself directly but makes himself elusive.

And why is God elusive? Precisely because he is the truth, and by being elusive desires to keep men from error. The observer of nature does not have a result immediately set before him, but must by himself be at pains to find it, and thereby the direct relationship is broken. But this breach is precisely the act of self-activity, the irruption of inwardness, the first determination of the truth as inwardness.[62]

In this way God both protects the individual's subjectivity and prevents himself from being reduced to an idol.

The aesthetic approach, then, is inadequate on three grounds. First, it reduces God to an idol. Secondly, it misunderstands the nature of God's revelation. Thirdly, it annihilates the subjectivity essential for a genuine God-relationship. For these reasons, it must be rejected as a viable method of acquiring knowledge of God.

(b) *The Hegelian approach.* For Hegel, God is immanent in the world, unfolding and developing himself in the various historical epochs through which the world progresses. As Kierkegaard puts it, 'God becomes in a fantastic sense the soul in a process.'[63] If we conceive of God in this way, the various historical epochs can all be understood as manifestations of God's self-development. Consequently, by examining history we can come to know God as he unfolds himself in ever higher forms.

Kierkegaard, however, rejects the argument that world-history can provide us with knowledge of God on three counts. First, Hegel's position annihilates the transcendence of God. For Kierkegaard, if God is to be God, he must be 'sovereign'. He is above and beyond existence, and 'world-history is the royal stage where God is spectator'.[64] To reduce God to a world-soul, however, is to rob him of this sovereignty. God is then no longer transcendent of the world but is dependent upon, indeed imprisoned within, it: 'In the

---

[59] *CUP* 35 n.   [60] *CUP* 424, cf. 220.   [61] *CUP* 219, cf. 218.
[62] *CUP* 218; cf. E/O ii. 15.   [63] *CUP* 140.   [64] *CUP* 141.

world-historical process God is metaphysically imprisoned in a conventional straitjacket, half metaphysical and half aesthetic-dramatic, that is, the immanental system. It must be the very devil to be God in that manner.'[65] To rob God of his sovereignty means, in Kierkegaard's opinion, not only that we do not know God but also that God completely disappears from us. As he puts it, 'if [God] is not seen as sovereign he is not seen at all.'[66]

Secondly, history does not allow itself to be viewed according to Hegel's immanental principles. There are two reasons for this.

(i) The human being is unable to occupy the necessary position for observing history in this way. This criticism of Kierkegaard's was dealt with in some detail in Chapter 2 and need not be repeated here, except to say that whereas for God world-history is a theatre in which he is the only spectator, the human being is an actor in this theatre and consequently is incapable of viewing the 'play' as a whole.[67]

(ii) Any immanent development we might detect in history is an illusion. The Hegelian approach forgets that the people that make up a historical epoch were once alive. As such they lived, as we do, in the present tense and in what Kierkegaard calls a 'possibility-relationship' to God.[68] Like us, they were faced with choices and called upon to decide in *freedom*. Hegel, by understanding everything 'behind-hand' forgets this, with the result that 'in the world-historical process the dead are not recalled to life, but only summoned to a fantastic-objective life'.[69] That is, he does not deal with real human beings but with what we might call 'sanitized' human beings. Those elements which determine human beings as human beings and which lead in turn to the occurrence of historical epochs, are eliminated. In other words, in order to employ world-history as a source of the knowledge of God, Hegel must first transform it into a form that is accessible to immanental principles. If, however, it is necessary first to transform world-history into something it is not, then history cannot serve as the basis for the knowledge of God.

Thirdly, all arguments that God can be known in the world are based on the assumption that the world is neutral. This, however, overlooks the fact that the world is corrupted by sin. This makes it impossible for God to reveal himself directly.

[65] *CUP* 140.   [66] Ibid.   [67] *CUP* 141.   [68] *CUP* 139.
[69] *CUP* 140.

To assume that God is related directly to the world of appearance . . . would also involve us in the difficulty of having to assume that this world is a splendid world. The sensate man who thinks that this is a splendid world thinks therefore that the nearness of God is related directly to appearance: the more phenomena, the nearer God is. But Christianity teaches that this world lies in sin, which implies that God is related paradoxically to appearance, only tangentially, just as one may be able only to touch something but nevertheless can gear into it decisively, yet without being in continuity with it.[70]

Knowledge of God, then, cannot be acquired through history.

If God does not make himself known either in the form of a direct revelation to the individual or by means of a direct manifestation of himself in the historical process, how, then, does the human being come to acquire knowledge of him? In Kierkegaard's opinion, God does indeed reveal himself to the human being. God does this, however, in an indirect and elusive way which prohibits a direct appropriation of his revelation and the acquisition of objective knowledge. Kierkegaard cites three different but closely related ways in which God reveals himself. In all of these we shall note that God reveals himself in a way which only becomes intelligible when the individual *responds* to this revelation. The onus is thus placed not on God providing the human being with a direct revelation of himself but on the human being developing into a form which is responsive to God.

(a) *God reveals himself in creating the human being as a free being.* As Kierkegaard puts it, 'He communicates in creating, so as by creating to *give* independence over against himself.'[71] God, then, does not create mere ciphers, creatures which blindly follow his will, but autonomous beings capable of both responding to and rejecting his will. But why should God's gift of freedom constitute a revelation? Kierkegaard is not explicit on this, presumably because an explanation of the revelatory nature of human freedom would transform revelation into a direct form. Nevertheless, he does give us a partial explanation in the following passage.

Not even God, then, enters into a direct relationship with derivative spirits. And this is the miracle of creation, not the creation of something which is nothing over against the Creator, but the creation of something which is something, and which in true worship of God can use this something in order by its true self to become nothing before God.[72]

God is revealed, then, when the human being employs the freedom bestowed upon him as a means of constructing a God-relationship. This means becoming nothing before God, a process which, as we saw in Chapter 5, entails renouncing finitude and temporality in favour of the infinite and eternal dimension of the self. Freedom reveals, or at least has the potential to reveal, God, because it is the means by which the individual acquires a genuine relationship to God.

(b) *God reveals himself in the individual's development as a self.* Kierkegaard holds that the self is grounded in God or, as he puts it, is 'a relation and relates itself to that which established the entire relation'.[73] Consequently, in developing as a self, the human being also develops a God-relationship. As Kierkegaard puts it, 'the true autodidact is precisely in the same degree a theodidact'.[74] God is revealed to the human being, then, according to the extent in which the latter becomes a genuine self.

(c) *God reveals himself to the human being in ethics.*[75] This occurs in two ways.

First, God communicates with the human being and makes himself known in the world by setting each individual an ethical task. In carrying out this task *we* are revealed to God.

The ethical development of the individual constitutes the little private theatre where God is indeed a spectator, but where the individual is also a spectator from time to time, although essentially he is an actor, whose task is not to deceive but to reveal, just as all ethical development consists in becoming apparent before God.[76]

In this process of revealing ourselves to God, God comes to be revealed to us. As Kierkegaard puts it in a journal entry:

In paganism God was regarded as the unknown. More recently it has been assumed presumptuously that to know God is a trifle. Nevertheless, although God has revealed himself, he has taken some precautions, for one can know God only in proportion to one's being known, i.e. in proportion to one's acknowledging that he is known.[77]

---

[72] *CUP* 220.   [73] *SD* 13.   [74] *CA* 162; cf. *E/O* ii. 271.
[75] 'Ethics' is here employed in the general sense and does not refer to the ethical sphere of existence.
[76] *CUP* 141.   [77] *JP* ii. 1351, cf. 1362, 1372, 1373.

In fulfilling our ethical task, then, we are known by God, and in being known by God we come to know him. Kierkegaard is not explicit here on *how* we know God. He refers to God speaking through the human being's conscience[78] but does not go into detail as to how this occurs. If, however, we link this with the relationship Kierkegaard posits between self-knowledge and God-knowledge, then a likely answer would seem to be that in fulfilling his ethical task the individual penetrates so far into himself that he becomes aware of his basis in and dependence upon God.

Secondly, God reveals himself through the actions performed by his ethically motivated creatures. We saw earlier that Kierkegaard rejects Hegel's conception of God because it makes God dependent upon the world. By working through the ethical relationship of each individual, however, God reveals himself in the world without abdicating his sovereignty or revoking human freedom. This does not take the form of a direct intervention in human affairs, however. God stands in a 'possibility-relationship' to the world, in which he is able to make use of many different instruments to carry out his plans. As Kierkegaard puts it in his journal, 'No miracles are needed; God who holds everything in his hand at every moment has possibilities to burn.'[79] This does not mean, however, 'that God would contradict himself, that he would create and then refuse to use'.[80] Each individual is provided with his task, but God retains both the freedom to fulfil his plans by other means and respects the individual's freedom to thwart these plans. God is thus indeed sovereign but a benevolent sovereign who respects the autonomy of his subjects. It is, then, through his interaction with the human being and through the human being's free response that God acts in the world and reveals himself.

True revelation takes place, then, not in dramatic theophanies or mystical experiences but in the individual's inward and ethical self-development to the point where God becomes an essential reality for him. As Kierkegaard puts it, 'only for the existing person is God present, i.e. he can be *present* in faith.'[81] Once the individual has faith, he sees God everywhere.[82]

This does not mean, however, that when we have faith it becomes

---

[78] *JP* ii. 1382.   [79] Ibid.   [80] *CUP* 140.
[81] *JP* ii. 1347 (original emphasis); cf. iii. 3615.   [82] *CUP* 218, 220–1.

possible to perceive God *directly*. This is excluded for two reasons. First, our knowledge of God is dependent upon our relationship with him. This means that if we do not establish a genuine relationship with him, it becomes possible to overlook the Divine Presence altogether. Similarly, if we establish such a relationship but then revert to aesthetic conceptions of God as an external object, the relationship collapses and with it our knowledge of God.

Secondly, even when we have faith and can see God everywhere, our vision of God is not direct and objective but indirect and subjective. Indeed, the mark of God's presence for the believer becomes his apparent absence. The more external appearance seems to exclude the possibility of God's presence, the more he is in fact present for the believer.

The law for God's nearness and remoteness is as follows: The more the phenomenon, the appearance, expresses that here God cannot possibly be present, the closer he is; inversely, the more the phenomenon, the appearance, expresses that God is very near, the farther away he is.[83]

Faith, then, does not allow us to return to aesthetic conceptions of God. God is *always* hidden and, indeed, must remain so if the autonomy of the human being is to be protected and the possibility of a genuine God-relationship held open. Knowing God means knowing him in *relationship*, a point that is succinctly expressed by George Price.

We know Him only in direct personal encounter, in an 'I-Thou' relationship. As it is sometimes put: God cannot be legitimately 'objectified'—He cannot be known when we study him as an object, and talk about Him in the third person in an 'I-It' relationship, for He then eludes all our words and categories.[84]

Once again, then, the inherent apophaticism of Kierkegaard's thought has become apparent. God, for Kierkegaard, is the hidden God who, in revealing himself, does so in a way which protects his hiddenness.

Summing up this chapter, we can see that apophatic motifs are very prominent in Kierkegaard's understanding of God. In our analysis of Kierkegaard's treatment of the concept of God, we saw how he prefaces all attempts to conceptualize God with an emphasis upon

---

[83] *JP* iii. 3099; cf. ii. 1425; iii. 3100; *SD* 114.   [84] Price, *Narrow Pass*, 122.

the essential incomprehensibility of God and upon the precedence of relationship over conceptuality. Only when these two principles have been accepted is it legitimate to go on to a consideration of possible terms and descriptions of God. These terms and descriptions, of course, never grasp the essence of God. They merely provide us with a point of departure for our articulation and development of an already present God-relationship.

In our consideration of Kierkegaard's treatment of the arguments for God's existence, we ascertained that he holds all such arguments to be both inadequate and illegitimate. Such arguments would only be viable if we stood above God and were able to treat him as an object. Since God is transcendent of both the world and our reasoning faculties, however, these arguments are doomed to failure. In addition to this, such arguments are existentially invalid because they distract us from the true task of establishing a *relationship* with God.

Finally, we saw that God does not remain in his transcendence but communicates with human beings. He does this in an elusive and indirect way, however, in order to protect his own transcendence and to avoid overriding the individual's freedom. This means that if we reject his subtle overtures, if we do not develop as selves towards the relationship of faith, it can appear as if God were absent or indeed did not even exist at all.

7

Christology

IN the previous chapter we pointed out that Kierkegaard holds that there is both a general and a special revelation of God. In this chapter we intend to examine God's special revelation—namely, his revelation of himself in his Son, Jesus Christ. This chapter, then, will be devoted to a consideration of Kierkegaard's Christology.

It is a subject of some dispute amongst scholars whether a Christology can in fact be attributed to Kierkegaard. They point out that many traditional Christological terms are lacking in Kierkegaard's works. There is little or no discussion of the relationship between the divine and human natures in Christ, no discussion of the relationship between the Second Person and the other Persons of the Trinity, and no detailed treatment of the titles applied to Jesus in the New Testament.[1] This, however, is too narrow a definition of Christology. Christology is *Christ-logos*, that is, discourse on Christ. Since a large proportion of Kierkegaard's literary output was devoted to discourse on Christ, we can, I believe, speak of a Kierkegaardian Christology.

Nevertheless, it remains true that Kierkegaard's Christology lacks elements present in more conventional Christologies. There are two reasons for this. First, Kierkegaard's Christology is coloured by his antipathy to the three dominant Christological trends of his day. As Hannay points out:

Kierkegaard's discussion as a whole is directed at what was, in his view, an unholy alliance between two main contemporary currents in religious thought: one a renewed interest in the historical Jesus as the source of true human value . . . and the other the Hegelian belief that significant historical events occur with a retrospectively discernible necessity.[2]

---

[1] Trinitarian terminology does occasionally appear in Kierkegaard's works but this is minimal and no attempt is made to develop a Trinitarian doctrine. See Kierkegaard's description of Christ as 'the Only Begotten Son' (*TC* 79–80, 134–5, 167; *JP* i. 298) and the Son of God (*TC* 243); cf. also Kierkegaard's description of God as Father in the previous chapter.

[2] Hannay, *Kierkegaard*, 97.

To these we ought also to add a third contemporary trend attacked by Kierkegaard, namely, the reduction of Christ to a teacher of doctrine.[3] The result of Kierkegaard's anxiety to combat these three trends is that Christological terms which are not of direct relevance to his attack retreat into the background.

Secondly, Kierkegaard's primary concern is with Christ's *existential* significance. He simply accepts the Christ-event as a brute fact and then attempts to work out the existential consequences of this fact. The decisive issue is not 'Who or what is Christ?' but 'What does Christ mean to me?' Consequently, issues such as the relation between Christ's divinity and humanity, etc., recede into the background.[4]

Despite the anomalies caused by his specific interests, however, Kierkegaard does indeed have a Christology. In the following pages we wish to examine in detail the apophatic structure of this Christology, beginning first with his understanding of the Incarnation before moving on to consider his soteriology.

I. THE INCARNATION

We have already discussed some of Kierkegaard's most important Christological terms, namely, the absolute paradox, the God-in-time, and the God-man. For this reason it is not necessary to discuss these here. We wish here to concentrate on the other terms employed by Kierkegaard. This will involve an analysis of his version of the kenotic theory and his development of the concept of contemporaneity. In the course of our discussion we will attempt to ascertain to what degree apophatic motifs are present.

1. *Kenosis*

Kierkegaard develops his version of the kenosis theory by way of analogy. He asks us to envisage a king who wishes to marry a maiden far below his station. A genuine love-relationship is only possible,

---

[3] *TC* 123, 127, 135.

[4] Kierkegaard does at times touch upon traditional Christological problems such as Christ's foreknowledge (*TC* 106–7, 163, 170, 184; *JP* i. 286, 308, 315; iii. 3442) and pre-existence (*TC* 81, 167, 171; cf. *PF* 26–30). However, he simply asserts these principles and makes no attempt to justify them or incorporate them into his Christology.

Kierkegaard holds, on the basis of equality. If one of the partners is inferior to the other, then the relationship becomes unhappy.[5] If his relationship with the lowly maiden is to succeed, the king must thus establish equality between himself and the maiden. There are two ways of achieving this.

(a) *Equality established on the basis of the king's position.* This can take two forms. First, the king can elevate the maiden to his own level. This, however, is an inadequate approach. There are three reasons for this. (i) It is a deception. This is because the equality the maiden's elevation establishes is based on a change of costume.[6] She now has the *appearance* of equality but beneath her finery she still remains the lowly maiden. The equality is thus a deception with no basis in reality. (ii) The danger arises of the maiden's coming to believe herself to be loved not for her own sake but for the sake of her costume. Such a thought would result in her utter demoralization.[7] (iii) 'Love . . . does not change the beloved but changes itself.'[8] If the king genuinely loves the maiden, he will not attempt to change her but will change himself.

Secondly, 'the king could have appeared before the lowly maiden in all his splendour . . . and let her forget herself in adoring admiration.'[9] This is unsatisfactory because the king 'did not want his own glorification but the girl's',[10] and because it would again base a relationship on the outward appearance of one of the parties in the relationship.

Equality, then, cannot be based on the king's position.

(b) *Equality established on the basis of the maiden's position.* Instead of elevating the maiden to his level, the king could descend to her level. This is achieved by the king's taking upon himself the same form as the maiden. Rather than clothing the maiden in the raiment of a queen, he clothes himself in the peasant garments to which she is accustomed. Thereby the maiden is protected from the king's glory and is able to respond not to the glory of the man she has before her but to the man himself.

In the Incarnation, God, motivated by the same principles as the king in Kierkegaard's analogy, adopts the second option. He does not exalt the human being, for, as we have seen, true love changes itself and not the loved one.[11] Nor does he appear in glory because

---

[5] *PF* 28.   [6] *PF* 29.   [7] *PF* 30.   [8] *PF* 33.
[9] *PF* 29; cf. *JP* ii. 2402.   [10] Ibid.   [11] *PF* 33.

this would simply be too much for the human being.[12] God respects the human being's frailty and autonomy, and for this reason reveals himself in human form. In Kierkegaard's opinion, 'For the god's love, any other revelation would be a deception.'[13]

In incarnating himself, however, it is not enough that God assume *any* human form. God wishes to address *all* human beings and thus, although 'it is not a greater humiliation for God to become a beggar than to become an emperor',[14] he takes the lowest common denominator as the basis for his Incarnation. Thereby 'no man will feel himself excluded or think that it is human status and popularity with men that bring a person closer to God'.[15] Consequently, the form God assumes in incarnating himself is that of a *servant*.[16]

Kierkegaard stresses that 'this form of a servant is not something put on like the king's plebeian cloak, which just by flapping open would betray the king'.[17] God's humanity is not a disguise but is 'his true form'.[18] It is 'not something put on but is actual, not a parastatic but an actual body'.[19] Kierkegaard, then, quite clearly rejects docetism.[20]

Thus far Kierkegaard is in line with the orthodox understanding of the kenotic theory. But, as H. Roos points out,[21] Kierkegaard goes a stage further than the orthodox position and introduces a new element, namely, that God is *bound* by his human form.

The god, from the hour when by the omnipotent resolution of his omnipotent love he became a servant, . . . has himself become captive, so to speak, in his resolution and is now obliged to continue (to go on talking loosely) whether he wants to or not. He cannot betray his identity; unlike that noble king, he does not have the possibility of suddenly disclosing that he is, after all, the king—which is no perfection in the king (to have this possibility) but merely manifests his impotence and the impotence of his resolution, that he actually is incapable of becoming what he wanted to become.[22]

The humanity of God is so real that once he has assumed human form he cannot remove it, but 'must suffer all things, endure all things, be tried in all things, hunger in the desert, thirst in his agonies, be

---

[12] Kierkegaard quotes with approval the statement in Exod. 33: 20 that 'to see the god was death' (*PF* 30).
[13] *PF* 33; cf. *JP* i. 301.   [14] *CUP* 528; cf. *TC* 43, 127.
[15] *SD* 128; cf. *PF* 31; *TC* 13, 63.
[16] *PF* 31; *SD* 128; cf. *TC* 13.   [17] *PF* 31-2.   [18] *PF* 32.   [19] *PF* 55.
[20] Cf. also *SD* 131, where Kierkegaard describes docetism as a form of offence.
[21] H. Roos, 'Søren Kierkegaard und die Kenosis-Lehre', *Kierkegaardiana*, i. 56.
[22] *PF* 55; cf. *TC* 131-2; *JP* iv. 4651.

forsaken in death, absolutely the equal of the lowliest of human beings'.[23] Far from being docetist, then, Kierkegaard is a vigorous advocate of the humanity of Christ. Indeed, Christ's humanity seems in danger of swallowing up his divinity.[24]

Here again, then, we can see the inherent apophaticism of Kierkegaard's thought rising to the surface. We have seen that Christ adopts the form of a servant in order to shield the human being from the overwhelming power of his divinity. The consequence of this is that God becomes absolutely unrecognizable. God, on becoming human, has adopted a form which is 'the greatest possible, the infinitely qualitative, remove from being God, and therefore the profoundest incognito'.[25] Furthermore, there is no direct transition from Christ's appearance to the assertion that he is God. Kierkegaard criticizes vigorously those who argue that 'Christ was God *to such a degree* that one could at once *perceive* it directly—instead of saying as they ought: he was very God, and therefore *to such a degree* God that he was unrecognizable, so that it was not flesh and blood, but the exact opposite of flesh and blood, which prompted Peter to recognize him.'[26] Indeed, Kierkegaard makes Christ's divinity dependent upon his unrecognizability since 'direct recognizableness is precisely the characteristic of the pagan god'.[27]

Apophaticism is present in Kierkegaard's Christology, then, in his emphasis on the fact that in revealing himself God conceals himself behind an incognito. As Hirsch puts it, 'the incarnated God is the God which is unknown in his Godhead'.[28] Even in revelation, then, God is hidden from the human being.

---

[23] *PF* 32–3; cf. *TC* 131.

[24] Nevertheless, it is unfair to argue, as Roos does ('Kierkegaard und die Kenosis-Lehre', 60), that Kierkegaard's position is a renunciation of the Chalcedonian formula that Christ is 'truly God and truly man...made known in two natures without confusion, without change'. As is indicated by his description of Christ as the God-man and as the absolute paradox of eternity's presence in time, Kierkegaard takes Christ's divinity seriously. Furthermore, Kierkegaard's acceptance of the Chalcedonian formula is made clear in a journal entry in which he states that 'At every moment Christ is God just as much as he is man—just as the sky seems to be as deep in the sea as it is high above the sea' (*JP* i. 284). Kierkegaard's apparent overemphasis of Christ's humanity is due to his concentration on Christ's existential and soteriological significance. An examination of the context of the 'servant passages' shows that these occur in the course of a discussion of Christ as *Teacher*. Since, in order to be a teacher, it is necessary that one find some common ground with one's pupils, it is only to be expected that Kierkegaard emphasizes Christ's humanity at this point.

[25] *TC* 127, cf. 131.   [26] *TC* 128 (original emphasis).

[27] *TC* 135, cf. 137.   [28] Hirsch, *Kierkegaard-Studien*, 705.

But if the human being is to come to respond to God, God cannot allow his incognito to be total. This would run the risk of the human being's completely overlooking God's revelation of himself in Christ. Kierkegaard writes:

He humbled himself and took the form of a servant, but he certainly did not come to live as a servant in the service of some particular person, carrying out his tasks without letting his master or his co-workers realize who he was—wrath such as that we dare not ascribe to the god.[29]

Christ, then, although hiding himself from the direct gaze of human beings by taking on the form of a servant, must nevertheless reveal himself in some manner. He does this in the following ways.

First, Christ can send someone ahead to attract the individual's attention. Clearly thinking of John the Baptist, Kierkegaard writes: 'Although the god is unable to send anyone in his place, he presumably is able to send someone in advance who can make the learner aware.'[30] Such a predecessor, however, cannot pre-empt the god's mission in any way. He 'cannot know what the god wants to teach',[31] but must merely create an atmosphere of expectation and awareness.

Secondly, Christ's unconventional life-style makes people take notice of him. He does not strive to accumulate wealth, he shows a lack of concern for house and home, he is unmarried, etc.[32] 'This exalted absorption in his work', Kierkegaard writes, 'will already have drawn to the teacher the attention of the crowd.'[33]

Thirdly, Christ 'makes his appearance under circumstances which are bound to fix very especial attention upon him'.[34] Thus he allows himself to be born into a nation which 'looks forward to an Expected One who will usher in a golden age for his land and nation'.[35] Although he appears in a way that contradicts the expectations of the people, the situation is such that attention is inevitably focused upon him.

Fourthly, Christ may hint at his special status by performing 'signs and wonders which are talked about in the whole land'.[36]

Finally, as we shall see shortly, Christ can reveal himself through indirect communication.

In revealing himself in these ways, however, Christ retains his hiddenness. This is to avoid endangering the servant form and

---

[29] *PF* 56; cf. *PV* 16; *JP* iii. 3077, 3081.   [30] *PF* 55; cf. *TC* 44, 97.   [31] Ibid.
[32] *PF* 56.   [33] *PF* 57.   [34] *TC* 44.   [35] Ibid.   [36] Ibid.

jeopardizing the human being's autonomy. Contradictory as it sounds, Christ can only reveal himself in a way which sustains his hiddenness. As Kierkegaard puts it, Christ 'is willing, it is true, to be recognized, but not *directly*'.[37] Thus Christ's apparently open manifestation of his divinity does not reveal him as God or allow a direct relationship to him. This is because there is no direct transition from the fact that he performs miracles to the conclusion that he is God. Miracles themselves, Kierkegaard argues, do not prove anything.[38] Indeed, 'a miracle is a very uncertain thing'.[37] It is only the passage of time, the two thousand years since Christ's death, that allows us the deceit of believing that we would have perceived Christ's divinity on the basis of his miracles.[40] In the situation of contemporaneity, however, miracles cannot reveal anything directly but merely 'make one attentive', thrusting the observer into 'a state of tension'.[41] The onus of how to interpret them, however, is on the individual himself.

The same is the case with Christ's employment of indirect communication. We saw in Chapter 2 that the purpose of indirect communication was to confront the recipient with key existential issues without the interference of the personality of the communicator. With regard to Christ, however, indirect communication acquires a different form. Because Christ himself is the 'teaching', he cannot withdraw himself from the communication. However, to protect the human being's autonomy and to make genuine choice possible he must nevertheless communicate himself in an indirect manner. This he does, first, by adopting the form of a servant and, secondly, by stating openly and directly that he is God. Although the latter is a direct statement, the fact that it is made by a human being transforms it into indirect communication.

When one says directly, 'I am God; the Father and I are one,' that is direct communication. But when he who says it is an individual man, quite like other men, then this communication is not just perfectly direct; for it is not just perfectly clear and direct that an individual man should be God— although what he says is perfectly direct.[42]

Christ's revelation of himself in the direct statement of his true status is thus a revelation that is rooted in hiddenness. As Kierkegaard puts it, it 'can only serve, like the miracle, to make people attentive'.[43]

[37] *TC* 128 (original emphasis).   [38] *TC* 99.   [39] *TC* 54.
[40] *TC* 44–5.   [41] *TC* 99.   [42] *TC* 134, cf. 135, 175.   [43] *TC* 135.

The onus for accepting or rejecting this revelation is again with each individual.

For Kierkegaard, then, even God's revelation of himself in his Son Jesus Christ remains rooted in the principle of hiddenness. Once again, then, the inherent apophaticism of Kierkegaard's thought has become apparent.

Before going on to deal with Kierkegaard's concept of contemporaneity, it is necessary to ask whether later generations, armed with the knowledge that Christ was God, can dispense with the servant Christology and relate solely to the exalted Christ. In Kierkegaard's opinion, this is an illegitimate, indeed blasphemous, move. The servant form and the divinity of Christ are tied together in a 'dialectical knot' which no human being should presume to untie.[44] Although Christ is now in glory, his words of invitation to the human being were spoken not in glory but in a state of humiliation. If we treat them otherwise we transform them from truth into untruth. Even after his exaltation, it continues to be the servant that speaks.[45] The tension that existed in his lifetime between his words and his guise as a servant thus remains in force and will only be revoked in the Parousia, when Christ returns to earth in glory. Consequently, the risen Christ remains just as hidden, ambiguous, and opaque to human comprehension as the Christ who was stumbling-block to the Jews during his lifetime.

2. Contemporaneity

The concept of contemporaneity is Kierkegaard's attempt to solve the problem of how an event which occurred almost two thousand years ago can be of any significance for us today. In working out his solution Kierkegaard takes as his starting-point Lessing's remarks in *Über den Beweis des Geistes und der Kraft* that 'accidental truths of history can never become proof of necessary truths of reason'.[46] That is, a general truth, i.e. a truth which is not bound to a particular historical event or epoch but has universal significance for every generation, cannot be proved to be such on the basis of its appearance in a historical event. History, as subject to arbitrariness and contingency, cannot serve as evidence for necessary, immutable truths.

If this is the case, then what sense can we make of the Incarnation?

[44] *TC* 36.   [45] *TC* 27.   [46] See *CUP* 86, 89.

Here we have, according to Christianity, absolute truth manifested in a specific historical individual at a specific point in time. How can we know this to be the case if this event is now long past and how can it be of any significance for later generations? Lessing's position is that it was only Christ's immediate contemporaries who were in the position to answer this question. They were able personally to witness Christ's miracles and the other activities which indicated his special status. Later generations, however, have to rely on the reports of these witnesses, which, according to Lessing, are insufficient evidence upon which to base a judgement on the divine nature of Christ.

Kierkegaard takes up this argument but unlike Lessing seeks to show that every generation, no matter how far removed from the historical event of the Incarnation, has the possibility of establishing a relationship to it or, as Kierkegaard expresses it, of becoming 'contemporary with Christ'.

Kierkegaard develops his concept of contemporaneity by first making clear what contemporaneity is not. This he does by showing the inadequacy of both immediate contemporaneity and historical evidence as the basis for a relationship with Christ. He then goes on to describe the nature of true contemporaneity.

(a) Immediate Contemporaneity

The argument that the immediate contemporaries of Christ, i.e. those who were able personally to witness the activity of the historical Jesus, have a decisive advantage over later, non-contemporary generations is vigorously attacked by Kierkegaard. In his opinion, the fact that an individual may have been physically in the presence of Christ is of merely incidental significance. It cannot make the individual a follower of Christ and Kierkegaard criticizes sharply those who 'live . . . in the vain persuasion that, had they lived contemporary with Christ, they would at once have known and recognized him in spite of his unrecognizableness'.[47] Kierkegaard's reasons for denying any significance to immediate contemporaneity are as follows.

(a) Immediate contemporaneity is impossible. For immediate contemporaneity to be valid it must be total. That is, the individual must be constantly in Christ's presence from birth to death. If the in-

[47] *TC* 127.

dividual is only occasionally contemporary with Christ, however, his knowledge is approximate, and approximate knowledge, as we saw in Chapters 3 and 5, is not a sufficient basis for becoming a follower of Christ. Indeed, the gaps in our knowledge can place in jeopardy the limited knowledge we do have. According to Kierkegaard, 'we can let ignorance step in here, let ignorance, so to speak, destroy one fact after the other, let it historically demolish the historical.'[48] If we are consistent in our advocation of immediate contempoɩaneity, then, only one single person could become a follower of Christ, namely, Mary, since, 'if we insist upon absolutely exact historical knowledge, only one human being would be completely informed, namely, the woman by whom he let himself be born'.[49] Because of the impossibility of acquiring absolute immediate contemporaneity, the significance of being physically present at the Christ-event falls away.

The significance of immediate contemporaneity is further undermined by the fact that all knowledge of an event, even if based on absolutely complete first-hand information, is inherently uncertain. There are two reasons for this. First, the Christ-event is 'historical to the first power'.[50] That is, like all other historical events, it has come into existence. As we saw in our analysis of Kierkegaard's epistemology, 'coming into existence' is a transcendent 'leap' that is inaccessible to reason. The result of this inaccessibility is that a vital part of the information necessary for the construction of knowledge is lacking. This lack of information places our knowledge as a whole in doubt. In this the contemporary is in no better a position than the non-contemporary. For both the transition of coming into existence is inaccessible. As Kierkegaard puts it: 'With respect to the directly historical, it holds true that it cannot become historical for immediate sensation or cognition, no more for the contemporary than for someone coming later.'[51] This places contemporary and non-contemporary on the same footing, thereby annulling the advantage of immediate contemporaneity. Secondly, unlike other historical facts, the Christ-event 'is indeed no simple historical fact'[52] but is what Kierkegaard calls an 'absolute fact'.[53] As Holm rightly points out,[54] this is best understood as the unity of a simple historical fact and an eternal fact. A simple historical fact is a fact which is wholly conditioned by and dependent upon a particular epoch. It has no

48 *PF* 59.   49 Ibid.   50 *PF* 87.   51 Ibid.   52 *PF* 92.
53 *PF* 99.   54 Holm, *Kierkegaards Geschichtsphilosophie*, 71.

existence independent of this epoch. An eternal fact, on the other hand, is not dependent upon a particular historical epoch but is the common possession of all generations. 'Every age is equally close to it,'[55] and history plays no role in determining the individual's relationship to it. As a combination of historical and eternal facts, then, the absolute fact is a universal truth that has become present at a particular point in time.

The unique composition of the absolute fact annuls the significance of contemporaneity for two reasons. The first reason is that as eternal, the absolute fact cannot be limited to a specific point in time. It is a fact which, although present in history, is not bound to or dependent upon history but speaks to each of us regardless of the era in which we live. Only one tense is applicable, namely, the present.[56] Decisive is not the historical point at which the eternal has entered time, but the fact that it should have entered time at all. With this, the eternal has become present in the medium of existence, a medium common to human beings of all generations. Consequently, immediate contemporaneity with the point at which the eternal entered time is of no significance. Indeed, Kierkegaard writes that 'the follower, if he understood himself, would have to wish that it would be terminated by the departure of the god from the earth,'[57] in order that he might not 'be tempted to run around to see with his physical eyes and to hear with his mortal ears'.[58]

The second reason for the irrelevance of contemporaneity is the paradoxical nature of the absolute fact. It has 'a unique quality in that it is not a direct historical fact but a fact based upon a self-contradiction'.[59] In the absolute fact, two contradictory elements are conjoined, namely, God and the human, eternity and time. This is just as much a paradox for the contemporary as it is for later generations, even if he should spend his whole life in Christ's presence. This paradoxicality cancels out the advantages of contemporaneity and places contemporary and non-contemporary on equal footing,[60] since 'face to face with a self-contradiction and the risk entailed in assenting to it, immediate contemporaneity is no advantage at all'.[61]

(b) *There is no direct progression from immediate contemporaneity to becoming a follower of Christ.*[62] The reason for this is

---

[55] Ibid. 70.   [56] TC 67.   [57] PF 105; cf. CUP 536.   [58] PF 106.
[59] PF 87.   [60] PF 88.   [61] PF 87.   [62] PF 59.

that Christ's status is not immediately obvious. As we saw earlier, the historical person Jesus of Nazareth is extremely ambiguous. On the one hand, certain actions seem to indicate that he is more than a mere man. On the other hand, his appearance is that of an ordinary human being. This ambiguity makes impossible any conclusion of the type: 'This man has this or that quality or has performed this or that action, therefore he must be God.' Consequently, contemporaneity is of no advantage.

The contemporary learner possesses an advantage for which, alas, the subsequent learner, just in order to do something, will very much envy him. The contemporary can go and observe that teacher—and does he then dare to believe his eyes? Yes, why not? As a consequence, however, does he dare to believe that he is a follower? Not at all, for if he believes his eyes, he is in fact deceived, for the god cannot be known directly. Then may he close his eyes? Quite so. But if he does, then what is the advantage of being contemporary?[63]

Immediate contemporaneity, then, is of no significance. As Kierkegaard puts it, 'the historical in the more concrete sense is inconsequential,'[64] and the person who holds on to it reduces Christ to a merely historical event.[65]

(c) *It would be unjust of God if immediate contemporaneity were of decisive significance.* This is because his saving work would then be directed not at all humankind but at one particular generation.

Would the god allow the power of time to decide whom he would grant his favour, or would it not be worthy of the god to make the reconciliation equally difficult for every human being at every time and in every place, equally difficult because no human being is capable of giving himself the condition (but neither is he to receive it from another human being and thereby produce new dissension), equally difficult, then, but also equally easy—inasmuch as the god gives it.[66]

(d) *The individual only acquires faith when Christ provides him with the condition.* If, as we saw in Chapter 5, it is the condition that is decisive in the God-relationship, then immediate contemporaneity can play no significant role in bringing the human being to faith. God can grant the condition of faith at all places and at all times. Consequently, immediate contemporaneity is of no importance for faith in Christ.

[63] *PF* 63, cf. 66–7.   [64] *PF* 59.   [65] *PF* 60.
[66] *PF* 106–7; cf. *CUP* 89.

(b) The Follower at Second Hand

If the contemporary has no advantage over the non-contemporary, does the non-contemporary perhaps possess an advantage over the contemporary? Can the weight of history aid him in becoming a follower or, as Kierkegaard formulates it in *Training in Christianity*, 'Can one prove from history that Christ was God?'[67]

In Kierkegaard's opinion, these questions must be answered in the negative. Just as the immediate contemporary possesses no advantage over the later follower, so too does the later follower possess no advantage over the immediate contemporary. Kierkegaard's reasons for this are as follows.

(*a*) *Faith cannot be based on historical knowledge.* As we saw earlier, no matter how extensive and reliable historical knowledge may be, it can never provide a sufficient basis for faith. 'For faith cannot be distilled from even the finest detail.'[68] In addition to this, the historical approach misunderstands the nature of the Christ-event. The Christ-event is more than a simple historical event. It is an event which has decisive existential significance. Consequently, to respond to it by demanding reliable historical information is a misunderstanding. To do so is to intellectualize an event which should be understood existentially. As Kierkegaard puts it, 'the passion of faith, that is, the passion that is just as intense as faith,' had taken a wrong turn toward the *purely historical*.'[69] The true response to the Christ-event is faith. Since this is true both of the contemporary and the latest generation, neither has an advantage over the other.

(*b*) *The Christ-event is paradoxical.* History cannot help to remove this, since God's presence in time remains just as paradoxical two thousand years after the event as it was when it occurred.

> If that fact came into the world as the absolute paradox, all that comes later would be of no help, because this remains for all eternity the consequences of a paradox and thus just as definitively improbable as the paradox, unless it is assumed that the consequences (which, after all, are derived) gained retroactive power to transform the paradox, which would be just as acceptable as the assumption that a son received retroactive power to transform his father.[70]

---

[67] *TC* 28.   [68] *PF* 103.   [69] *PF* 92 (emphasis added).
[70] *PF* 94–5, cf. 98; *TC* 28, 36, 38, 40.

Kierkegaard concludes that 'History . . . has nothing whatever to do with Christ. . . . He is the paradox, which history can never digest or convert into a common syllogism.'[71] If this is the case, then the member of a later generation is, despite the abundance of historical knowledge, in no better a position than the immediate contemporary.

(c) *The Christ-event is inaccessible to proof.* According to Kierkegaard, 'To "prove" is to demonstrate something to be the rational reality it is.'[72] As the paradox, however, the Christ-event is not accessible to reason. One can only prove that it is at variance with reason. This also applies to the proofs often cited in support of Christ's divinity, namely, the miracles, the resurrection, and the ascension. These too are paradoxical and therefore inaccessible to reason. They exist only for faith and thus fail as 'proofs' of Christ's divinity.[73] Once again, then, the later follower's advantage disappears.

(d) *The consequences of Christ's life cannot serve as proof of his divinity.* There are five reasons for this.

(i) The most that Christianity's impact on the world can prove is that Christ was a great man.[74] We cannot prove on this basis, however, that Christ was God. There is no ascending scale of greatness to a point where human greatness becomes divinity. A new quality cannot be derived from a different quality unless the latter already contains the former.[75] Consequently, 'one cannot, without being guilty at one point or another of a μετάβασις εἰς ἄλλο γένος, arrive suddenly by an inference at the new quality . . . God.'[76] Furthermore, if there were a relationship between divinity and greatness, Christ's divinity would become dependent upon his influence on the world. This would lead to the absurdity that Christ's divinity is more certain in the nineteenth century than in earlier centuries, and confront us with the question of how many centuries are required to establish divinity.[77]

(ii) The argument that Christ's divinity is proved by the consequences of his life, is based upon the principle of a fundamental kinship between God and humankind. However, as we have seen, Kierkegaard holds that there is a qualitative difference between God and the human being. The result of this is that, 'if God exists, and consequently is distinguished by an infinite difference of quality from

71 *TC* 33.   72 *TC* 29.   73 Ibid.   74 Ibid.   75 *TC* 30.
76 Ibid.   77 Ibid.

all that it means to be a man, then neither can I nor anybody else, by beginning with the assumption that he was a man, arrive in all eternity at the conclusion, "therefore it was God".'[78]

(iii) It is Christ himself and not the historical consequences of his life that is decisive. God's presence on earth is the 'in-and-for-itself noteworthy'[79] and would continue to be so even if it had had no historical consequences whatsoever.[80] Indeed, to consider Christ in terms of his historical consequences is blasphemy.[81] It is 'impious heedlessness, which reduces sacred history to profane history, Christ to a mere man!'[82]

(iv) History distorts Christ. As we saw earlier, Christ came in the form of a lowly servant. If we stress the consequences of his life, however, Christ becomes a glorious figure of world-historical significance. Thereby 'we put Christ's humiliation in an accidental relation to him, i.e. we make him out to be a man, a distinguished man to whom this happened through the impiety of his age, a thing which for his part he was very far from wishing, for he would fain (that is human) have been something very great in the world—whereas on the contrary Christ freely willed to be the lowly one'.[83] Christ will indeed return in glory[84] but we should never forget that he came as the Servant and the Humiliated One. If we forget this, our understanding of Christ and his mission is distorted.

(v) It is not history's task to examine Christ, but to let itself be examined by him. As Kierkegaard puts it, 'It is not he that, after letting himself be born, and making his appearance in Judaea, has presented himself for an examination in history; it is he that is the Examiner, his life is the examination, and that not alone for that race and generation, but for the whole race.'[85]

For these reasons, then, the attempt to prove Christ's divinity on the basis of the consequences of his life is doomed to failure. Consequently, any advantage the later follower may have on the basis of his awareness of these consequences disappears.

In conclusion, then, there is no essential difference between the immediate contemporary and the follower at second hand. Both are faced with the problem of becoming a follower and in this their position in time is of no significance.

---

[78] *TC* 31.   [79] *TC* 34.   [80] Cf. *TC* 26.   [81] *TC* 32.
[82] *TC* 36.   [83] *TC* 37, cf. 34.   [84] *TC* 27, 33–4, 36–7, 198.
[85] *TC* 37.

(c) True Contemporaneity: Faith

If neither immediate contemporaneity nor the weight of history are of any significance, how can we become contemporary with Christ? Kierkegaard's answer is that there is only one way of becoming truly contemporary with Christ, namely, faith.

> So long as there is a believer, such a one must, in order to become such, have been, and as a believer must continue to be, just as contemporary with his presence on earth as were those [first] contemporaries. This contemporaneousness is the condition of faith, and more closely defined it is faith.[86]

Faith makes Christ real to me here and now. His presence in time is not a past event but is a living reality.[87]

But, as we saw earlier, the individual cannot attain faith by means of his own powers but requires divine assistance. God gives this assistance by providing the human being with the condition of faith. In providing this condition, God is restricted neither by time nor by location. He can grant it to the contemporary and the non-contemporary alike. Consequently, one's position in history is irrelevant. Immediate contemporaneity and historical reports at best serve only as the *occasion* by which the human being may be prompted to think about Christ.[88] But whatever the source of his confrontation with the Christ-event, whether through first-hand experience or through the reports of others, every human being is confronted with the same question as Peter: 'Who do you say that I am?'[89] If Christ provides the condition, then both the contemporary and the non-contemporary can reply, 'You are the Christ. I believe in you.' In conclusion, then, 'there is not and cannot be any question of a follower at second hand, for the believer (and only he, after all, is a follower) continually has the *autopsy* of faith; he does not see with the eyes of others and sees only the same as every believer sees—with the eyes of faith'.[90]

What, then, is the significance of the concept of contemporaneity for our consideration of Kierkegaard as negative theologian? In my opinion, the underlying apophatic structure of Kierkegaard's Christology can be detected in his denial that we can acquire knowledge of Christ either through immediate contemporaneity or on the

---

[86] *TC* 9.   [87] *TC* 67–8; cf. *PF* 87.   [88] *PF* 100.   [89] Matt. 16: 15.
[90] *PF* 102 (original emphasis), cf. 69–70.

basis of reliable historical information. We cannot 'know' Christ, first, because he is the paradox,[91] and, secondly, because 'he declines to be judged in a human way by the consequences of his life.'[92] Christ is simply inaccessible to those principles upon which knowledge is constructed. Consequently, history cannot provide us with knowledge of Christ.[93] Only by believing in Christ do we come to 'know' him, albeit in a non-epistemological way. As Kierkegaard puts it, 'About him nothing can be known, he can only be believed,'[94] and 'the God-man exists only for faith.'[95] In this transferral of knowledge of Christ from the epistemological sphere to the realm of faith, the underlying apophaticism of Kierkegaard's thought again becomes apparent.

This brings us to the close of our discussion of Kierkegaard's treatment of the Incarnation. We have established, I hope, that a strong apophatic strand runs through his Christology. We have seen that Kierkegaard develops a version of the kenotic theory which stresses Christ's incognito. We have also seen that Kierkegaard stresses what we might call the 'trans-historicity' of the Incarnation. It is an ever-present event, available to all those who *believe*. Finally, we can, I believe, detect apophatic motifs in the basic structure of Kierkegaard's Christology. We have seen that in developing his Christology Kierkegaard always has the existential consequences of the Incarnation uppermost in his mind. He is not concerned with establishing a coherent and rational doctrine of the Incarnation— something he would reject as 'speculation'—but with making clear its significance for the life of each individual human being. In the shift of emphasis from an intellectual to an existential approach we can again detect the apophaticism of Kierkegaard's thought.

We wish now to examine more closely Kierkegaard's treatment of Christ's existential significance. This will entail a detailed examination of Kierkegaard's soteriology.

II. SOTERIOLOGY

Just as Kierkegaard accepts the two-natures doctrine without attempting to justify it doctrinally, so too does he accept Christ's

[91] *TC* 28.   [92] *TC* 26.   [93] *TC* 26, 28, 36, 40.   [94] *TC* 28.
[95] *TC* 122.

saving work as a given fact and does not attempt to examine its
doctrinal validity and coherence. His antipathy towards 'objective'
analyses of Christ's saving work is made clear in his statement that
'Christ did not establish any doctrine; he acted. He *did not teach* that
there was redemption for men, but *he redeemed men.*'[96] Consequently, just as we found the existential aspect to be dominant in
Kierkegaard's treatment of the Incarnation, so too will we find that
Kierkegaard considers soteriology exclusively from the perspective
of Christ's effect upon *my* personal existence.

This emphasis on the existential dimension of Christ's saving
work leads, in the opinion of some scholars, to a serious deficiency in
Kierkegaard's soteriology. Taylor complains that, 'For Kierkegaard,
salvation does not involve the reformation of the structures of the
historical-natural process, but removes the self from historical
travail to a realm that lies beyond the world of space and time.'[97]
That is, salvation consists not in sanctifying existence as a whole but
in lifting the self out of existence. Schröer[98] criticizes Kierkegaard
for not indicating whether Christ participates in our sinful nature
and for not making clear whether Christ is identical with us or offers
us only solidarity. Schröer also notes that the concepts of Christ as
both Lord and brother seem to be of no significance for Kierkegaard.
Another scholar who is unhappy with Kierkegaard's soteriology is
George Price. He writes that 'for a religious thinker who wrote so
penetratingly about sin and human weakness, the absence of any
new insight into the meaning of atonement is a great disappoint-
ment'.[99] Price complains that Kierkegaard simply does not express
what he means by atonement. He attributes this failure to Kierkegaard's refusal to treat Christ metaphysically. Such treatment is
necessary, he argues, if we are to come to an understanding of
Christ's person and his saving work.

These scholars have indeed noted an anomaly in Kierkegaard's
soteriology. There is certainly very little reference to certain traditional soteriological concepts in Kierkegaard's thought. Consequently, if we ourselves regard soteriology as being the development
of these concepts, then Kierkegaard's soteriology will necessarily
appear inadequate.

However, there are indeed traditional soteriological elements

[96] *JP* i. 412 (original emphasis).
[97] Taylor, *Kierkegaard's Pseudonymous Authorship*, 362.
[98] Schröer, *Denkform*, 66.   [99] Price, *Narrow Pass*, 198.

present in Kierkegaard's thought. We find, however, that they remain in the background, appearing only when they have a direct bearing upon the existential aspect of Christ's saving work. This will become particularly clear in the section entitled 'Christ the Atoner', where we will ascertain that Kierkegaard bases his exposition of Christ's existential significance on a traditional theory of the atonement. We now wish to consider Kierkegaard's soteriology in detail.

For Kierkegaard Christ's saving work comprises two parts. First, there is his work as Atoner. By his suffering and death he saves human beings from their sins. Secondly, there is his work as the 'Pattern'. Here Kierkegaard develops a version of the *imitatio Christi*. Christ is the example which we are called upon to follow.

1. *Christ the Atoner*

The first aspect of Christ's saving work is that he atones for our sins. When we attempt to ascertain the precise nature of this atonement, however, we run into difficulties. This is due not only to Kierkegaard's reluctance to deal with the atonement in objective doctrinal terms but, more importantly, to the paradoxicality of atonement itself. Kierkegaard writes:

Christianity . . . is as paradoxical on this point as possible; it seems to be working against itself by establishing sin so securely as a position that now it seems to be utterly impossible to eliminate it again—and then it is this very Christianity that by means of the Atonement wants to eliminate sin as completely as if it were drowned in the sea.[100]

The paradoxicality of the atonement does not, however, absolve the individual from the responsibility of attempting to comprehend it. On the contrary, Kierkegaard writes that, 'With all the strength of his mind, to the last thought . . . he must try to understand the forgiveness of sins, and then despair of the understanding.'[101] We saw in Chapter 5 that one of the prerequisites of faith is what Kierkegaard calls the 'crucifixion of the understanding'. Only when the understanding has been brought to a standstill in the attempt to comprehend the paradox of the God-man, does faith become a genuine possibility. Similarly, the prerequisite of receiving the gift of atonement is that the understanding comes to a standstill. This seems to have a twofold significance for the individual's reception of

---

[100] *SD* 100; cf. *CUP* 201, 203, 479n.; *JP* ii. 1215; iii. 3085.   [101] *CUP* 201.

the atonement. First, in coming to such a standstill, the individual ceases to seek salvation by means of his own powers. Thereby the individual becomes fully receptive to God's gracious gift of the forgiveness of sins.[102] Secondly, it produces the tension in which the leap of faith may take place. By means of this tension-filled leap the human being grasps the gift offered to him in the paradox of the atonement.[103]

In this emphasis upon the paradoxicality and incomprehensibility of the atonement the apophatic strand in Kierkegaard's thought again becomes apparent. Christ's gift of atonement can be received only in faith. Atonement is thus non-intellectual in nature. It addresses the whole human being and not merely his intellect.

Despite the paradoxicality of the atonement, however, Kierkegaard does devote some space to its consideration. The following is an attempt to sketch the outlines of his position on the basis of his scattered remarks on the subject.

The death of Christ occupies, as we would expect, a central position in Kierkegaard's understanding of the atonement. Indeed, Kierkegaard expands Christ's Passion to cover his whole life.[104] It was specifically 'in order to suffer and to die'[105] that Christ came to earth. According to Kierkegaard, it is this death that brings about the possibility of the human being's atonement. The question now arises as to how Christ's death is able to achieve this.

Kierkegaard explains the significance of Christ's death by means of the satisfaction theory of the atonement. He writes:

His death alters everything infinitely. Not that his death abolished the fact that at the same time he is the Pattern; no, but his death becomes the infinite guarantee with which the striver starts out, the assurance that infinite satisfaction has been made, that to the doubtful and disheartened there is tendered the strongest pledge—impossible to find anything more reliable!—that Christ died to save him, that Christ's death is the atonement and satisfaction.[106]

But Kierkegaard does not attempt to argue for this position. We find nothing of Anselm's juristic terminology in his deliberations on the atonement. Indeed, Kierkegaard would most certainly regard Anselm's attempts to describe the Godward or objective aspect of the

---

[102] *TC* 71, 269, cf. 7.   [103] *CUP* 201–2; *SD* 115; *TC* 79; *JP* ii. 1215.
[104] *TC* 168, cf. 169.   [105] *TC* 9.
[106] *TC* 270; cf. *JP* ii. 1223; *For Self-Examination*, 22.

atonement as illegitimate speculation. In his opinion, 'the forgiveness of sins is the *paradoxical* satisfaction by virtue of the absurd'.[107] Satisfaction has indeed been made, but the manner in
which this has occurred remains a mystery. We must simply accept
that Christ has made satisfaction for our sins and gratefully receive
this gift in faith.[108]

However, Kierkegaard does give us some idea of the subjective
side of the atonement. This consists of God's *overlooking* our sins.
Through his 'vicarious satisfaction', Kierkegaard argues, 'Jesus
Christ covers with his *holy body* thy sin'.[109] This means that in
making satisfaction for our sins, Christ does not actually eradicate
them. They remain in force, the difference being that God is now
prepared not to take them into account.[110]

Apophatic elements emerge in Kierkegaard's treatment of atonement in his argument that Christ cannot offer himself *directly* as
Saviour. There are two reasons for this. First, if Christ were to offer
atonement directly, it would override human freedom. Openly confronted by such an offer, the human being would simply be unable to
resist. But Christ does not wish to override human freedom. As
Kierkegaard puts it, 'He will draw all to himself—*draw* them to
himself, for he would *entice* no one.'[111] In offering himself as
Saviour, then, Christ respects and protects the freedom of the human
being. Secondly, Christ's saving work is aimed at effecting a *change*
in the human being. According to Kierkegaard there is an element in
human nature which the individual must put aside if he is to become
a genuine self.[112] The direct gift of atonement, however, would
hinder such a change. It would be an accommodation to what the
human being *is*, instead of aiding him in becoming what he *should*
be. The individual could simply accept atonement and carry on as
before. He would feel no inclination to improve himself. Why should
he? Christ has atoned for his sins, making unnecessary any effort on
his part.[113]

For these reasons Christ chooses to make his offer of atonement
indirectly. This he does, as we saw earlier, by assuming the form of a
servant. The paradox of being offered atonement by such a figure
acts as a repellent to the individual. The invitation is certainly in-

---

[107] *CUP* 479 n. (emphasis added).   [108] *TC* 271.
[109] *For Self-Examination*, 22 (original emphasis); cf. *TC* 20.
[110] *JP* ii. 1205, cf. 1201, 1222; iii. 3637; *Gospel of Sufferings*, 45–6.
[111] *TC* 153 (original emphasis).   [112] Ibid.; cf. *CA* 119; *SD* 38–41.
[113] Cf. *JP* i. 83.

viting but the Inviter who makes it is singularly unattractive. This ambiguity places the individual before the choice: offence or faith. This both protects the human being's autonomy and opens up the possibility of effecting a change in the self. It protects the human being's autonomy because the onus is now on him. He must decide whether to have faith and to accept Christ's offer of salvation or to be offended by the fact that this offer is made by a lowly servant.[114] Similarly, a change is effected in the self because to accept Christ and his offer of atonement, the individual must let go of his previous mode of existence and make the leap of faith into the sphere of Christian religiousness. In this emphasis upon the *indirectness* of atonement and upon the *ambiguity* of the Atoner, the apophatic structure underlying Kierkegaard's Christology again becomes apparent. It is simply impossible to establish a direct relationship with the Atoner and to appropriate as a matter of course his gift of atonement.

2. *Christ the Pattern*

As well as offering us atonement Christ shows us what it is to be truly human.[115] The term Kierkegaard employs to describe this aspect of Christ's work is *Forbilledet*, that is, Christ is the 'Pattern', 'Prototype', or 'Paradigm' for our own lives.[116] As Kierkegaard puts it, 'Christ's life here upon earth is the paradigm; it is in likeness to it that I along with every Christian must strive to construct my life.'[117] In expressing the truly human and thereby becoming the paradigm for human existence, Christ, Kierkegaard argues, is also the fulfilment of the law. Indeed, in Kierkegaard's opinion, he is its perfect embodiment: 'Christ as the prototype is still a form of the law, yes, the law raised to a higher level.'[118] We no longer have, then, a set of rules and regulations according to which we must structure our lives, but a perfect expression of the law in human form. It is this perfect human form that we are called upon to emulate.

Kierkegaard stresses, however, that the likeness towards which we must strive is not that of Christ's divinity.[119] This would be blasphemy. Similarly, our attempt to emulate Christ should not be

---

[114] *TC* 101, 107, 137.   [115] *JP* ii. 1848; *SD* 127; cf. *TC* 182.
[116] *TC* 109, 111, 183, 198; *JP* ii. 1848.   [117] *TC* 109, cf. 108, 232; *JP* ii. 1867.
[118] *JP* ii. 1654, cf. 1484, 1905.   [119] *JP* i. 693.

based on the exalted Christ. A Christology which views Christ only as the Exalted One is, as we saw earlier, a misrepresentation of the Person of Christ. Establishing a true likeness with Christ means, Kierkegaard asserts, emulating the *earthly Christ*. This requires first and foremost that the Christian be prepared to undergo the suffering that Christ underwent in his earthly life. This does not mean, however, that the Christian should indulge in self-torture[120] or regard general earthly adversity[121] as true emulation of Christ. Rather it means 'to suffer ill at the hands of men because as a Christian or by being a Christian one desires and strives after the Good, so that one could avoid the suffering by ceasing to will the Good'.[122] If a human being is prepared to undergo such suffering for his faith, 'he thus resembles the pattern as nearly as it is possible for a man to resemble it'.[123] Suffering for Christ's sake, then, constitutes genuine emulation of Christ. This is the true *imitatio Christi*.

Many of the apophatic elements contained in Kierkegaard's concept of the Pattern have already been considered with reference to other aspects of Kierkegaard's Christology. Thus we find the apophaticism implicit in the servant form repeated in the Pattern. There is one area, however, where a form of apophaticism arises that is unique to the Pattern. As Malantschuk rightly points out,[124] Kierkegaard's emphasis on imitation of the Pattern revokes the qualitative dialectic in force in the earlier works. The demand is no longer that one's *Christsein* be concealed in the 'hidden inwardness' of subjectivity but that one openly confess one's adherence to Christ. It might seem here, then, that Kierkegaard is beginning to reject the apophatic strand in his thought. This, however, is not the case. Kierkegaard does not replace the negativity of hiddenness with the positivity of direct expression but with another form of negativity. This negativity appears in the inverse dialectic he establishes between being a Christian and being in the world. That is, the mark of the Christian is not success in the world but suffering. The Christian is recognizable, then, but this is a 'paradoxical recognizability', where the Christian is recognized 'as the direct opposite of the directly human'.[125] In this opposition to what is 'directly human' another apophatic motif comes to the fore.

---

[120] *JP* ii. 1904, 1905.   [121] *TC* 110–11, 173.   [122] *TC* 173.
[123] *TC* 117.   [124] Malantschuk, *Kierkegaard's Thought*, 367–8.
[125] *JP* vi. 6933.

We have now come to the close of our discussion of Kierkegaard's Christology. It has become clear, I believe, that apophaticism is a factor in Kierkegaard's understanding of Christ. We have seen that in assuming human form Christ conceals his divinity so radically that he cannot reveal it, even if he should wish to do so. In our discussion of contemporaneity we saw that knowledge acquired either immediately or historically is insufficient with regard to the paradox that is Christ. We cannot know him intellectually, we can know him only in faith. In Kierkegaard's soteriology apophatic motifs appeared in the emphasis upon the humanward aspect of the atonement and in his rejection of attempts to ascertain the relationship between the Divine Persons in the atoning process. Apophatic motifs were also seen to be present in Kierkegaard's emphasis upon the paradoxicality of Christ's saving work and in the fact that it is not offered to the human being directly but in a manner which places him before the choice: offence or faith. Finally, the apophatic strand in Kierkegaard's thought was made apparent in Kierkegaard's emphasis on the Christian's imitation of Christ and his participation in his suffering. Through this suffering the Christian is 'paradoxically recognizable' through being the direct opposite of society's conception of a valid and successful human life.

8

Kierkegaard
as Negative Theologian

WE have established that apophatic motifs are present in Kierkegaard's pseudonymous works. Although not always explicitly present, apophaticism is an underlying factor in his thought. We might compare it to an underground stream, which, although always present, is mostly hidden and only occasionally rises to the surface. In this final chapter we wish to consider whether this implicit apophaticism allows us to speak of Kierkegaard as a negative theologian.

The first point we should make, however, is that the negative theologians stand in a very different tradition from Kierkegaard. The motivating force in the theologies of the negative theologians is not Kierkegaardian existentialism but Neoplatonism with its emphasis upon the One and the problem of multiplicity. This bears a closer resemblance to Hegel's position than to Kierkegaard's. Indeed, as Friedrich Heer points out, Eckhart's Commentary on John 'can be read as an introduction to idealist philosophy'.[1] This fundamental difference between Kierkegaard and the negative theologians manifests itself above all in the ontological foundations upon which their thought is based. As we saw in Chapter 1, the negative theologians base their theology upon the principle of a procession from and return to God. In Kierkegaard's thought, however, this principle is completely lacking. Indeed, if we understand Hegel's philosophy as a modern expression and development of this principle, we can interpret Kierkegaard as vigorously attacking the basic position adopted by the negative theologians.

On the basis of this fundamental difference, it might be argued that it is invalid to interpret Kierkegaard as a negative theologian. Indeed, it would appear that it is not Kierkegaard but Hegel who

[1] F. Heer, *Meister Eckhart: Predigten und Schriften* (Frankfurt am Main, 1956), 40.

most closely resembles the negative theologians.[2] If, however, we concentrate not on the presuppositions that underlie the thought of the negative theologians but on the 'results' to which these presuppositions give rise, we will notice interesting parallels with certain aspects of Kierkegaard's thought. Indeed, it is my contention that it is not only possible to understand Kierkegaard as a negative theologian but to argue that he is *more apophatic* than the negative theologians. We turn now to a comparison of the 'results' of negative theology with the apophatic elements of Kierkegaard's thought in order to justify this claim.

Perhaps the most basic feature Kierkegaard has in common with the negative theologians is his emphasis upon the transcendence of God. The negative theologians we have discussed stress that, lying behind our conception of God, there is an 'Absolute Godhead' or 'a God beyond God'. Although not adhering to the principle of a God beyond God, Kierkegaard is a vigorous advocate of God's transcendence, arguing that there exists a 'qualitative difference' between God and humankind.

This common emphasis on God's transcendence leads to a similar position on the problem of the knowledge of God. Because God is utterly transcendent of the world, the conceptual tools we employ in order to know anything, such as reason and language, break down. As Dionysius puts it, 'The Supreme Cause of every conceptual thing is not itself conceptual.'[3] Consequently, if we are to make progress in our relationship with God we have to abandon the concepts and names with which reason provides us.

Kierkegaard's position is strikingly similar. Like the negative theologians, he wishes to limit the competence of reason and language with regard to God. This limitation occurs, as we have seen, in a number of different ways. First, God is the Unknown which reason is unable to grasp. To be able to grasp God, reason would have to be above God. Since, however, God is absolutely transcendent, he is above and *eo ipso* inaccessible to reason. As Kierkegaard puts it, God 'is this unknown against which the understanding in its paradoxical passion collides'.[4]

---

[2] Despite standing in a similar tradition to the negative theologians, Hegel does not progress to their conclusion that God is unknown and unknowable. God reveals himself wholly in the world and in this act of revelation does not keep anything of himself back. See R. Williamson, 'The Mystery of God in Hegel's Philosophy', *Prudentia: Supplementary Number 1981*, ed. D. W. Dockrill and R. Mortley, 107–15.

[3] Dionysius, *MT* v (1045D).   [4] *PF* 39.

Secondly, Kierkegaard sets the God-relationship above the concept of God. Our concept of God is not constructed on a rational basis but flows from an existential relationship. The concept of God thus has a non-epistemological basis.

Thirdly, when developing a concept of God, we must remember that God is not to be explained by means of comparison and contrast with other things but can only be discussed by exploring the inner permutations of the concept. Because God is absolutely transcendent any other method is invalid. This bears an interesting similarity to Nicolas of Cusa's position. According to Nicolas, human knowledge is based on the comparison of objects in the world. Because God is the highest that there is, however, he is not subject to this principle. Nicolas writes: 'Every enquiry . . . consists in a relation of comparison that is easy or difficult to draw; for this reason the infinite as infinite is unknown, since it is away and above all comparison.'[5]

Fourthly, Kierkegaard argues that the highest form of knowledge is when knowledge breaks down. This seems to resemble the thought of the negative theologians in general and Nicolas's concept of 'learned ignorance' in particular. Both Nicolas and Kierkegaard stress that ignorance is the only correct existential attitude towards the mystery that is God.[6]

Fifthly, there is an interesting similarity between Kierkegaard and Eckhart on the importance of paradox. Both argue that the purpose of paradox is to drive the human being beyond the confines of reason to that mysterious and hidden place where God dwells. Furthermore, both speak of this process as 'crucifixion'. For Kierkegaard, the human being's acceptance of paradox is, as we saw earlier, 'crucifixion' or 'martyrdom of the understanding'. Similarly, for Eckhart the human being undergoes a crucifixion of the will, which he understands as 'detachment', as well as crucifixion of language and thought.[7]

Another area where there is some degree of similarity between Kierkegaard and the negative theologians is Christology. This similarity consists not so much in their understanding of Christ's office as in the common emphasis upon his hiddenness. Dionysius, for example, stresses that although Christ is the 'supreme theophany', he does not negate but retains God's apophatic character. He writes:

---

[5] Nicolas Cusanus, *Of Learned Ignorance*, trans. Germain Heron (London, 1954), ch. 1, p. 8.   [6] Ibid., ch. 26, pp. 59–61.   [7] Smith, *Way of Paradox*, 26–7.

'But he [Christ] is hidden even after this revelation, or, if I may speak in a more divine fashion, is hidden even amid the revelation.'[8] Similarly, Kierkegaard argues that Christ, despite being the revelation of God, remains hidden. First, Christ is the absolute paradox which contradicts human reason. Secondly, Christ adopts the incognito of the servant form. Although Christ is thereby revealed to human beings, the servant form conceals this revelation behind an appearance that is incommensurable with Christ's divinity. The consequence of this is that a direct and immediate relationship with Christ becomes impossible. In addition to this, there is, as Hirsch points out,[9] a similarity between Kierkegaard's emphasis upon Christ as the absolute paradox which unites God and the human, eternity and time, and Nicolas of Cusa's concept of the *coincidentia oppositorum*. In this emphasis upon Christ's hiddenness, there again seems to be a strong similarity between Kierkegaard's thought and that of the negative theologians.

Another similarity between Kierkegaard and negative theology can perhaps be observed in the former's use of indirect communication. If we look at the works of the negative theologians we can detect in certain areas a similar technique at work. Thus the manner in which Eckhart employs paradox bears some degree of resemblance to indirect communication. Eckhart makes impossible a direct appropriation of the truth by continually negating the positive statements he makes. In this way, it is impossible to take a statement at face value.[10] It may also be possible that Dionysius the Areopagite employed a form of indirect communication. Some scholars— including Thomas Aquinas—have suggested that the difficulty of Dionysius' works is due to his wish to conceal the truth from those unworthy of it.[11] The clearest parallel between Kierkegaard's doctrine of indirect communication and the thought of the negative theologians, however, is to be found in the argument of Clement of Alexandria that the Bible was deliberately written in symbols in order that the truth might be concealed from those not worthy to receive it.[12] Kierkegaard cites Clement's position with approval,

---

[8] Dionysius, Letter Three (1069B).

[9] Hirsch, *Kierkegaard-Studien*, 792–3.

[10] Smith, *Way of Paradox*, 27.

[11] Rutledge, however, disagrees with this. In his opinion, Dionysius' obscurity is not deliberate but is due to the difficulty of the themes with which he is dealing (*Cosmic Theology*, p. xi).

[12] *Str.* vi. 126. 1–127. 4 (ii. 378–9), cf. v. 20. 1 (ii. 233), v. 21. 4 (ii. 234).

stating that Constantin Constantius, the pseudonymous author of *Repetition*, 'very properly joins Clement of Alexandria in writing in such a way that the heretics are unable to understand it'.[13] Now although Kierkegaard does not apply Clement's principle to the Bible, he does make use of it with reference to his own works. As we saw in Chapter 2, he deliberately expresses the truth in an indirect and concealed form in order to make immediate and straightforward appropriation of the truth impossible.

Summing up our discussion so far, it seems clear that there is a strong affinity between Kierkegaard and the negative theologians in their conception of God, treatment of the knowledge of God, Christology, and employment of indirect communication. On this basis, it would seem that, despite differing ontological presuppositions, it is possible to regard Kierkegaard as a negative theologian.

In addition to this affinity between Kierkegaard and the negative theologians, there are several areas in Kierkegaard's thought which, although not directly corresponding to anything in negative theology, certainly seem to be written in an apophatic spirit. A prime example is Kierkegaard's epistemology. Kierkegaard not only adopts, as we have already seen, a negative position towards the knowledge of God but also attacks the viability of knowledge *as a whole*. In Chapter 3 we saw how Kierkegaard drives the gap between sense data and knowledge so far apart that knowledge becomes an impossibility. Furthermore, other apophatic motifs became apparent in his emphasis that this epistemological impasse is overcome not by the acquisition of more information but by *belief*. Knowledge thus ceases to be something intellectual and becomes an *existential* category.

Similarly, Kierkegaard's conception of truth also seems to be in the spirit of negative theology. Here apophatic motifs are present above all in Kierkegaard's rejection of objective truth. Truth for the human being is not a sum of propositions but a subjective disposition and relationship. Furthermore, we saw that truth in its absolute form is hidden from the human being. In his rejection of objective truth and his emphasis on hiddenness Kierkegaard certainly seems to be in harmony with the interests of negative theology. Indeed, this extension of the principles of negative theology to epistemology and truth in general, would seem not only to justify our contention that Kierkegaard can be understood as a negative theologian but would seem

---

[13] R 225; cf. CA 18; JP ii. 1724.

to indicate that he is more apophatic than the negative theologians themselves.

Our thesis that Kierkegaard is not only a negative theologian but actually outdoes the negative theologians is lent further weight when we examine the *differences* between Kierkegaard and negative theology.

The first difference is the manner in which they regard the relation between essence and existence. As we saw earlier, the negative theologians assume a fundamental continuity between God and creation. Creation is the 'spilling over' of the Godhead into the universe. Thus although an entity's divine origin may be obscured in existence, it is never cancelled. Put in philosophical terms, there is a fundamental continuity between essence and existence. For Kierkegaard, however, coming into existence involves a *breach*. In existence the being or reality of a thing does not correspond to its thought or idea, but has fallen away from it. There is thus not a continuity but a fundamental *dis*continuity between essence and existence.

To cope with this breach Kierkegaard adopts a mode of thought that, in contrast to the negative theologians, does not function according to the principle of immanence or continuity but according to the principle of discontinuity. This mode of thought is 'qualitative' or 'existential dialectics'.

In this dialectics discontinuity and contradiction are taken seriously. They are overcome not by immanent and continuous progression but by a passionate 'leap'. This leap, however, does not cancel out the contradiction but merely temporarily brings together the disparate elements of thought and being in the moment of passion. In this stress on contradiction and discontinuity, then, Kierkegaard goes further than the negative theologians. In his dissolution of the relationship between essence and existence, thought and being, as well as his development of a dialectics based on their separation, we can argue that Kierkegaard is *more* apophatic than the negative theologians.

Another fundamental difference between Kierkegaard and the negative theologians is their understanding of the relationship between God and the human being. We saw earlier that one of the similarities between Kierkegaard and the negative theologians is that they all stress God's transcendence. Despite this transcendence, however, the negative theologians hold that there is a fundamental affinity between God and humanity. Although God is transcendent of the human being, a continuity is present between them by virtue of the fact that, like all creation, the human being is the product of God's spilling over into the universe. It is this that makes possible the progression towards the Godhead by means of the *via negativa*. By negating our terms and concepts we can ascend back to the Divine Source from which we have proceeded. Thus, although transcendent of the human being, God is not so transcendent that there is no affinity or continuity between himself and humankind.

For Kierkegaard, however, there is no continuity underlying God's transcendence. God remains the unknown, even when the understanding 'risks a sortie through *via negationis*'.[14] God and humankind are separated by a qualitative abyss, an abyss that is made all the greater by the human being's sin. This means that the progression towards God by means of the *via negativa* is not possible. Such a progression does not lead to the knowledge of God but, as we saw in our discussion of subjectivity in Chapter 4, to a more profound understanding of the sinful and flawed nature of the human self. The principle espoused by the negative theologians that, 'To the extent that I am close to God, so to that extent God utters himself into me,'[15] is thus invalid. Indeed, it is paganism. Because of the qualitative abyss between God and the human being, it is not proximity but *distance* that is determinative of the God-relationship. Consequently, as we saw in our examination of religiousness A and B, it is *dis*relationship that constitutes relationship with God.

Following on from this, there is a considerable difference between Kierkegaard and the negative theologians on the question of the role of knowledge with regard to God. We saw earlier that one of the similarities between Kierkegaard and the negative theologians is their emphasis on the limitation of human knowledge. Despite this, there is, however, a fundamental difference which again seems to add weight to our argument that Kierkegaard is more apophatic than the negative theologians. This difference is that although the negative theologians place a limitation upon knowledge they nevertheless conceive of the human being's God-relationship in epistemological terms. This comes to the fore in two ways. First, the *via negativa* is employed not as a means of making knowledge impossible but of enabling the individual to progress beyond the confines of human knowledge to a mystic union in which he knows God non-

14 *PF* 44.
15 Eckhart, Sermon 53 (*Essential Sermons*, trans. Colledge and McGinn, 204).

conceptually and non-linguistically. As Dionysius puts it, 'This quite positively complete unknowing is knowledge of him who is above everything that is known.'[16] Despite imposing limitations upon knowledge, then, negative theology does not place knowledge as such in question but merely substitutes a higher for a lower form of knowledge. Secondly, many of the negative theologians place knowledge *above* faith. Thus Clement of Alexandria argues that although faith is sufficient for simple believers,[17] for the true believer or 'gnostic' it provides only the starting-point for his development towards the higher gnosis.[18] Faith that remains undeveloped, he says, is 'inert and alone'.[19] Indeed, Clement writes that if knowledge of God and eternal salvation were separable and we were forced to choose between them, the gnostic would without hesitation choose knowledge.[20] Similarly, Eckhart understands knowledge to be superior to faith by virtue of the fact that it articulates *explicitly* what is present only *implicitly* in faith.[21] In the thought of Nicolas of Cusa, this predominance of knowledge over faith becomes even more apparent. For Nicolas faith merely provides the presupposition upon which knowledge is constructed.[22]

Kierkegaard, however, differs in four important respects. First, he makes no attempt to develop a higher form of knowledge. The closest approximation we find to such an idea in Kierkegaard's thought is his theory of the stages of existence. The knowledge gained here, however, is not that of a higher, intuitive comprehension of God but of human inadequacy. The individual acquires knowledge not of the 'divine mysteries' which transcend human understanding but of his distance from the truth and his inability to sustain a genuine God-relationship.

Secondly, faith is not an inferior form of knowledge but is a response of the *whole* human being. It encompasses *all* the dimensions of the human self, of which the epistemological faculty forms only *one* aspect. The idea that faith is merely the foundation for the development of a higher knowledge, as Clement of Alexandria would have us believe, would therefore be anathema to Kierkegaard.

---

[16] Dionysius, Letter One (1065A–1065B); cf. *MT* i. 1 (997A), 3 (1001A).
[17] *Str.* vii. 95. 9 (ii. 478); cf. vii. 55. 1 (ii. 446); vii. 57. 3–4 (ii. 447).
[18] *Str.* v. 5. 2 (ii. 223).   [19] *Str.* v. 11. 1 (ii. 227).
[20] *Str.* iv. 136. 5 (ii. 203).   [21] Smith, *Way of Paradox*, 23.
[22] H. Bett, *Nicolas of Cusa* (London, 1932), 202.

Thirdly, for Kierkegaard knowledge is the enemy of faith. As we saw in Chapter 2, Kierkegaard believes that it is knowledge which is responsible for the spiritual malaise of his age. Knowledge robs faith of the tension of uncertainty. Without this tension the passion that prompts the individual to make the leap of faith and which in turn sustains him in faith is eliminated, thereby robbing him of his relationship with God. It is for this reason that Kierkegaard makes use of indirect communication. As we saw in Chapter 2, his intention is to *decrease* the amount of knowledge at the individual's disposal. It is not knowledge—not even 'transcendent knowledge'—that leads the human being to God. Only epistemological uncertainty and the passion it evokes can prompt the individual to make the leap of faith and thus sustain a relationship to God.

Fourthly, Kierkegaard rejects the idea of mystic union. There is no idea in Kierkegaard's works of the individual being absorbed into the Godhead. Whereas for the negative theologians God can become so near that the distinction between the human and the divine can be broken down, for Kierkegaard God is and will always remain beyond our grasp. In addition to this, Kierkegaard attacks mysticism for its selfishness, its inadequate conception of sin, and its desire to escape existence and take refuge in a personal relationship with God.[23] Furthermore, Kierkegaard rejects, as we saw in our discussion of his attitude to Hegel in Chapter 2, all notion of the human being coming to perceive the world *sub specie aeternitatis*. The Eckhartian idea that the human being can come to participate in the thinking of God's thoughts would thus be anathema to him. But perhaps the main reason for Kierkegaard's antipathy to the concept of mystic union is its threat to the two concepts he sees as absolutely essential to Christianity, namely, the transcendence of God and the single individual. These two concepts come together not in a mystic union but in a paradoxical relationship in which both retain their independence and yet exist in a relationship of unparalleled intimacy.

Once again, then, Kierkegaard seems to be more apophatic than the negative theologians. Although all are concerned to emphasize the limitations of knowledge, Kierkegaard goes further than the negative theologians in his refusal to develop a higher, spiritual form of knowledge. In addition to this, he places faith above knowledge, thereby again placing a firm limitation upon the competence of

[23] *E/O* ii. 241–50.

knowledge. In this limitation of knowledge and in the precedence he attributes to faith, Kierkegaard's thought can be said to be more apophatic than that of the negative theologians.

Another difference between Kierkegaard and the negative theologians is the role they attribute to subjectivity. At first sight there does in fact seem to be a certain degree of similarity. Thus Kierkegaard's emphasis on subjectivity with its demands for self-annihilation and 'dying away' would seem to correspond to Dionysius' stress on the necessity of the individual's plunging into the depths of his spirit in order to discover the Super-Essential.[24] Similarly, there is a resemblance between Kierkegaard's position and Eckhart's demand that the individual penetrate to the 'ground of the soul' by means of 'detachment'. Despite this similarity, however, Kierkegaard's position differs fundamentally from that of the negative theologians. The negative theologians have basically an optimistic approach to the process of subjective development. The true self to which they penetrate is one which stands in union with God. Indeed, it is the mirror image of God, and the place where we meet God and become one with him.[25] For Kierkegaard, however, the true self which subjectivity uncovers is a sinful self. Far from leading to an awareness of a fundamental affinity with God, then, Kierkegaard's concept of subjectivity leads to a consciousness of the human being's utter separation from God. By severing the bond that exists for the negative theologians between God and the human being in the ground of the soul and replacing it with the radical separation of sin, Kierkegaard again appears to be more apophatic than the negative theologians.

This leads us on to another distinction between Kierkegaard and the negative theologians, namely, the difference in their understanding of sin. Although emphasizing the destructiveness of sin and the separation it causes between God and the human being, sin is treated primarily epistemologically by the negative theologians. Thus Clement of Alexandria writes that 'the sources of all sin are but two, ignorance and inability.'[26] As he puts it in an earlier passage, 'Sinning arises from being unable to determine what ought to be done, or being unable to do it; as doubtless one falls into a ditch either through not knowing, or through inability to leap across through feebleness of body.'[27]

[24] Rolt, *Dionysius the Areopagite*, 25, 35.   [25] Smith, *Way of Paradox*, 50–1.
[26] *Str.* vii. 101. 6 (ii. 482).   [27] *Str.* vii. 62. 3 (ii. 39).

But perhaps the most significant difference between Kierkegaard and the negative theologians and the point at which the inherent apophaticism of Kierkegaard's thought shows up most clearly is Christology. For the negative theologians, God's revelation of himself in Christ, although not undermining the hiddenness of God, is nevertheless intended to reveal something concrete about the nature of God. Thus for Clement of Alexandria, Christ is the means by which we gain an insight into the Unknowable that is God.[28] Similarly, Dionysius, who, as we saw earlier, emphasizes that God remains hidden even in his revelation of himself in Christ, nevertheless writes that in Christ 'the transcendent has put aside its own hiddenness and has revealed itself to us by becoming a human being'.[29] For Eckhart, Christ's purpose is the divinization of the human being. He writes: 'Why . . . did God become man?—I would answer, in order that God may be born in the soul, and the soul be born in God.'[30] In allowing himself to be incarnated, God enters the ground of the soul of the man Jesus and *eo ipso* our soul. Consequently, in entering into the ground of our soul we meet Christ, and through him God.[31] God's purpose in becoming human, then, was to allow himself to be born mystically in all subsequent generations.[32] For Nicolas of Cusa, Christ seems to perform three different functions. First, he provides us with information concerning immortality. This he does in his Death and Resurrection.[33] Secondly, Christ reveals the hidden God that lies behind our concepts and modes of thought.[34] Thirdly, as the most perfect 'contraction' of the universe, Christ is complete fullness. In coming to earth he offers us participation in this fullness.[35]

Now despite the diversity of ways in which the negative theologians interpret Christ and his mission, they always understand him as either providing humankind with some sort of divine knowledge or with offering the human being a share in his divinity. This is the point where a considerable divergence can be seen between

[28] Theill-Wunder, *Die archaische Verborgenheit*, 137.
[29] Dionysius, Letter Three (1069B).
[30] *Eckhart: Sermons*, trans. Walshe, i. 29. 215.
[31] Smith, *Way of Paradox*, 54.   [32] Ibid. 76–7.
[33] J. Pelikan, 'Negative and Positive Theology: A Study of Nicolas Cusanus De pace fidei', *Prudentia*, 75–6.
[34] Ibid.; J. Hopkins, *A Concise Introduction to the Philosophy of Nicolas of Cusa* (2nd edn., Minneapolis, 1978), 40.
[35] Hopkins, *Concise Introduction*, 38–9; cf. Bett, *Nicolas of Cusa*, 191–7.

Kierkegaard and the negative theologians. For Kierkegaard Christ does not provide the human being with knowledge of the divine mysteries. Nor does he offer the human being the means of diviniza-tion. Far from alleviating the division between God and humankind, Christ makes it *absolute*. By entering into time he posits the human being as a sinner, thereby driving God and the human being as far apart as is possible. Unlike the negative theologians, then, Kierke-gaard continues the movement *away* from God that is set in motion by God's transcendence, understanding Christ not as arresting or redirecting it but as furthering it. It is only on the basis of the radical disrelationship posited by sin that Christ is prepared to supply the condition necessary to overcome it and to enable the human being to establish a relationship with God.

In his concept of Christ's radical widening of the breach between God and the human being, it again becomes clear, I believe, that Kierkegaard not only can be interpreted as a negative theologian but is in fact more apophatic than the negative theologians.

In conclusion, then, we are justified in saying, first, that apophaticism is an inherent element in Kierkegaard's thought and, secondly, that this gives rise to a number of interesting similarities with negative theology. Does this allow us, however, to speak of Kierkegaard as a negative theologian? If we limit this description to those thinkers who stand in the Neoplatonist tradition, then the answer must be 'no'. If, however, we are prepared to apply this term to those thinkers who stress God's hiddenness, then it seems to me that we must include Kierkegaard in the first rank of negative theo-logians. Indeed, we can go further than this and argue that because Kierkegaard does not make the transition to the *via mystica* but stops at the *via negativa* he is more apophatic than the negative theo-logians themselves.

BIBLIOGRAPHY

1. Søren Kierkegaard

Samlede Værker, 2nd edn., eds. A. B. Drachmann, J. S. Heiberg, and H. O. Lange, I–XIV, Copenhagen, 1920–31.

Papirer, 1st edn., P. A. Heiberg, V. Kuhr, and E. Torsting, I–XI³, Copenhagen, 1909–48.

The Concept of Irony, trans. L. M. Capel (London, 1966).

Either/Or, trans. H. V. and E. H. Hong, i–ii (Princeton, NJ, 1987).

Fear and Trembling/Repetition, ed. and trans. H. V. and E. H. Hong, (Princeton, NJ, 1983).

Philosophical Fragments/Johannes Climacus, ed. and trans. H. V. and E. H. Hong (Princeton, NJ, 1985).

Philosophical Fragments, trans. D. F. Swenson (Princeton, NJ, 1962).

The Concept of Anxiety, ed. and trans. R. Thomte in collaboration with A. B. Anderson (Princeton, NJ, 1980).

Stages on Life's Way, trans. H. V. and E. H. Hong (Princeton, NJ, 1988).

Concluding Unscientific Postscript, trans. D. F. Swenson and W. Lowrie (Princeton, NJ, 1941).

Abschließende unwissenschaftliche Nachschrift, trans. H. M. Junghans, i–ii (Gütersloh, 1982).

The Sickness unto Death, ed. and trans. H. V. and E. H. Hong (Princeton, NJ, 1980).

Training in Christianity, trans. W. Lowrie (Princeton, NJ, 1972).

For Self-Examination and *Judge for Yourselves!*, trans. W. Lowrie (Princeton, NJ, 1941).

Edifying Discourses, trans. D. F. and L. M. Swenson, i–iv (Minneapolis, 1943–6).

Christian Discourses, trans. W. Lowrie (Princeton, NJ, 1971).

Gospel of Sufferings, trans. A. S. Aldworth and W. S. Ferrie (Cambridge, 1955).

The Point of View, trans. W. Lowrie (London, 1939).

Armed Neutrality and *An Open Letter*, trans. H. V. and E. H. Hong (Bloomington, Ind., 1968).

On Authority and Revelation, trans. W. Lowrie (New York, 1966).

Journals and Papers, trans. H. V. and E. H. Hong, i–vii (Bloomington, Ind., 1967–78).

Auktionsprotokol over Søren Kierkegaards Bogsamling, ed. H. P. Rohde (Copenhagen, 1967).

The Kierkegaard Indices, compiled A. McKinnon, i–iv (Leiden, 1970–75).

2. Clement of Alexandria

Clemens Alexandrinus, ed. O. Stählin (Die griechischen christlichen Schriftsteller der ersten drei Jahrhunderte), i (2nd edn., Leipzig, 1936), ii (3rd edn., Berlin, 1960), iii (Leipzig, 1909).

The Writings of Clement of Alexandria, i–ii, trans. W. Wilson, Ante-Nicene Christian Library (Edinburgh, 1867–89).

3. Dionysius the Areopagite

Pseudo-Dionysius, *The Complete Works*, Classics of Western Spirituality, trans. Colm Luibheid (London, 1987).

Dionysius the Areopagite: The Divine Names and the Mystical Theology, trans. and intro. C. E. Rolt (London, 1940).

4. Meister Eckhart

Sermons and Treatises, i–ii, trans. and ed. M. O'C. Walshe (Shaftesbury, Dorset, 1979).

The Essential Sermons, Commentaries, Treatises and Defense, Classics of Western Spirituality, trans. and intro. E. Colledge and B. McGinn (London, 1981).

5. General

ADORNO, T., *Kierkegaard: Konstruktion des Ästhetischen* (Frankfurt am Main, 1962).

ALLEN, E. L., *Kierkegaard: His Life and Thought* (London, 1935).

ANZ, W., *Kierkegaard und der deutsche Idealismus* (Tübingen, 1956).

——'Philosophie und Glaube bei S. Kierkegaard: Über die Bedeutung der Existenzdialektik für die Theologie', in H.-H. Schrey (ed.), *Søren Kierkegaard*, 179–239.

ARNOLD, G., *Unparteysche Kirchen- und Ketzer-Historie* (Frankfurt am Main, 1699–1700).

BAADER, F. VON, *Sämmtliche Werke* (16 vols.; Leipzig, 1851–60).

BEJERHOLM, L., *'Meddelelsens Dialektik': Studier i Søren Kierkegaards teorier om språk, kommunication och pseudonymitet* (Copenhagen, 1962).

——'Abstraction', *Bibliotheca Kierkegaardiana*, 3 (Copenhagen, 1980).

BERNARD OF CLAIRVAUX, *Opera* (Basle, 1566).

BETT, H., *Nicolas of Cusa* (London, 1932).

BLASS, J. L., *Die Krise der Freiheit im Denken Sören Kierkegaards: Untersuchungen zur Konstitution der Subjektivität* (Ratingen bei Dusseldorf, 1969).

BÖHRINGER, F., *Die Kirche Christi und ihre Zeugen oder die Kirchengeschichte in Biographien*, i–vi (Zurich, 1842–55).

BONAVENTURE, *Opusculorum*, i–ii (Lugd., 1647).

CARNELL, E. J., *The Burden of Søren Kierkegaard* (Exeter, 1965).

CARRIERE, M., *Die philosophische Weltanschauung der Reformationszeit in ihren Beziehungen zur Gegenwart* (Stuttgart, 1847).

COLLINS, J., *The Mind of Kierkegaard* (Princeton, NJ, 1983).

DAUB, C., 'Die Form der christlichen Dogmen- und Kirchen-Historie', in *Die Zeitschrift für spekulative Theologie*, i (1836).

DIEM, H., *Kierkegaard's Dialectic of Existence*, trans. H. Knight (Edinburgh, 1959).

DUNNING, S. N., *Kierkegaard's Dialectic of Inwardness* (Princeton, NJ, 1985).

EDWARDS, P., 'Kierkegaard and the "Truth" of Christianity', in P. Edwards and A. Paps (eds.), *A Modern Introduction to Philosophy* (3rd edn., New York, 1973), 505–22.

ELROD, J. W., *Being and Existence in Kierkegaard's Pseudonymous Works* (Princeton, NJ, 1975).

FAHRENBACH, H., *Kierkegaards existenzdialektische Ethik* (Frankfurt am Main, 1968).

GARDINER, P., *Kierkegaard* (Oxford, 1988).

GARELICK, H. M., *The Anti-Christianity of Kierkegaard* (The Hague, 1965).

GÖRRES, J. VON, *Die christliche Mystik*, i–iv (Regensburg, 1836–43).

GUARDINI, R., 'Der Ausgangspunkt der Denkbewegung Sören Kierkegaards', in Schrey, *Sören Kierkegaard*, 52–80.

GUERIKE, H. E. F., *Handbuch der Kirchengeschichte*, i–ii (3rd edn., Halle, 1838). ET: *A Manual of Church History*, trans. W. G. T. Shedd (Edinburgh, 1857).

HAECKER, T., 'Der Begriff der Wahrheit bei Sören Kierkegaard', in *Opuscula* (Munich, 1949), 153–223.

HANNAY, A., *Kierkegaard* (London, 1982).

HASE, K., *Hutturus Redivivus oder Dogmatik der Evangelisch-Lutherischen Kirche* (7th edn., Leipzig, 1848).

——*Kirkehistorie*, trans. C. Winther and T. Schorn (Copenhagen, 1837). ET: *A History of the Christian Church*, trans. C. E. Blumenthal and C. P. Wing (London, 1855).

HEER, F., *Meister Eckhart: Predigten und Schriften* (Frankfurt am Main, 1956).

HEGEL, G. W. F., *Geschichte der Philosophie*, i–iii, ed. L. Michelet (Berlin, 1836). ET: *Hegel's Lectures on the History of Philosophy*, trans. E. S. Haldane and F. H. Simson, i–iii (London, 1955).

——*Vorlesungen über die Philosophie der Religion*, ed. P. Marheineke, i–ii (2nd edn., Berlin, 1840). ET: *Lectures on the Philosophy of Religion*, trans. E. B. Speirs and J. Burdon Sanderson, i–iii (London, 1895).

——*Wissenschaft der Logik*, i–ii (Frankfurt am Main, 1969).

——*Hegel's Logic*, trans. W. Wallace (Oxford, 1975).

HELFFERICH, A., *Die christliche Mystik in ihrer Entwickelung und in ihren Denkmalen*, i–ii (Gotha, 1842).

HENRIKSEN, A., *Methods and Results of Kierkegaard Studies in Scandinavia* (Copenhagen, 1951).

HEYWOOD THOMAS, J., *Subjectivity and Paradox* (Oxford, 1957).

HIRSCH, E., *Kierkegaard-Studien*, i–iii (Gütersloh, 1930–3).

HOLM, S., *Søren Kierkegaards Geschichtsphilosophie*, trans. Günther Jungbluth (Stuttgart, 1956).

HOPKINS, J., *A Concise Introduction to the Philosophy of Nicolas of Cusa* (2nd edn., Minneapolis, 1978).

JOLIVET, R., *Introduction to Kierkegaard*, trans. W. H. Barber (London, 1950).

KEMPIS, T. À., *De imitatione Christi* (Paris, 1702).

——*Om Christi Efterfølgelse*, i–iv, trans. J. A. L. Holm (3rd edn., Copenhagen, 1848).

——*Rosengaarden og Liliehaven*, trans. M. Boyesen (Copenhagen, 1849).

KHAN, A. H., *Salighed as Happiness? Kierkegaard on the Concept Salighed* (Waterloo, Ont., 1985).

KIRCHHOFF, A., *Plotini De Virtutibus et adversus gnosticos libellos* (Berlin, 1847).

KLEMKE, E. D., *Studies in the Philosophy of Kierkegaard* (The Hague, 1976).

LOSSKY, V., *The Mystical Theology of the Eastern Church* (Cambridge, 1957).

MACQUARRIE, J., *In Search of Deity: An Essay in Dialectical Theism* (London, 1984).

MALANTSCHUK, G., *Kierkegaard's Thought*, ed. and trans. H. V. and E. H. Hong (Princeton, NJ, 1971).

——'Begrebet Fordobelse hos Søren Kierkegaard', in *Kierkegaardiana*, ii (Copenhagen, 1957), 43–55.

MARBACH, G. O., *Geschichte der Philosophie des Mittelalters* (Leipzig, 1841).

MARTENSEN, H., *Mester Eckhart. Et Bidrag til at oplyse Middelalderens Mystik* (Copenhagen, 1840).

MURPHY, A. E., 'On Kierkegaard's Claim that "Truth is Subjectivity"', in J. H. Gill (ed.), *Essays on Kierkegaard* (Minneapolis, 1969), 94–101.

NEANDER, A., *Der heilige Bernhard und sein Zeitalter* (2nd edn., Hamburg, 1848).

NEANDER, A., *Denkwürdigkeiten aus der Geschichte des christlichen Lebens* (4th edn., Gotha, 1865).

NICOLAS CUSANUS, *Of Learned Ignorance*, trans. G. Heron (London, 1954).

PATRICK, J., *Clement of Alexandria* (Edinburgh 1914).

PELIKAN, J., 'Negative and Positive Theology: A Study of Nicolas Cusanus De pace fidei', *Prudentia: Supplementary Number 1981*, ed. D. W. Dockrill and R. Mortley, 65–77.

PERKINS, R., 'Kierkegaard: A Kind of Epistemologist', *History of European Ideas*, 12/1 (1990), 7–18.

POJMAN, L. P., *The Logic of Subjectivity: Kierkegaard's Philosophy of Religion* (Tuscaloosa, Ala., 1984).

PRICE, G., *The Narrow Pass: A Study of Kierkegaard's Concept of Man* (London, 1963).

QUINT, J., *Meister Eckhart: Deutsche Predigten und Traktate* (Munich, 1979).

REIMER, L., 'Die Wiederholung als Problem der Erlösung bei Kierkegaard', in Theunissen and Greve, *Materialien zur Philosophie Sören Kierkegaards*, 302–46.

RICHTER, L., *Der Begriff der Subjektivität: Ein Beitrag zur christlichen Existenzdarstellung* (Würzburg, 1934).

RITSCHL, D., 'Kierkegaards Kritik an Hegels Logik', in Schrey, *Søren Kierkegaard*, 240–72.

ROHRMOSER, G., 'Die Metaphysik und das Problem der Subjektivität', in *Emanzipation und Freiheit* (Munich, 1970), 159–96.

ROOS, H., 'Søren Kierkegaard und die Kenosis-Lehre', *Kierkegaardiana*, i (Copenhagen, 1955), 54–60.

RUTLEDGE, D., *Cosmic Theology—The Ecclesiastical Hierarchy of Pseudo-Denys: An Introduction* (London, 1964).

SCHLEIERMACHER, F., *Der christliche Glaube nach den Grundsätzen der evangelischen Kirche*, i–ii (3rd edn., Berlin, 1835).

——*The Christian Faith*, ed. H. R. MacKintosh and J. S. Stewart (Edinburgh, 1989).

SCHREY, H.-H. (ed.), *Søren Kierkegaard* (Darmstadt, 1971).

SCHRÖER, H., *Die Denkform der Paradoxalität als theologisches Problem* (Göttingen, 1960).

SCHULZ, W., 'Sören Kierkegaard: Existenz und System', in Schrey, *Søren Kierkegaard*, 173–239.

SLØK, J., *Die Anthropologie Kierkegaards* (Copenhagen, 1954).

SMITH, C., *The Way of Paradox: Spiritual Life as taught by Meister Eckhart* (New York, 1987).

SONTAG, F., 'The Role of Repetition', *Bibliotheca Kierkegaardiana*, 3 (Copenhagen, 1980), 283–94.

Sponheim, P., *Kierkegaard on Christ and Christian Coherence* (Westport, Conn., 1968).

Stack, G. J., *Kierkegaard's Existential Ethics* (Tuscaloosa, Ala., 1977).

Stengren, C., 'Faith', *Kierkegaardiana*, xii (Copenhagen, 1982), 81–92.

Suso, H., *Leben und Schriften*, ed. M. Diepenbrock (2nd edn., Regensburg, 1837).

Tauler, J., *Predigten*, ed. E. Kuntze and J. H. R. Biesenthal, i–ii (Berlin, 1841–42).

——*Nachfolgung des armen Lebens Christi*, ed. W. Casseder (Frankfurt am Main, 1821).

Taylor, M. C., *Kierkegaard's Pseudonymous Authorship: A Study of Time and the Self* (Princeton, NJ, 1975).

——*Journeys to Selfhood: Hegel and Kierkegaard* (Berkeley, Calif., 1980).

Tennemann, W. G., *Geschichte der Philosophie,* i–xi (Leipzig, 1798–1819).

Theill-Wunder, H., *Die archaische Verborgenheit* (Munich, 1970).

Theunissen, M., and Greve, W. (eds.), *Materialien zur Philosophie Sören Kierkegaards* (Frankfurt am Main, 1979).

Thompson, J., 'The Master of Irony', in J. Thompson (ed.), *Kierkegaard: A Collection of Critical Essays* (New York, 1972).

Thulstrup, M. M., 'Kierkegaard's Acquaintance with Various Interpretations of Christianity: Studies of Pietists, Mystics, and Church Fathers', *Bibliotheca Kierkegaardiana*, 1 (Copenhagen, 1978).

Thulstrup, N., *Kierkegaard's Relation to Hegel*, trans. G. L. Stengren (Princeton, NJ, 1980).

Trendelenburg, A., *Logische Untersuchungen* (Berlin, 1840).

Utterback, S. W., 'Kierkegaard's Inverse Dialectic', *Kierkegaardiana*, xi (Copenhagen, 1980), 34–54.

Weisshaupt, K., *Die Zeitlichkeit der Wahrheit: Eine Untersuchung zum Wahrheitsbegriff Sören Kierkegaards* (Freiburg, 1973).

Williamson, R., 'The Mystery of God in Hegel's Philosophy', *Prudentia: Supplementary Number 1981*, ed. D. W. Dockrill and R. Mortley, 107–15.

INDEX

Abraham 135 n., 139, 140, 141, 147
absolute, the 51, 53
absolute disjunction 52
absolute good 101, 102, 138
absolute *telos* 101 n., 102, 129, 130,
    133, 134, 138, 142
abstract, abstraction 40, 41, 42, 47,
    48, 50, 51, 55, 84, 105, 140
abstract thought 39–45, 49, 54–5, 57,
    58, 105, 140
    see also objective reflection; pure
    thought; reflection; thought
absurd, absurdity 120 n., 137, 139,
    141, 146 n., 148, 155–6, 202
action 82–4, 110
actuality 35 n., 39 n., 43–5, 46, 50, 79,
    80, 82–4, 85, 147
Adorno, Theodor 35 n., 37
aesthetic principle 83
aesthetic sphere 65, 83, 124–6, 127,
    138, 142, 174–5, 180
Albert the Great 31 n.
Alexandrians 24
Allen, E. L. 91–2
analysis 10–12
Anderson, Albert B. 26 n.
angels 14
Anselm 201
anxiety 35 n.
Anz, Wilhelm 6, 35 n., 38 n., 50, 115 n.
apophaticism:
    definition of 1
    of Kierkegaard 34, 52, 53, 57, 64–5,
        68–70, 81, 84–5, 88–9, 100, 101–3,
        112, 114, 117, 123, 125–6, 127–8,
        132, 135, 136–7, 138–9, 140, 142,
        147–8, 149–51, 155, 158–61, 162,
        163–7, 173, 180–1, 186, 189,
        197–8, 201, 202–3, 204–5, 206–17
    see also apophatic theology; negative
    theology
apophatic theology 1, 16, 17, 23, 25
    see also apophaticism; negative
    theology
appropriation 60, 62, 66, 67–8, 69,
    70, 96, 97, 106, 110, 119–20, 121,
    123, 143, 209–10

approximation 74, 75, 79, 80, 84, 104,
    106, 109, 191
argument from design 171–3
Arnold, Gottfrid 25, 29, 30, 31, 33, 34
ascension 195
ascent 17
Aristotle 31 n., 41, 84
atonement, *see* satisfaction; soteriology
autonomy 60–1, 66, 179, 180, 185,
    188, 203
    see also freedom

Baader, Franz von 30, 31, 33
Basil 29
becoming 43, 44, 46, 53, 54, 87, 104,
    109
being 14–15, 17, 18–19, 43, 46, 50, 53,
    54, 55, 56, 58, 104–5, 108, 168, 211
    empirical 104–5, 168 n.
    factual 42 n., 168, 171
    ideal 42 n., 168, 171
    pure 41–2, 43, 45
Bejerholm, Lars 39 n., 40 n., 42 n.,
    64 n.
belief 85–9, 124, 151, 153, 169, 210
    and faith 153–4
Bernard of Clairvaux 32
Bett, Henry 213 n., 216 n.
Bible 17, 107, 209–10
biographical–psychological method 3
birth of the Son in the soul 22, 216
Blass, Joseph L. 100–1 n.
Bohlin, Torsten 6
Böhringer, F. 27–8, 29, 30, 32
Bonaventure 31 n., 32
both–and 48
bourgeois philistinism 141
bullitio 19
bürgelin 19

Carnell, E. J. 91
Carriere, M. 32 n., 33, 34
cataphatic theology 10, 16–17, 20–1,
    23
category 73–4
cause 77–8
celestial hierarchy 14

certainty 54, 74, 76, 77, 79, 80, 85, 86, 87, 106–7, 111 n., 120, 121, 138, 140, 148, 151, 153, 159
Chalcedon 186 n.
choice 47, 88, 120, 126, 127, 128, 157, 188
  see also decision
Christ 10–13, 19, 22, 145–6, 150, 152, 182–205, 208–9, 216–17
  as Atoner 200–3
  divinity of 186, 188, 189, 195–6
  as Exalted One 189, 203–4
  humanity of 186
  as Inviter 189, 202–3
  as Pattern 200, 201, 203–4
  as Servant 185–9, 196, 202–3, 204, 209
  as Teacher 186 n.
Christendom 37–8, 95
Christianity 38, 49, 61–2, 71, 95, 103 n., 113, 115, 118, 121, 146 n., 154, 200, 214
Christian religiousness, see religiousness B
Clement of Alexandria 8–13, 26–8, 34, 209–10, 213, 215, 216
coincidentia oppositorum 34, 209
Colledge, E. 18 n., 19 n., 22 n., 212 n.
Collins, James 87, 91, 93, 111 n.
coming into existence 77–80, 81, 86, 87, 129, 149, 191, 211
commitment 60, 67, 69, 72, 87, 88, 96, 120, 122
communication:
  breakdown of 140–1
  existential 62, 95, 121, 154
  indirect 4–5, 28, 34, 36, 58, 62–9, 187, 188, 209–10, 214
  objective 58–62, 66
condition 143, 144, 149, 156–8, 193, 197, 217
contemporaneity 188, 189–98, 205
content method 3
continuity 143, 211–12
contradiction 35 n., 36, 37, 41, 42, 44, 46, 47–8, 50, 53, 55–7, 58, 61, 116, 124–5, 127, 128, 129–30, 134, 145, 151–2, 159–60, 192, 211
Corsair 132 n.
creation 14–15, 19, 23, 177–8, 211, 212

Daub, Carl 85 n.
deceit 65

decision 35 n., 47, 67, 72, 82, 84, 87–8, 113, 122, 151, 158
  see also choice
deduction 16, 155, 168–9, 170, 172
deification 12–13, 22, 216–17
descent 16, 17
descriptive–thematic method 3–4
despair 107, 126, 128, 131
detachment 20, 21–2, 208, 215
dialectics 35–9, 44, 45, 56 n., 58, 63, 67, 69–70, 113, 117, 128, 143–4, 150, 151–2, 159, 175, 204
  aesthetic 125
  anthropological 57
  existential 36, 37, 50–5, 211
  of inwardness 114, 117
  qualitative 35 n., 36, 52–3, 84, 204, 211
  quantitative 35 n., 36, 39, 52
Diem, Hermann 6, 37, 40, 63, 94, 96–7
differentiation 14
Dionysius the Areopagite 1, 7, 13–18, 30–1, 207, 208–9, 213, 215, 216
discontinuity 211
disrelationship 135, 150, 212, 217
divine vision 12
divinization, see deification
division of thought and being 50, 52, 53, 55–7, 69, 116, 124, 127, 168
docetism 185–6
double reflection 65–6, 69
doubt 87–8, 126
Dunning, Stephen N. 7, 36, 39 n.
dying away 131, 132 n., 133, 134, 215
  see also nothingness before God; self-annihilation

earnestness 163
ebullitio 19
ecclesiastical hierarchy 14
Eckhart, Meister 8, 18–22, 23, 31–3, 206, 208, 209, 212 n., 213, 214, 215, 216
Edwards, Paul 91, 92, 94
either–or 42, 47–8
Elrod, John W. 71 n.
elusiveness 54, 61, 84, 175, 177
empiricism 75, 76
enjoyment 125
epistemology, see knowledge
essence 35, 42–3, 80, 171, 211
eternal, eternity 42 n., 43, 45, 53, 56–7,

61, 100–1 n., 116, 124, 129–30, 134, 137, 143–4, 145–7, 148–9, 152, 154, 155, 156, 166, 167, 168, 192
eternal consciousness 130
eternal happiness 100–3, 106–7, 122, 125–6, 134, 138, 143–4, 151–2
ethical principle 83
ethical sphere 82 n., 126–8, 129, 130, 133, 142, 178
ethics 46–9, 55, 82 n., 119, 127, 178–9
existence 35, 37, 38, 42–7, 49–57, 58, 61, 70, 72, 104, 108, 124, 129–30, 133–4, 137, 143–4, 145–6, 148–9, 158, 167–8, 171, 192, 211
existential issues 120–1

facts 94, 123
  absolute 191–2
  eternal 191–2
  historical 121–2, 191–2
Fahrenbach, Helmut 56–7
faith 51, 71, 86, 97, 105 n., 121, 131, 132, 137–40, 141, 142, 151–60, 172, 173, 179–80, 194, 203, 205
  and belief 153–4
  and the condition 156–8
  as contemporaneity 197–8
  and inwardness 155–6
  and knowledge 153, 194, 213–15
  movement of 131, 132, 136
  sensu strictissimo 86, 153–5
  and will 154–5, 158
Feuerbach, Ludwig 35
finite, finitude 35 n., 43, 44, 53, 56–7, 61, 115 n., 116, 124, 127, 129–30, 134, 135, 136, 137, 145–6
follower at second hand 191–2, 194–6
Forbilledet 203
foreshortened perspective 59
forgiveness of sins 157–8, 201–2
freedom 47, 62, 77, 78, 79, 87, 176, 177–8, 179, 181, 202
  see also autonomy

Gardiner, Patrick 71 n., 75 n.
Garelick, Herbert 59, 91, 93, 164
general religiousness, see religiousness A
German idealism 33, 35 n., 38 n.
  see also Hegel
God, Godhead 8–23, 26, 103, 107, 121, 127, 131, 135, 139, 146–7, 150, 151, 155, 157, 184–5, 195–6, 197, 202, 207, 208, 211–12, 214, 215, 216–17

concept of 16, 162–7, 180–1, 208
existence of 121, 167–73
knowledge of 10–12, 16–17, 23, 173–81, 207–8, 212–13, 216–17
  as object 180, 181
  sovereignty of 175–6, 179
God-man, God-in-time 145, 146, 157, 158, 186 n., 198, 200
God-relationship 61, 103, 107, 109, 125–6, 127, 128, 129–30, 131–2, 133–5, 138–9, 140, 142, 143, 149, 150, 159–60, 161, 163–5, 170, 173, 174–5, 176, 177–9, 180, 181, 208, 211–12, 214, 217
Görres, J. von 31, 32
grace 154 n.
Gregory of Nazianzus 30
Gregory of Nyssa 29–30
Greve, W. 111 n.
ground 77–8
ground of the soul 21–2, 215, 216
Grundtvig, N. F. S. 37 n.
Guardini, Romano 94, 96
Guerike, H. E. F. 25, 28, 29, 30
guilt 113, 133–5, 137, 142, 150

Haecker, Theodor 91
Hannay, Alistair 35, 56, 72, 78, 83 n., 93–4, 100 n., 111, 182
Hase, K. 25–6 n., 28, 29, 30, 31, 33, 34
Heer, Friedrich 206
Hegel, Hegelianism 25, 28, 31, 33, 35, 37–50, 52, 69, 72, 115 n., 174, 175–6, 179, 182, 206–7
Heiberg, J. L. 27, 39 n.
Helfferich, A. 31, 32
Henriksen, Aage 3
heretics 26–7 n., 210
Heywood Thomas, John 94, 97
hiddenness 2, 9, 15, 31, 142, 161, 166–7, 173, 180, 186, 187–9, 204, 208–9, 210, 216, 217
highest good, see absolute good
Hildegard 32
Hirsch, Emanuel 94, 95, 115 n., 186, 209
historian 79, 86
historical–comparative method 3–4
historical, history 35 n., 48, 77, 78, 86, 121–2, 143, 146, 151–3, 154, 175–7, 189, 191–6, 197, 198
Høffding, H. 96
Holm, Søren 36, 191

Hong, E. H. 24, 26n., 29n., 32n., 85n.
Hong, H. V. 24, 26n., 29n., 32n., 85n.
Hopkins, J. 216n.
'how' the 91, 93, 109, 110, 111, 113–14, 118, 122
Hugo of St Victor 31n., 32
human being 44, 116, 136, 167, 176
Hume, David 75n., 92
humility 131
humour 112–13

idea 35n., 45, 67, 140, 145
ideality, the ideal 82, 83, 173
identity of thought and being 41, 44, 45–6, 47, 50, 56–7, 104–5, 108, 114, 117
ignorance 137, 156, 191, 208, 215
    see also learned ignorance
illusiveness 78, 79
imitatio Christi 200, 203–4, 205
immanence 84, 112, 143–4, 148, 149, 175–6, 211
immediacy 125, 131
impossible, impossibility 136, 137, 158
Incarnation 72, 77, 103, 121–2, 145, 151–2, 161, 174, 183–98, 216
incognito 65, 132, 141, 186–7, 198, 209
incommensurability 112–13, 141, 209
indirect communication, see communication, in direct
individual 107–8, 115n., 141, 143, 214
induction 169, 171–2
infinite, infinitude, infinity 35n., 43, 53, 54, 56–7, 61, 109, 114, 115n., 116, 119, 124, 127, 129–30, 134, 135, 136, 137, 145–6, 166, 167, 208
intellect, see reason
intellectual principle 83
interest 106, 109, 160
interpretation of Kierkegaard's thought 4–5
inwardness 36, 51, 53, 59, 68–9, 109, 110–13, 119, 128, 132, 140, 141–2, 143, 144, 155, 156, 159, 160
    hidden 112–13, 132n., 204
    and subjectivity 100–11
    as truth 112, 174–5

Jesus, see Christ
Job 136

John the Baptist 187
Jolivet, Regis 6, 37, 64, 91, 93
Junghans, H. M. 115n.
just man, the 22

Kempis, Thomas à 32
kenosis 183–9, 198
Khan, Abrahim H. 71n., 101n.
Kirchhoff, A. 25
Klemke, E. D. 37–8n., 94, 95
knight of faith 139, 140–1
knight of resignation 130, 139
knowledge 10, 38, 51, 68–9, 71–89, 99, 118, 161, 191, 205, 208, 210, 213–15, 216
    of Christ 197–8
    empirical 75
    ethical 73, 82–5
    and faith 153–4, 213
    historical 72, 77, 79–80, 103, 107, 154, 194–5
    objective 62, 85, 113, 177
    religious 73
    of self 85
    of sin 149–50
know thyself 55

language 9, 23, 59, 141, 207, 208
law 203
leap 35n., 46, 77, 79, 84, 121, 140, 149, 152, 154, 155, 169, 174, 191, 201, 203, 211, 214
learned ignorance 34, 208
Lessing 189–90
literary method 3
logic 39, 40, 42, 45, 46, 52, 155
Lossky, V. 23
Luther 36

McGinn, B. 18n., 19n., 22n., 212n.
Macquarrie, John 15
Malantschuk, Gregor 6, 50n., 110n., 204
Marbach, G. O. 24, 25, 28, 31
marriage 120, 127
Martensen, H. L. 32–3, 37–8n.
martyrdom 32n.
marvel 137, 139, 141n.
Marx, Karl 35
Mary 191
meaning 99–100
mediation 36, 39, 40, 47, 49, 50, 53, 141

μετάβασις εἰς ἄλλο γένος,
    metabasis eis allo genos 34, 195
methodology 3
Middle Ages 31
miracles 187–8, 195
moment, the 35 n.
movement 42, 45–6, 84
    of faith 131, 132, 136, 141 n.
    immanent 45, 46
    of infinity 130, 136, 137
    paradoxical 139
    quantitative 45
    of resignation 130, 136
Murphy, Arthur E. 91, 92
Mynster, J. P. 37 n.
mystical theology 16, 18
mysticism, mystics 31–3, 214, 217

Napoleon 172–3
nature 172–3
Neander, August 28, 29, 30, 32
necessity 56, 72, 77, 79–80, 85
negation 17–18, 21–2, 23, 44, 45
negativity, the negative 1 n., 43–4, 53,
    54, 56, 58, 61, 67, 69, 88, 132, 134,
    138–9, 150–1, 159, 204
negative theology, negative theologians
    8–24, 24–34, 163, 206–17
    see also individual negative
    theologians
Neoplatonism 24–5, 206, 217
Nero 126 n.
Nicolas of Cusa 31 n., 33–4, 208, 209,
    213, 216
non-being 79
Nonna 30
nothingness before God 131–2, 142,
    178

object:
    of faith 154, 159
    of knowledge 88
    relationship to 114, 117
    of truth 96, 105–7, 118–23
    see also God, as object
objective reflection 39, 54–6, 60, 82–3,
    105–7
    see also abstract thought; pure
    thought; thought
objective thought, see objective
    reflection
objectivity 36, 52, 60, 92, 93, 94, 95–8,
    109, 118–23
occasion 197

offence 158 n., 185 n., 203, 205
omnipotence 166
oneness, the One 13, 14, 206
ontological argument 170–3
ontology 40

paganism 49, 175, 186, 212
paradox, paradoxicality 21, 26, 35 n.,
    36, 112–13, 122, 135–7, 139, 141,
    149–50, 152, 158, 159, 161, 194–5,
    198, 200, 202, 204, 205, 207, 208,
    209, 214
    absolute 122, 144–8, 149, 151, 153,
    154, 155–6, 158, 186 n., 194, 209
    objective 145–7
    subjective 145, 147–8
Parousia 189
particularity 14, 43, 44, 124, 126, 127,
    140, 141, 147
passion 49, 51–2, 57, 72, 86, 88, 89,
    91, 106, 109, 114, 119, 140, 156,
    159, 160, 162, 194, 207, 211, 214
Patrick, J. 13 n.
Pelikan, J. 216 n.
perception 1 n., 78
perfection 149, 170–1
Perkins, Robert 71 n., 94, 97
personality 35 n., 126, 127
Plato 24, 63, 129
Plotinus 24–5
plurality 13, 14
Plutarch 99 n.
poetic the 83
Pojman, Louis P. 6, 71 n., 88, 94,
    97–8, 108
Porphyry 25 n.
positivity, the positive 1 n., 43–4, 53,
    54, 67, 88, 132, 134, 138, 150–1,
    159, 204
positive theology, see cataphatic
    theology
possibility 35 n., 44, 46, 55, 56, 64,
    79–81, 83–4, 85, 87, 147, 176, 179
prayer 164
presuppositionless beginning 41
Price, George 6, 111 n., 154 n., 180,
    199
procession from God 19, 23, 206
Proclus 25
proof 94, 121, 195
prophet in reverse 85–6
pseudonymity 4–5, 63–5
psychological method 3

pure thought 39, 40 n., 42
    see also abstract thought; objective
        reflection; thought

qualitative difference 167, 186, 195,
    207, 212
Quint, J. 19 n., 22 n.

reality, see actuality
reason 21, 23, 137, 148, 149, 153, 154,
    155, 163, 164, 168–9, 171–2, 195,
    207, 208, 209
recollection 35 n., 129, 145, 148–9
redemption, see soteriology
reduplication 82, 110
reflection 41, 74, 76, 81, 111
    see also abstract thought; objective
        reflection; thought
Reimer, L. 136
relation 56, 111, 116, 178
religiousness, see religiousness A
religiousness A 113, 129–42, 143–4,
    145, 146, 147, 148, 149, 151 n., 161
religiousness B 103, 113, 120, 143–61
repellence 135, 137
repetition 136–7, 139
resignation 130, 131, 136
results 45, 48, 49, 54, 60, 68, 110,
    141–2
resurrection 195, 216
return to God 19, 21, 23, 206
revelation 11, 127, 172, 174–5, 176–9,
    181, 182, 185, 186–9, 209, 216
Richard of St Victor 32
Richter, Liselotte 94, 95–6
riddles 67
risk 159, 192
Ritschl, Dietrich 35 n.
Rohrmoser, Günter 94, 95
Rolt, C. E. 13 n., 15, 215 n.
Roos, H. 185, 186 n.
Rutledge, D. 13 n., 14 n., 209 n.

Salighed 100 n., 101 n.
satisfaction theory of atonement 201–2
scepticism 81, 82–3, 84, 87
    anthropological 73–7, 81
    Greek 76, 87
    ontological 73, 77, 81
Schleiermacher, F. 28, 29, 30, 31
Schrey, H.-H. 35 n.
Schröer, Henning 36, 135 n., 199
Schulz, Walter 7, 94, 96

selfhood, the self 21, 35 n., 36, 56–7,
    96, 100–1 n., 115–17, 124–8,
    129–30, 131, 133, 134, 136, 144,
    150, 152, 160, 161, 178, 202–3,
    212, 215
self-annihilation 131–2, 134, 144, 215
Simon Tornacensis 31 n.
sin 26, 116, 148–51, 152, 156, 157, 158,
    160, 161, 167, 176–7, 200, 212,
    215, 217
Sløk, Johannes 6, 101 n.
Smith, Cyprian 21 n., 208 n., 209 n.,
    213 n., 215 n., 216 n.
society 127
Socrates 55, 63, 66, 120 n., 129, 135 n.,
    137, 156
Son of God, see Christ
Sontag, F. 136 n.
soteriology 103, 193, 198–205
soul 19, 20, 22, 216
speculative philosophy, see Hegel
Spinoza 40 n., 171
spirit 35 n., 115 n., 126, 157
Sponheim, Paul 7, 38 n., 64 n.
Stack, G. J. 83 n.
stages of existence 102–3, 124–61,
    162 n., 213
Stählin, Otto 8–9 n.
Stengren, C. 154 n.
Stiglmayr 13 n.
striving 54, 57, 96, 113–14, 174
subject 106–7, 115–16
subjective thinker 50, 51, 52, 53, 54
subjective reflection 40 n., 54–5, 57,
    82–3, 107
subjective thought, see subjective
    reflection
subjectivism 91–3, 95, 96, 97, 122
subjectivity 36, 37, 52, 54, 59, 62–3,
    81, 84, 106, 108, 117–19, 160, 175,
    204, 215
    and inwardness 110–12
    and objectivity 118–23
    as relationship 108–14, 116–17
    as selfhood 108, 115–17
    as truth 72, 90–8, 109, 114, 124,
        134, 149, 156, 174
    as untruth 115–16, 149, 156
sub specie aeterni/aeternitatis 22,
    39–40, 42, 46, 214
suffering 125, 131–2, 137, 138, 142,
    204, 205
suicide 49

Super-Essential, the 13–18, 22, 215
Suso, H. 32
Swenson, David F. 85 n.
synteresis 19
synthesis 35 n., 43–4, 56–7, 61, 115 n.,
116–17, 136, 146
systematic structure of Kierkegaard's
works 5–8

task 178–9
Tauler, Johann 32
Taylor, Mark C. 3, 6, 7, 8, 39 n.,
63–4, 94, 96, 100 n., 103, 154 n.,
174, 199
temporality, the temporal 43, 44, 53,
56–7, 61, 116, 124, 129–30, 134,
143, 145–7, 152, 192, 197
Tennemann, W. G. 25, 28, 29, 30, 31,
32 n., 34
Teresa of Avila 32
Theill-Wunder, Hella 17, 216 n.
Theunissen, M. 111 n.
Thomas Aquinas 209
Thompson, Josiah 6
Thomte, Reidar 26 n.
thought 45, 46, 47, 50, 51–2, 53, 54,
56, 58, 83, 108, 139, 147, 152, 208,
211
  medium of 39–40 n.
  breakdown of 140–1
  see also abstract thought; objective
  reflection; pure thought; reflection
Thulstrup, M. M. 30 n., 33
Thulstrup, N. 25–6 n., 39 n.
time, *see* temporality
transcendence 8–10, 13–15, 17, 18–19,
20, 22–3, 131, 146, 166–7, 168,
175–6, 181, 207–8, 211–12, 214,
216, 217
transformational criticism 35
transition 35 n., 42, 46, 77, 78, 80–1,
84, 86, 152
transparency 69, 82
Trendelenburg, A. 41 n.
Trinity, the 15, 19, 21, 182
Tro 86–7
truth 4, 38 n., 59–61, 62–3, 65, 66, 68,
69, 75, 96, 100, 125–6, 128,
129–30, 137, 142, 144, 146, 149,
151, 152, 157, 160, 161, 189–90,
192, 209, 210
  of Christianity 121

correspondence theory of 104–8, 114
existential and religious nature of
99–100
  object of 118–22
  objective 94, 95, 99, 105–6, 161, 210
  subjective 106–11, 119, 154, 210
  as subjectivity 72, 90–8, 116, 122–3,
124, 134, 149, 156, 174

uncertainty 50, 54, 72, 77, 79–81, 82,
85, 86, 87, 88, 89, 119–20, 122,
123, 124, 138, 140, 152, 153, 155–6,
159–60, 174, 191, 214
understanding, the 139, 162, 169, 200,
207, 212
  crucifixion of 155, 200, 208
  martyrdom of 155, 208
unintelligibility 126, 127–8, 132,
140–1, 148, 159
union 17, 18, 20, 22, 23–4, 212, 214,
215
universality, universal, the 14, 43,
127–8, 140–1, 147, 192
unknowing 18, 213
Unknown, the 11, 162–4, 178, 186,
207, 208, 212, 216
unrecognizability 141, 186, 190, 204,
205
untruth 115–16, 149, 156
Utterback, S. W. 37

verification 122–3, 160
via eminentiae 25 n., 26
via mystica 217
via negationis 25–6, 34, 212
via negativa 25, 212, 217
virtue 152
vünkelin 19–20

Walshe, M. O'C. 18 n., 19 n., 20 n.,
21 n., 22 n., 23 n., 216 n.
way, the 110
Weisshaupt, Kurt 101 n.
'what', the 91, 93, 109, 113, 118, 122
will 51, 76, 87, 88, 89, 105 n., 154–5,
158, 208
Williamson, R. 207
wonder 86, 155
works 172–3
world-historical, the 48–9, 118–19,
175–6
worship 51, 170, 178